First World War
and Army of Occupation
War Diary
France, Belgium and Germany

28 DIVISION
Headquarters, Branches and Services
Royal Army Medical Corps
Assistant Director Medical Services,
Commander Royal Engineers,
Deputy Assistant Director Ordnance Services,
Assistant Director Veterinary Services
15 December 1914 - 31 October 1915

WO95/2270

The Naval & Military Press Ltd
www.nmarchive.com
Published in association with The National Archives

Published by

The Naval & Military Press Ltd

Unit 10 Ridgewood Industrial Park,
Uckfield, East Sussex,
TN22 5QE England
Tel: +44 (0) 1825 749494

www.naval-military-press.com
www.nmarchive.com

This diary has been reprinted in facsimile from the original. Any imperfections are inevitably reproduced and the quality may fall short of modern type and cartographic standards.

© **Crown Copyright**
Images reproduced by permission of The National Archives, London, England, 2015.

Contents

Document type	Place/Title	Date From	Date To
Heading	WO95/2270/1		
Heading	28th Division Medical A.D.M.S. Dec 1914-Oct 1915		
War Diary	Winchester	24/12/1914	14/01/1915
War Diary	Borre	20/01/1915	31/01/1915
War Diary	Brandhoek	01/02/1915	04/02/1915
War Diary	Brandhoek Poperinghe	05/02/1915	05/02/1915
War Diary	Poperinghe	06/02/1915	31/03/1915
Heading	A.D.M.S. 28th Division April 1915		
War Diary	Poperinghe	01/04/1915	21/04/1915
War Diary	Vlamertinghe	21/04/1915	22/04/1915
War Diary	Poperinghe	23/04/1915	26/04/1915
War Diary	Near Proven	27/04/1915	30/04/1915
Heading	A.D.M.S. 28th Division May 1915		
War Diary	Near Proven	01/01/1915	01/01/1915
War Diary	Proven	02/05/1915	31/05/1915
Miscellaneous	Report of Work Performed By R.A.M.C., of The 28th Division From The 22nd April to The End of The Withdrawal To The Present Position.	06/05/1915	06/05/1915
Miscellaneous	Report of Work Performed By The R.A.M.C. Of The 28th Division From The 22nd April To The 10th May.	11/05/1915	11/05/1915
Miscellaneous	84th Field Ambulance. (2nd London T)		
Miscellaneous	85th Field Ambulance. (3rd London T)		
Miscellaneous	85th Field Ambulance (2nd North'bn T)		
Miscellaneous	No 15 Sanitary Section.		
Miscellaneous	Casualties Among Officers R.A.M.C., In Medical Charge of Combatant Units of The 28th Division.		
Miscellaneous	Honours And Rewards Administrative Staff.		
Heading	A.D.M.S. 28th Division		
War Diary	Watou	01/01/1915	13/05/1915
War Diary	West Outre	14/05/1915	30/05/1915
Heading	28th Division War Diary of A.D.M.S. 28th Division From July 1st 1915 To July 31st 1915 Vol I		
Miscellaneous	Map Has Been Ditached From July Diary & Attached to January		
War Diary	West Outre	01/07/1915	09/07/1915
War Diary	Woutre	09/07/1915	12/07/1915
War Diary	West Outre	13/07/1915	31/07/1915
Miscellaneous	Appendices For July.		
Miscellaneous	28th Division Expeditionary Force. Casualties in Six Months:- January 18th to July 18th 1915		
Miscellaneous	Cases Treated In Field Ambulances, January To 18th July 1915		
Miscellaneous	Honours And Rewards Administrative Staff.		
Heading	28th Division A.D.M.S. 28th Division Vol II August 15		
Heading	War Diary of A.D.M.S. 28 Division From August 1st To August 31st 1915		
War Diary	West Outre	01/08/1915	31/08/1915
Heading	A.D.M.S. 28th Div. Sep 1915 Vol II		
Heading	War Diary A.D.M.S. 28th Division. Period 1st To 30th September 1915 Volume No 9		

War Diary	West Outre	01/09/1915	22/09/1915
War Diary	Merris	23/09/1915	25/09/1915
War Diary	Merris-Merville-Bethune	26/09/1915	26/09/1915
War Diary	Bethune	27/09/1915	27/09/1915
War Diary	Sailly Labourse	28/09/1915	30/09/1915
Heading	A.D.M.S. 28th Division Oct 1st-21st 1915		
War Diary	Sailly Labourse	01/10/1915	05/10/1915
War Diary	Busnes	06/10/1915	16/10/1915
War Diary	Bethune	17/10/1915	20/10/1915
War Diary	Lillers	21/10/1915	21/10/1915
Miscellaneous	Summary of Medical Operations Of 28th Division, January-June 1915, Together With Apps., Maps, Etc		
Miscellaneous	Summary of Medical Operations Of 28th Div Jan-July 1915		
Miscellaneous			
Miscellaneous	28th Division. Summary A.D.M.S. Six Months January-July 1915		
Miscellaneous	Summary. Diary: A.D.M.S., 28th Division: January-July 1915		
Miscellaneous	28th Division Expeditionary Force. Nominal Roll of Officers R.A.M.C.	18/07/1915	18/07/1915
Miscellaneous	Officers In Medical Charge of Combatant Units.		
Miscellaneous	Circular Memorandum On Camp Sanitation.		
Miscellaneous	Time Table Convay Control Town Hall Poperinghe Evacuation night 3 of 4.5.15		
Miscellaneous	List of Appendices, War Diary, D.A.D.M.S., 28th Division.		
Miscellaneous	Appendices.		
Miscellaneous	Original Nominal Roll of Officers R.A.M.C., 28th Division.		
Miscellaneous	Officers In Medical Charge of Combatant Units.		
Miscellaneous	The D. M. S., 2nd Army.	03/03/1915	03/03/1915
Miscellaneous	Statement of Expenses 28th Divisional Bathing Establishment.	05/03/1915	05/03/1915
Miscellaneous	Detailed Cost of Items.	05/03/1915	05/03/1915
Miscellaneous			
Miscellaneous	D.M.S., 2nd Army.	13/03/1915	13/03/1915
Miscellaneous	Sanitation of The Trench Area.	17/03/1915	17/03/1915
Miscellaneous	Original Nominal Roll of Officers R.A.M.C., 28th Division.		
Miscellaneous	Officers In Medical Charge of Combatant Units.		
Miscellaneous	The A.D.M.S., 28th Division.	09/03/1915	09/03/1915
Miscellaneous	Routine Standing Orders For Convalescents On Admission Or Discharge.	08/03/1915	08/03/1915
Miscellaneous	Standing Orders For Convalescents.	08/03/1915	08/03/1915
Miscellaneous	Routine Standing Orders In Case of Fire.	08/03/1915	08/03/1915
Miscellaneous	The Most Urgent Need of The Hut Encampment of This Division Is The Suitable Form of Latrine.	24/03/1915	24/03/1915
Miscellaneous	A.D.M.S., 28th Division. (Repeated D.M.S., 2nd Army.)	25/03/1915	25/03/1915
Map	Ypres		
Miscellaneous	Position of Ambulances And Dressing Stations, 28th Division On The 11th April, 1915	11/04/1915	11/04/1915
Miscellaneous	Report On the Suggested Reduction of Rations During the Summer Months.		

Miscellaneous	Names of Officers And Other Names In Medical Unit 28th Division Recommended For Good Services.		
Miscellaneous	From O.C. 84th Field Ambulance	09/05/1915	09/05/1915
Map	Position of Medical Units O.C. 31st July 1915		
Map	Scheme of Evacuation Wounded February 1915		
Map	Scheme For Collection of Wounded 28th Div. April 11 1915		
Map	Scheme of Collecting Wounded 28 Division June 15-July 15 1915		
Map	28 Division Aid Posts May 5-8, 1915		
Map	Aid Posts Re April 20 1915		
Miscellaneous	To: O.C., 85th (3rd London) Field Ambulance. From: Captain H.A.T. Fairbank.	24/05/1915	24/05/1915
Miscellaneous	Water Supply of The 28th Division On 7th May 1915	07/05/1915	07/05/1915
Miscellaneous	The G.O.C., At His Inspection To-day Considered That Nothing Had Been Done In The Way of Cooking To Increase The Well-being of The Patients In The Field Ambulances.	06/06/1915	06/06/1915
Miscellaneous	A Localized Epidemic of Enteric Fever Has Broken Out In The Division of The Most Startling Intensity.		
Miscellaneous	Confidential Circular No 10		
Miscellaneous	As It Is Necessary To Take Every Possible Precaution Against An Outbreak of Enteris Fever.	25/06/1915	25/06/1915
Miscellaneous	28th Division Expeditionary Force. Casualties in Six Moths.- January 18th to July 18th 1915		
Miscellaneous	Cases Treated In Field Ambulances, January To 18th July 1915		
Heading	WO95/2270/2		
Heading	28th Division Divl Engineers C.R.E. Dec 1914-Oct 1915		
Heading	Hd Qrs: RE. 28th Division Vol I 18.12.14-28.2.15		
War Diary	Winchester	18/12/1914	18/01/1915
War Diary	Havre	19/01/1915	20/01/1915
War Diary	Hazebrouck	21/01/1915	21/01/1915
War Diary	Borre	21/01/1915	31/01/1915
War Diary	Vlamertinghe	01/02/1915	05/02/1915
War Diary	Poperinghe	06/02/1915	19/02/1915
War Diary		17/02/1915	17/02/1915
War Diary	Ypres	20/02/1915	28/02/1915
Heading	Hd Qrs RE. 28th Division Vol II 1-31.3.15		
War Diary	Ypres	01/03/1915	31/03/1915
Heading	Hd Qrs: R.E. 28th Division Vol III 1-29.4.15		
War Diary	Ypres	01/04/1915	29/04/1915
Heading	Hd Qrs R.E. 28th Division Vol IV 1-31.5.15		
War Diary	Ypres	01/05/1915	31/05/1915
Heading	28th Division Hd Qrs R.E. 28th Division Vol V 1-30.6.15		
War Diary	Watou	01/06/1915	30/06/1915
War Diary		20/06/1915	20/06/1915
Heading	28th Division Hd Qrs R.E. 28th Division Vol VI		
War Diary		01/07/1915	31/07/1915
War Diary		23/07/1915	23/07/1915
War Diary		15/07/1915	15/07/1915
Heading	28th Division Hd Qrs R.E. 28th Division Vol VII August 15		
War Diary		01/08/1915	31/08/1915

Heading	28th Division Hd. Qrs R.E. 28th Division Vol VIII Sept 15			
War Diary	Westoutre		01/09/1915	22/09/1915
War Diary	Merris		23/09/1915	23/09/1915
War Diary	Bethune		26/09/1915	26/09/1915
War Diary	Sailly-Labourse		27/09/1915	30/09/1915
Heading	C.R.E. 28th Divn Oct 15 Vol IX			
War Diary	Sailly-Labourse		01/10/1915	06/10/1915
War Diary	Busnes		06/10/1915	16/10/1915
War Diary	Le Quesnoy		17/10/1915	17/10/1915
War Diary	Bethune		18/10/1915	22/10/1915
War Diary	In The Train		23/10/1915	25/10/1915
War Diary	Marseilles		26/10/1915	31/10/1915
Heading	WO95/2270/3			
Heading	28th Division Divl Troops D.A.D.O.S. Dec 1914-Sep 1915			
Heading	28th Division DADOS. 28th Division Vol V 1914 Dec To 1915 August			
Heading	28th Division DADOS. 28th Division Vol I			
Heading	War Diary of D.A.D.O.S. 28th Division From 15-12-14 To 30-4-15 1-6-15 To 30-6-15			
War Diary			15/12/1914	01/01/1915
War Diary	Mobilization		03/01/1915	15/01/1915
War Diary	Winchester		15/01/1915	30/01/1915
War Diary	Bandehoek		01/02/1915	01/02/1915
War Diary	Poperinghe		06/02/1915	19/04/1915
War Diary	Ypres		19/04/1915	24/04/1915
War Diary	Caestre		28/04/1915	28/04/1915
Heading	DADOS. 28th Division Vol I 1-31.5.15			
War Diary			01/05/1915	31/05/1915
Heading	28th Division DADOS. 28th Division Vol III			
War Diary			01/06/1915	30/06/1915
Heading	28th Division D.A.D.O.S. 28th Division Vol IV			
Heading	War Diary of D.A.D.O.S. 28th Division (major Sainders Area) From 1.7.15 To 31.7.15			
War Diary	Westoutre		01/07/1915	29/07/1915
Heading	War Diary of D.A.D.O.S. 28th Division From Aug 1st To Aug 31st 1915 (Volume 1)			
War Diary	Westoutre		01/08/1915	31/08/1915
Heading	28th Division DADOS. 28th Division Vol VI Sept. 15			
Heading	War Diary Of DADOS 28th Division From Sept 1st To Sept 30th Volume I 1915			
War Diary	Westoutre		01/09/1915	26/09/1915
War Diary	Steenwerke		26/09/1915	26/09/1915
War Diary	Hazebrouk		27/09/1916	28/09/1916
War Diary	Fouquereuil		29/09/1916	30/09/1916
Heading	WO95/2270/4			
Heading	28th Division Divl Troops A.D. Vety Services 1915 Jan-1915 Oct			
Heading	ADVS. 28th Division Vol I Jan 1915			
War Diary	Borre		19/01/1915	31/01/1915
Heading	ADVS. 28th Division Vol II Feb 1915			
Heading	War Diary For February 1915			
War Diary	Brandhoek		01/02/1915	04/02/1915
War Diary	Poperinghe		05/02/1915	28/02/1915

Miscellaneous	No. 17, Mobile Veterinary Section. Sick State of Horses For Period From 30-1-15 To 5-2-15	06/02/1915	06/02/1915
Miscellaneous	No. 17, Mobile Veterinary Section. Sick State of Horses For Period From 6-2-15 To 11-2-15	12/02/1915	12/02/1915
Miscellaneous	No. 17, Mobile Veterinary Section. Sick State of Horses For Period From 12-2-15 To 18-2-15	19/02/1915	19/02/1915
Miscellaneous	No. 17, Mobile Veterinary Section. Sick State of Horse For Period From 19-2-15 To 25-2-15	26/02/1915	26/02/1915
Heading	A.D.V.S. 28th Division War Diary 31st March 1915		
War Diary	Poperinghe	01/03/1915	31/03/1915
Heading	ADVS. 28th Division Vol. III & IV 14-27.4.15		
Heading	A.D.V.S. 28th Division War Diary 1/30th April 1915		
War Diary	Poperinghe	01/04/1915	14/04/1915
War Diary	Vlamertinghe	21/04/1915	22/04/1915
War Diary	Poperinghe	23/04/1915	23/04/1915
War Diary	Proven	27/04/1915	27/04/1915
Miscellaneous	No. 17, Mobile Veterinary Section. Sick State of Horses For Period From 9-4-15 To 15-4-15	10/04/1915	10/04/1915
Miscellaneous	No. 17, Mobile Veterinary Section. Sick State of Horses For Period From 16-4-15 To 22-4-15	23/04/1915	23/04/1915
Miscellaneous	No. 17, Mobile Veterinary Section. Sick State of Horses For Period From 23-4-15 To 29-4-15	30/04/1915	30/04/1915
Miscellaneous	No. 17, Mobile Veterinary Section. Sick State of Horses For Period From 2-4-15 To 8-4-15	09/04/1915	09/04/1915
Heading	ADVS. 28th Division Vol V 1-31.5.15		
Heading	War Diary Month Ending 31st May 1915		
War Diary	Proven	04/05/1915	23/05/1915
War Diary	Watou	31/05/1915	31/05/1915
Miscellaneous	Work of Army Veterinary Services, 28th Division, From April 22nd, To May 13th 1915.	16/05/1915	16/05/1915
Miscellaneous	No. 17. M.V.S. A.V.C Sick State of Horses For Period From 30.4.15 to 6.5.15	07/06/1915	07/06/1915
Miscellaneous	No. 17. M.V.S. A.V.C Sick State of Horses For Period From 7.5.15 to 13.5.15		
Miscellaneous	No. 17. M.V.S. A.V.C Sick State of Horses For Period From 14.5.15 To 20.5.15	21/05/1915	21/05/1915
Miscellaneous	No. 17. M.V.S. A.V.C Sick State of Horses For Period From 28.5.15 To 28.5.15	28/05/1915	28/05/1915
Heading	28th Division ADVS. 28th Division Vol VI From 1st To 30th June 1915		
War Diary	Watou	01/06/1915	11/06/1915
War Diary	Westoutre	14/06/1915	30/06/1915
Heading	28th Division ADVS. 28th Division Vol VII 1-31.7.15		
Heading	War Diary for Month of July 1915		
War Diary	Westoutre	01/07/1915	31/07/1915
Miscellaneous	Sick State of Horses For Period From 25=6=15 To 1=7=15	02/07/1915	02/07/1915
Miscellaneous	Sick State of Horses For Period From 2=7=15 To 8=7=15	09/07/1915	09/07/1915
Miscellaneous	Sick State of Horses For Period From 9=7=15 To 15=7=15	16/07/1915	16/07/1915
Miscellaneous	Sick State of Horses For Period From 16=7=15 To 22=7=15	23/07/1915	23/07/1915
Miscellaneous	Sick State of Horses For Period From 23=7=15 To 29=7=15	30/07/1915	30/07/1915

Heading	28th Division ADVS. 28th Division Vol VIII August 15		
War Diary	Westoutre	12/08/1915	31/08/1915
Heading	28th Division War Diary of A.D.V.S. 28th Division From 1st Sept. 15 To 30th Sept. 1915 Vol IX		
War Diary	Westoutre	01/09/1915	22/09/1915
War Diary	Merris	23/09/1915	25/09/1915
War Diary	Bethune	26/09/1915	30/09/1915
Heading	A.D.V.S. 28th Div Oct Vol X		
War Diary	Bethune	01/10/1915	10/10/1915
War Diary	Busnes	11/10/1915	16/10/1915
War Diary	Bethune	17/10/1915	20/10/1915
War Diary	On Train Journey	21/10/1915	23/10/1915
War Diary	Marseilles	24/10/1915	31/10/1915

WD95/22270(1)

WD95/22270(1)

28TH DIVISION
MEDICAL

A. D. M. S.
DEC 1914-OCT 1915

Army Form C. 2118.

WAR DIARY
or
INTELLIGENCE SUMMARY.
(Erase heading not required.)

Instructions regarding War Diaries and Intelligence Summaries are contained in F.S. Regs., Part II and the Staff Manual respectively. Title pages will be prepared in manuscript.

Hour, Date, Place	Summary of Events and Information	Remarks and references to Appendices
3 P.M.	Arrived today to report to A.D.M.S. 28th Division deputed to S.O.E. 28th Division (Major General E. S. Bulfin C.V.O. C.B.)	
24th December 1914 Warwick	Major A.S. Roch R.A.M.C. introduced himself being (D.A.D.M.S) this afternoon. After my arrival I visited the J.A.D.M.S. in office of S.D.M.S. Southern Command - Salisbury. Visited the Territorial Field Ambulances being bivouac viz the 1st A.S.A Lines too stationary at Tinsley Park & the 2nd Northumbrian Field Amb. (on at Magdalen Hill These huts have so far no transport Mendzacan Medical Equipment and no picture of uniform trusting to R.A and Men having to hold.	

WAR DIARY

INTELLIGENCE/SUMMARY.

(Erase heading not required.)

Army Form C. 2118.

Instructions regarding War Diaries and Intelligence Summaries are contained in F.S. Regs., Part II. and the Staff Manual respectively. Title pages will be prepared in manuscript.

Hour, Date, Place	Summary of Events and Information	Remarks and references to Appendices
25/12/14 Midnight 10 am	Three Infantry Brigades (12 Battalions) are now here - the Divisional Artillery & Heavy Batteries & Howitzer Batty. and 2 Fd. Coys. R.E. have been affiliated to Divn. so far - + no cavalry. 1 Sqdn. 9.L. Telephones to s.o. units, transport, & the issues & receipt of highest quantity rations - was approved that step was being taken to supply them against issues.	
26/12/14 11 am	Inspected 20. War. Hampshire Field Ambulance. The units, horses + issues recently the units are reported as being of inferior quality. Have instructed G.O.C. to issue of hard clothing.	

Army Form C. 2118.

WAR DIARY
or
INTELLIGENCE SUMMARY.
(Erase heading not required.)

Instructions regarding War Diaries and Intelligence Summaries are contained in F.S. Regs., Part II. and the Staff Manual respectively. Title pages will be prepared in manuscript.

Hour, Date, Place	Summary of Events and Information	Remarks and references to Appendices
R. history 27th Dec 1914 Winchester.	Several officers I.M.S. having rejoined their unit & the [?] from India - the remainder have been left Winchester Barracks at the main office.	
28th Dec 1914	The wealthr has been very wet & wet - during the [?] days have been some in the camps but highly satisfactory. The Brahmins transport at Hursley Camps - they died [?] at work & ambulance transport in [?] in extra (300 horses). They have been interchanged between the brigades & the horses stabled in Winchester.	
11 am		
29th Dec 1914	Several officers of which 11 [?] this morning [?] with [?]	H.F.
11 am		

Army Form C. 2118.

WAR DIARY
or
INTELLIGENCE SUMMARY.
(Erase heading not required.)

Hour, Date, Place	Summary of Events and Information	Remarks and references to Appendices
10 am 30th Dec 1914 Nyndurli	Familiar faces (2 Capt R.A.M.C, 1 Capt R.A.M.C.(T) & 11 Lnds(TC)) have not been pulled of the various units & 9th Divison. The missing equipment is mostly being endeavoured to tap on contact - area filled. Spoke to Corps. The S.O.C is 2 Bn. Visited Sn. No Station J.A. at Nyndurli late letter accompanied by Major ADM.C. Telephone to W.O. Enquiries supply of new material & equipment for the F.A. & also the transport animals, which now 31 per annum. — there are 90 men in hospital.	
31st Dec 1914 11 am	Heavy rain again — the Survival Ammunition Column are holding aloft. D. have reported W.O. to send Br. H. & Kit. Bills. — The army Butler back which Capt Wyatt Deane broke and then took on behalf of anyone there to make a separate arrival transport (or J.A.) Received telegram from W.O. (31/12) stating that the radio ambulance would but for the British teu carried in France — than were to W.O. for the Junior Princip[al] to all Auto Nurses as he a Forgot with him clothes for an allowance for private dancer. Lance J.A. is receiving two an allowance for private dancer. still many applications sent in chiefs of by Cpl had service in the FA's	[signature]

WAR DIARY
or
INTELLIGENCE SUMMARY.
(Erase heading not required.)

Army Form C. 2118.

Instructions regarding War Diaries and Intelligence Summaries are contained in F.S. Regs., Part II. and the Staff Manual respectively. Title pages will be prepared in manuscript.

Hour, Date, Place	Summary of Events and Information	Remarks and references to Appendices
4 pm M/a 1915 Winchester	Wire received last night from 10 (Group 3?) stating that all the while manoeuvres —plans to finish for Sunday were first the Divine troubles — also complete but help. Weather conditions very wet & strong but in Infantry 15th — 6 horses belonging to 2nd C.A. & 1 horse belonging to 3rd horse A. Res. Reserve have since open to the movement order. The F.C. has orders that he is 63 & 85 & 836 Originals etc killed at Winchester. Summer manoeuvres —	

Army Form C. 2118.

WAR DIARY
or
INTELLIGENCE SUMMARY.
(Erase heading not required.)

Instructions regarding War Diaries and Intelligence Summaries are contained in F. S. Regs., Part II. and the Staff Manual respectively. Title pages will be prepared in manuscript.

Hour, Date, Place	Summary of Events and Information	Remarks and references to Appendices
APM 2nd January 1915 Mindelo	The 63rd & 85th Brigades are now billeted in Winchester. Visited the 2nd & 3rd Ludgun FA's this afternoon. Found them to be short of beds in the same area as 1st, 2nd, 3rd FA's. Sent Major Root DADMS to inspect & call to form O.E. & institute during FA. to bring the wing up to date & held a Parade. V= 85th Brigade horse — Have instructed FC OC. 1st Ambulance to inspect a spread supply of clothing & wishing the half of man anything for children & front. — Shortage of all Tetanus Vaccine & of Private 1st & 3rd FA — the sick in Hospital number 70 (say) — at 8 pm — There have been in the wear 9 Officers & 1 Helena amongst the Battalions which illness from different causes I sealed him to — Telephone has been upheld from 1st to 2nd AD — Send a terram Ross TG informed the various authorities & telegram to ADMS into division.	

Army Form C. 2118.

WAR DIARY
or
INTELLIGENCE SUMMARY.
(Erase heading not required.)

Instructions regarding War Diaries and Intelligence Summaries are contained in F. S. Regs., Part II. and the Staff Manual respectively. Title pages will be prepared in manuscript.

Hour, Date, Place	Summary of Events and Information	Remarks and references to Appendices
6 p.m. 3rd Jan 1915 Winchester	Owing to unforeseen [delays?] there has been a hitch about the Sets being in the [?] for the [?] into the valley [?] & hills. The R.F.A. plus ammunition column are being transferred to that at [Knightsbridge], Sheen, Bushy & the village in the neighbourhood of Winchester. Arrangements have now been made for distribution of Service Ammunition to all units. There are still considerable deficiencies in the ordnance equipment of all three field Ambulances. The artillery of 2nd [?] F.A. is now complete — two of the musical equipments for [?] for known [?] for F.A.'s is now informed in [?] from W.O. that if no [?] it has — Sub in latitude 157 — (There are a few very close to — [?] balance efficiently in it. 18 R.G.y.L Infantry — †) † of balance especially in it. 18 [?] ammunition to artillery than are in addition to extract them	

Army Form C. 2118.

WAR DIARY
of
INTELLIGENCE SUMMARY.
(Erase heading not required.)

Instructions regarding War Diaries and Intelligence Summaries are contained in F.S. Regs., Part II. and the Staff Manual respectively. Title pages will be prepared in manuscript.

Hour, Date, Place	Summary of Events and Information	Remarks and references to Appendices

6 p.m.
4 Jan 1915
Windmill

Marta [illegible]
The 8th Brigade are once also coming in to billets. Consequently a small brigade in 3rd Division FA - there appears the brigadier being away the Sgt Maj[?] took FA officers are Brigade-wide un[der] the Command Ammunition Column. I am sent to ascertain the of the brigadier - I am given 3 lorries after 9.15 I go to where the A.A. Column had set out of the the 2nd Ambulance A.A. Column has been a kind out of the lorries. They had come up, and it was found that where within the area of the brigade behind it had been conforming affiliated while in Camp - there is also unable to mobilize the F.A. with the Ammunition and the brigade transport an attempt on my own less-than more than sure to consider the J.A. as final brigade must [illegible] organisation - I hand of the brigades organisation - visited 2nd Durham F.A. in billets at St Aunine and Shuttd[?] his clothing stuff wants, things is now complete he been given a laundry show sheet we are all expecting [illegible] in the Bayne Spitfire on the other

Note Brother half has pushed the podsol [illegible] [signature]
Forms/C.2118/10e that the pockets between are distributed - side without 16st - Sept 12

Army Form C. 2118.

WAR DIARY
or
INTELLIGENCE SUMMARY.
(Erase heading not required.)

Instructions regarding War Diaries and Intelligence Summaries are contained in F. S. Regs., Part II. and the Staff Manual respectively. Title pages will be prepared in manuscript.

Hour, Date, Place	Summary of Events and Information	Remarks and references to Appendices
5.10 pm 5th Jan 1915 Winterste	There has been considerable progress made in the Mobilization & the 3 Field Ambulances during the last 24 hours viz:— 22 Mobilization F.A. — CMT's now complete — advance equipment to issued — 2 horse Ambulance Wagons have been drawn — Supply has been issued — hospital harness. 2nd Home Field Ambulance — CMT's not complete — technical equipment not complete — Harness received — 3rd Horse Field Ambulance is still behindhand, but part of their technical equipment has been issued — all their horses have been received from the army to air. Milroy Group Last night proceeded a Telegram from Selentee how their clothing that all the received equipment in F.A.'s has been given up, that dated that day. Q.M. to hospital 161 — detached 15. — Pte. Y. O.Y. of Infants 5 State shows the unit sick 20. this Date also received recently from Sevagne	ffk

Army Form C. 2118.

WAR DIARY
INTELLIGENCE SUMMARY.
(Erase heading not required.)

Instructions regarding War Diaries and Intelligence Summaries are contained in F.S. Regs., Part II. and the Staff Manual respectively. Title pages will be prepared in manuscript.

Hour, Date, Place	Summary of Events and Information	Remarks and references to Appendices
5.45 p.m. 6th Jan 1915 Winchester	The medical equipment for Field Amb. arrived today. Gun harness has been under ordering - tin the outfits of vehicles. There is a improvement in the numbers on hospital strength. Sick in hospital = 169. Detached 34. There are also 6 under instruction in Royal Victoria Hospital Netley.	X.
6 p.m. 7th Jan 1915 Winchester	The Field Ambulances have also been provided with medical equipment - the 2nd London F.A. are still short of a heavy draught horse - the 2nd Westminster F.A. still require 9 draught horses. 9 officer horses also the men's horses have been obtained from Remounts. On the 2nd & 3rd London F.A's the horses is still inoculated against horse sickness in Winchester 179 - Cheesehill 21. & Bleinheim 35.	X.

Army Form C. 2118.

WAR DIARY
or
INTELLIGENCE SUMMARY.
(Erase heading not required.)

Instructions regarding War Diaries and Intelligence
Summaries are contained in F. S. Regs., Part II.
and the Staff Manual respectively. Title pages
will be prepared in manuscript.

Hour, Date, Place	Summary of Events and Information	Remarks and references to Appendices
5.45 pm 9th Jan 1915	There is still considerable difficulty in regard however with 3 Field Ambulances & all some deficiencies in horses & equipment but the [?] are improving. One [?] of armoured Panniers was sent to Portsmouth Reg[?] as reported as having been lost in convoy on its way to arrival & taken back - 3 hours after this was ascertained to be [?] having been taken. The 2 huntsmen 2A (two now re-ceived all their horses. [?] is thought at Winchester 144, at Hitty 21, at Wessin (Essex) 26 B.A. 46 = 267. — we have of 1st M Roy[?] Bns of Yeomanry in hospital.	
5.45 pm	Field Officers of O.C.'s Field Ambulances Etc). There is	
9 Jan 1915	general complaint that officials [?] them [?] so — these brought (on to leave — there seem to be many deficiencies in O.I. Damp Equipment — this is in most cases no complete & the duty to supply a conference of this this, Unit [?] for of field & up of yeoman [?] instruction regarding them being carried [?]. (Br. Z. R. hospital in Westerham 160, at Hitty 21 — at [?] (U) eq. before at 1 F.A. 3 Reg.	M.A.R.

(73989) W4141—463. 400,000. 9/14. H.&J.Ltd. Forms/C. 2118/10.

WAR DIARY
or
INTELLIGENCE SUMMARY.

(Erase heading not required.)

Army Form C. 2118.

Instructions regarding War Diaries and Intelligence Summaries are contained in F.S. Regs., Part II. and the Staff Manual respectively. Title pages will be prepared in manuscript.

Hour, Date, Place	Summary of Events and Information	Remarks and references to Appendices
6.45 p.m. 16 Jan 1915 Windmill	Some further preparis has been taken in the militia clair of the Fred Ambulance — Influenza in eight hours after sent in all three F.A.'s also the regt. a number of these cases of pneumonia reported. Sick in hospital in Windmill 149 — at billets 91 — (Alsea (VI) 31 — detained 60 = 261	YP
5.45 p.m. 11 Jan 1915	Four hours visit to F.A. am suffering from Pneumonia & one has died of influenza — there is still a shortage of harness — the Fred Ambulance has supplies on equip. ambulance in the 2nd hutzbacher F.A. has not yet been supplied. Sick in hospital in Windmill 146 — at billet 21 — Alsea (VI) 37 — Det. 58 = 264	

(73989) W4141—463. 400,000. 9/14. H.&J.Ltd. Forms/C. 2118/10.

WAR DIARY
or
INTELLIGENCE SUMMARY.
(Erase heading not required.)

Army Form C. 2118.

Hour, Date, Place	Summary of Events and Information	Remarks and references to Appendices
5.45 p.m. 12th Jan 15/15 Winchester	His Majesty the King inspected the Division in Marley Down today. The Inspection of H.E. 3 Fred Amm. Columns were presented but the transport of the fuel ambulance be complete in horses, limbers & harness (who some minor exceptions). The 2nd Ambulance is still very short of [?]. Motor vehicles & a number of small items in short supply. Motor vehicles & a number of small items in option to supplies to Winchester 131 - at Netley 21 - to Sick in hospital at Winchester 50 = 192 at Netley 52 = 192. o/c
6.5 p.m. 13th Jan 13/15	Good progress has been made in completing the mobil- -ization. Field ambulances. The Families have not yet been supplied. The base. Sick in hospital Winchester = 147. Netley 57.	s/o

Army Form C. 2118.

WAR DIARY
or
INTELLIGENCE SUMMARY.
(Erase heading not required.)

Instructions regarding War Diaries and Intelligence Summaries are contained in F.S. Regs., Part II. and the Staff Manual respectively. Title pages will be prepared in manuscript.

Hour, Date, Place	Summary of Events and Information	Remarks and references to Appendices
7.30 pm 14th Jan 1915 [illegible]	I inspected the 3 Field Ambulances this afternoon. The office is closed here for tonight. Named Roll Medical Officers who had met with division attached	[initials] App. 16.

Army Form C. 2118.

WAR DIARY
or
INTELLIGENCE SUMMARY.
(Erase heading not required.)

Instructions regarding War Diaries and Intelligence
Summaries are contained in F. S. Regs., Part II.
and the Staff Manual respectively. Title pages
will be prepared in manuscript.

Hour, Date, Place	Summary of Events and Information	Remarks and references to Appendices
6.30 p.m. 20th Jan 1915 Bonn	Heavy rainstorm meant to concentration of Division in Havre — left Winchester Friday 15th inst: arrived at HAVRE 16th inst (next morning) but was not got into dock there until midnight and brought into harbour across of West. to night. Entrained at 8 a.m. at MEREADISE for western destination. The train was made up of — train — 26 T.B. - 9th Divn. S.A. & Sigs (Res. Sqdn. any Cavalry Divnl. Train) Arrived at ST OMER (Sunday afternoon) were sent on by Staff officer to obtain at CASSEL — Owing to them. F.A. etc. at the same manner then billets were taken at HAZEBROUCK and arrived at … on the night …was fitted back of this Sunday round — three Note did not [the O.C. 7 A. Informed me afterwards] had been ill made. The F. & D. Ambulance arrived at billets held by … not any — … me kept slipped 3 a.m. which turn the 6 am … an easy start of the application. The march afforded outside in the C.O. & his friend & … It was known a some strain. Improper stomach trouble. Mr. Allen had gone with the General and staff who had left on Sunday to Winchester after … to the sea journey. Tonight the S.A.D.MS. O'Howard will accompany & … ordered the rations for them him to R. afternoon. & I.p.R not complete	

Army Form C. 2118.

WAR DIARY
or
INTELLIGENCE SUMMARY.
(Erase heading not required.)

Hour, Date, Place	Summary of Events and Information	Remarks and references to Appendices
6.45 pm 21/Feb 1915 Doris.	The 2nd Army HAZEBROUCK continuing. There was offensive Cavinells today in sections of this area billeted in the nights of HAZEBROUCK - including on further billets area of STRAZEELE the morning. Owing to the manner in which the news of the 9 Corps our planes were on any this a day he shows of himself. He Germany any news to know in— but thought infant threats remained trips. Some are enveloped at the head of programme shirts in his system but is action of 2nd Division has been shut on a strong fragment wounded to 6th. It switch accounted of the side at its unity of infants Brigade of Somme twenty time owing in the unfidence who was the end of the fixed machine with change with the— this has led to a close enterprise shell or to his depth they to let with— for one of Small down devoted as being removed every d/c. the news of C™ division Pt to in them reports that 2 can 4 extra-April transports be covered in on of 15C technicals to Ammunitin Park 29/45. as as well is therefore, the west not to observed.	

Army Form C. 2118.

WAR DIARY
or
INTELLIGENCE SUMMARY.
(Erase heading not required.)

Instructions regarding War Diaries and Intelligence Summaries are contained in F.S. Regs., Part II. and the Staff Manual respectively. Title pages will be prepared in manuscript.

Hour, Date, Place	Summary of Events and Information	Remarks and references to Appendices
8.30 a.m. 22nd Jan 1915 Borre	2nd North'n T.F. marched to billets at CAESTRE from I visited the headquarters of 27th Division	MR P.
6 p.m. 23rd Jan 1915	Visited 9 H.Q. the day.	JR
24 Jan 1915	Lt. Col. S.G. ALLEN was admitted to Casualty Clearing Hospital (No. 3) at HAZEBROUCK this day, suffering from Laryngitis & Bronchitis.	JSR
25 Jan Borre	Most of the day was devoted to administration of the Division. It has been necessary to organise a system of Sanitation. As each Brigade Billeting area an officer has been detailed by a field Ambulance as Sanitary Officer. He is assisted by an N.C.O. and one Private from 16 London Sanitary Section to act as Sanitary Inspectors and assist Regimental medical officers in Sanitation matters.	JSR

Army Form C. 2118.

WAR DIARY
or
INTELLIGENCE SUMMARY.
(Erase heading not required.)

Instructions regarding War Diaries and Intelligence Summaries are contained in F. S. Regs., Part II. and the Staff Manual respectively. Title pages will be prepared in manuscript.

Hour, Date, Place	Summary of Events and Information	Remarks and references to Appendices
26. Jan. 1915. BORRE.	The 27th Division is taking our Brigade for the first time supports Divisionally from a form of front line of four. I met the Officers Commanding the Field Ambulances and the Medical Officers in charge of Units to discuss the question of endeavouring to prevent the recent heavy incidence of sick in this Division. Whole it has been found 6 battalions and it is hoped that by feet, rubbing feet and legs with thus once by making socks and boots with the assistance of Corps Mobile Baths before entering the Trenches & reducing the time spent in them to a minimum that a good deal may be done to diminish the numbers of cases.	None
27. Jan. 1915.	The So/Div. MOTOR AMBULANCE WORKSHOP Unit under Lt. D. L. HEWETT reports for duty. The Cars of 3rd London F. Amb. (85) have been attained to undergo some slight alterations (allow fitting of stretchers) as also the 14 Cars available have been temporarily distributed between the three Field Ambulances. Visited all Field Amb & taken advanced Depot Medical Sms.	None

(73989) W4141—463. 400,000. 9/14. H.&J.Ltd. Forms/C. 2118/10.

WAR DIARY
or
INTELLIGENCE SUMMARY

Army Form C. 2118.

Hour, Date, Place	Summary of Events and Information	Remarks and References to Appendices
January 28. 1915. BORRE	Lt. Col. N.C. FERGUSON/BUCHANAN. Took over duties of A.D.M.S. 28th Division. Interviewed Surg: Gen. Pike — D.M.S. 2nd Army at HAZEBROUCK and Major Gen. C. Bulfin commanding 28th Division.	JKR
Tues. 29. BORRE	Visited the three Field Ambulances of the Division and interviewed their Commanding Officers. The Medical units of the Division are formed by the Territorial Force. 1/4th 2nd London Field Ambulance — Lt. Col. W. Salisbury SHARPE. 1/5th 3rd " " " — Lt. Col. J.T. WHAIT. 1/6th 2nd Northumbrian " — Lt. Col. A.D CAMERON. No 15. Sectn. 1st London Sanitary Company. Lieut. C.J. DRAYCOTT.	JKR
Jan. 30. BORRE	Visited proposed sites for Field Ambulances at OUDERDOM and YPRES, with O.C. 3rd F. Amb. and an officer from Northumbrian F.A. At former place the Northumbrian F. Amb. will be established. In the former none small house for use of sick of the troops in the "resting area". In YPRES the 2nd London F.A. will be established.	JKR

Army Form C. 2118.

WAR DIARY
or
INTELLIGENCE SUMMARY.
(Erase heading not required.)

Instructions regarding War Diaries and Intelligence Summaries are contained in F. S. Regs., Part II. and the Staff Manual respectively. Title pages will be prepared in manuscript.

Hour, Date, Place	Summary of Events and Information	Remarks and references to Appendices
Jan. 30. 1915 BORRE.	at the Gymnasium and Riding School, Cavalry Barracks, and the 3rd in the Lunatic Asylum, part of the building is already being used as a hospital for violent cases. During the luncheon by the "French". Branch of the Red Cross Society. Discussed arrangements for water supply & troops with Officer i/charge Water Intendant. The water will be purified by addition of chlorinated lime in the Iron swimming bath which has a capacity of 12 million gallons	JAM
Jan. 31. 1915 BORRE.	Visited YPRES with O.C. 2nd London Field Ambce explaining portion the area by his limit on arrival tomorrow, and scheme for collection of wounded.	JAM
Feb. 1. 1915 BRANDHOEK	Three miles from BORRE to BRANDHOEK school on POPERINGHE - VLAMERTINGHE Road - Accompanied 2 London F. Ambce from their Rendezvous into their position in YPRES.	JAM

WAR DIARY
or
INTELLIGENCE SUMMARY.

(Erase heading not required.)

Army Form C. 2118.

Instructions regarding War Diaries and Intelligence Summaries are contained in F.S. Regs., Part II. and the Staff Manual respectively. Title pages will be prepared in manuscript.

Hour, Date, Place	Summary of Events and Information	Remarks and references to Appendices
Feb. 2. 1915. BRANDHOEK.	Visited YPRES - Inspected the two Field Ambulances there - Arranged for evacuation of cases from YPRES and OUDERDOM to HAZEBROUCK by No 4 Motor Ambulance Convoy - Six Ambulance wagon cars will call at 9 A.M. daily at each hospital - Arranged with Civil contracts in YPRES for conveyance of places to be occupied by troops there. Northumbrian Field Ambulance arrived at OUDERDOM today. Casualties not arrived.	JSL
Feb. 3. 1915. "	Inspected the troops Field Ambulance in YPRES, both are established here now. - The second London Ambulance Casualties Arm 83? Brigade last night - D.M.S. Army visited Head Quarters. here is approves in obtaining permission from Brook authorities King Ambulance Train KPOPERINGHE - ✗ Casualties wounded evacuated 30. died no - remaining 8.	JSL
Feb. 4. 1915. "	Visited Field Ambulances at OUDERDOM - Interviewed O.C. 1st London Sanitary Section with him discussed details of establishing a Divisional washing place here - Submitted requisition Department Concerned for material required for North West Field Ambulances at YPRES.	JSL

Army Form C. 2118.

WAR DIARY
or
INTELLIGENCE SUMMARY.
(Erase heading not required.)

Instructions regarding War Diaries and Intelligence Summaries are contained in F.S. Regs., Part II. and the Staff Manual respectively. Title pages will be prepared in manuscript.

Hour, Date, Place	Summary of Events and Information	Remarks and references to Appendices
Feb. 4. (Cont.) BRANDHOEK.	This afternoon, when turning back the Hearse used to carry the Medical Unit our Motor car driven by a very fast pace collided with an YPRES, a Belgian car driven at a very fast pace collided with an Motor Car in a ditch & the seriously damaged the repaired locally. (See Army No M. 95.) — Reports & Reports of Transport G.H.Q. requisitioned for new Car. —	JSR
Feb. 5. – BRANDHOEK. POPERINGHE	Visited YPRES this morning and arranged for the extension, if necessary, of 3rd London Field Ambulance established at the Lunatic Asylum — to hold No 15 Section London Sanitary Company. — Got out the Schools at BRANDHOEK. Administrative Head Quarters moved to 27 Rue de BOESCHEPPE - POPERINGHE No. 3. Casualty Clearing Station is now established at POPERINGHE and will be the main through dock and any seriously wounded sent forward to HAZEBROUCK will be evacuated.	JSR
Feb. 6. POPERINGHE	Visited Field Ambulance at OOSTERDOM and Sanitary Section at BRANDHOEK. to arrange details of bathing establishment. —	JSR
Feb. 7. "	Visited YPRES in the morning and ABEELE and STEENVOORDE in afternoon with Administrative Staff in Army Corps. Relief with 1st	JSR

WAR DIARY
or
INTELLIGENCE SUMMARY.
(Erase heading not required.)

Army Form C. 2118.

Instructions regarding War Diaries and Intelligence Summaries are contained in F.S. Regs., Part II. and the Staff Manual respectively. Title pages will be prepared in manuscript.

Hour, Date, Place	Summary of Events and Information	Remarks and references to Appendices
POPERINGHE 7/2/14.	Convalescent Depot for the Division.	
" 8/2/14.	Visited Medical Units at OVERDOM. Arranged for Treatment of native details of Artillery Brigade from India there. Her O.C. is Sanitary Section and arranged details of Battery establishment. This will be worked tomorrow. Discussed Sany. Gen. O'Donnell in afternoon – All Field Ambulances have up to establishment with Ambulance Cars.	ASD
" 9.2.14	A Belgian Brigade of Artillery is to be attached to the Division. With the Brigade there is an Establishment of the Medical Officers & 2 Other ranks and Five Motor Cars for Ambulance work – Discussed Medical arrangements for the new Unit with the M.O. decided to attach it as an Extra Section to the 3rd London Field Ambulance – Went to YPRES with Offr i/c Medical Charge. Belgian Artillery explain "arranged" with hospital accommodation refugee.	ASD
10. 2. 14.	Interviewed Surg. Gen. Pike D.M.S. 2. Army. in morning. arranged to visit establishment of Convalescent Depot at STEENVOORDE. In afternoon arranged details with O.C. Antwerpian Field Ambulance for taking over fatoes to draw equipment &c. The detachment 90 m.p. tomorrow.	ASD

Army Form C. 2118.

WAR DIARY
or
INTELLIGENCE SUMMARY.
(Erase heading not required.)

Instructions regarding War Diaries and Intelligence Summaries are contained in F.S. Regs., Part II. and the Staff Manual respectively. Title pages will be prepared in manuscript.

Hour, Date, Place	Summary of Events and Information	Remarks and references to Appendices
11. 2.15. POPERINGHE	Visited bathing place at BRANDHOEK, located supplies at YPRES with O.i/c 49 Army Corps.— In afternoon visited STEENVOORDE, the buildings selected there for the Convalescent Depôt were the Boys' school, Hospice for old men and the Girls' school. A great many of men are suffering from frost bitten feet in parts of the Convalescent Depôt, getting well without oil, evidence of trenching being given in re up D'mington Pet. P. I. the top brigade in the trenches. There were 371 cases.—	MOL
12. 2.15.	Visited YPRES, arranged for new buildings the next by 2nd Lontin Field Ambulance '3' HOSPICE BELLE, ORPHANAGE ST ELIZABETH and HOSPICE O'TEAU and GYMNASIUM One Section of the Ambulance shall working Each building as a separate unit.— In afternoon visited STEENVOORDE Convalescent Station	KR
13. 2.15	Interview with ADMS RMD in question of that the offic Evacuation for Beth Ambulances and the possibility of taking the further buildings as present occupied by 3298 the French for the 3rd Clearing Hospital	MOL

WAR DIARY
or
INTELLIGENCE SUMMARY.
(Erase heading not required.)

Army Form C. 2118.

Instructions regarding War Diaries and Intelligence Summaries are contained in F. S. Regs., Part II. and the Staff Manual respectively. Title pages will be prepared in manuscript.

Hour, Date, Place	Summary of Events and Information	Remarks and references to Appendices
14-2-15 POPERINGHE	Iron rations furnished by Field Ambulances. Made no report in numbers to Corps - found like other Cases of Sickness had up in Rest until in the Division since they have 'gone into' the Trenches. In the afternoon interviewed M.O.M.S. 3rd Cavalry Division re the Evacuation of the wounded. The Division are working on an (plane, ideally) but division has lorries. Received at Col. Cameron C.E. 2nd Northumbrian R.E. Ambulance re Ambulance Wagons. At night, he of the Brigades of the Division were making an attack and heavy Casualties were expected. Went out to the 2/3 London Field Ambulance, Wangen near the Brewery & the Kearsney & Fusilier Ambulance Cars requisitioned by the bearer Subdivision of the Northumbrian F Ambly if necessary should all other means in which most frightly was expected - Brewers at YPRES through the Major to Supervise Collection. Casualties 20 wounded S.R. sick (including frost bite feet)	JSL
15.2.15 "	Interview with C.D.M.S. 2nd army, in question of Orderlies in view of increased number of troops billeting the room billeted here. A Servant sent our to YPRES as our bypass was attacked in P.M.	JSL

Army Form C. 2118.

WAR DIARY
or
INTELLIGENCE SUMMARY.
(Erase heading not required.)

Instructions regarding War Diaries and Intelligence Summaries are contained in F. S. Regs., Part II. and the Staff Manual respectively. Title pages will be prepared in manuscript.

Hour, Date, Place	Summary of Events and Information	Remarks and references to Appendices
16.2.15. POPERINGHE	Visited Convalescent Depôt at STEENVOORDE. The first patients were transported to the establishment today – Visited bathing establishment at ROUSBRUGGE and 2nd London Fd. Ambulance – arranged for immediate clearance by M.A.C. from Ambulance Convoy if cases taken in during the day, during the next 3 days.	JCA
17.2.15. "	Visited STEENVOORDE. Convalescent Rest Station – Visited field ambulances at YPRES, arranged retaining empty Motor Lorries with units on a good many occasions here today in case to carry the day – An attack is being made this evening on a good many Casualties may be expected unless the Grenn Subdivision of Northumbrian Field Ambulances are brought up (exists) in sharing wounded. Advanced Divisional Commander explained Medical arrangements to the attack. Lieut Campbell RAMC (Flying Corps) M.O. 4. 2. East Yorks was killed in action today.	KM
18.2.15. "	Visited YPRES Estd. D.M.S. 2nd Army inspected water supply, conservancy arrangements and 2nd London – Fd. Ambulance – Capt Hyatt RAMC senior in Mc Aneen with 28th Division being quilling Lt. A.W. Kuffer RAMC (Temp Comm) named for duty – Posted to 2 East York Regt.	KM
19.2.15. "	Inspected Convalescent Station at STEENVOORDE –	
	A.D.M.S. Vernon-Taylor (joined the Division and took over medical charge)[signature]	AV

WAR DIARY
or
INTELLIGENCE SUMMARY.
(Erase heading not required.)

Army Form C. 2118.

Hour, Date, Place	Summary of Events and Information	Remarks and references to Appendices
POPERINGHE 19-2-15	146 Battery RFA on discharge nr.ly Lieut W. McINTOSH who joined No 3 Casualty Clearing Station. Lt T. D. Inch (SR) joined the Division as Interpreter. Field Ambulances (T.C.) 1/5 & 1/6 Transferred and despatched to Poperinghe. Their missing unit awaits arrival of 84th (2nd Loan) Field Company reconnaissance	ASR
" 20.2.15	Inspected Chateaux Rest Station. Staff-working Satisfactorily and history of water for bath &c. Distribution of Products, Clothing and supply of water for bath &c.	ASR
" 21.2.15	Visited YPRES. Inspected Ambulances, arrangements and water supply. 13th Infantry Brigade joined the Division on lyf passing the 83rd in the Trenches Wednesday 24th inst. Lieut D. R. ROBERTS R.A.M.C. (Temp.Com.) arrived for duty and is posted at Poperinge July 1/86 (Northumbrian) Field Ambulance	ASR
22-2.15.	Visited YPRES. Inspected 84th (2nd Loan) Field Ambulance, and made arrangements for their Horses. Re billetted near the Asylum. W. of YPRES. They are at present occupying the Riding School in YPRES which is required for other military purposes.	ASR

WAR DIARY or INTELLIGENCE SUMMARY

Army Form C. 2118.

(Erase heading not required.)

Instructions regarding War Diaries and Intelligence Summaries are contained in F. S. Regs., Part II. and the Staff Manual respectively. Title pages will be prepared in manuscript.

Hour, Date, Place	Summary of Events and Information	Remarks and References to Appendices
POPERINGHE 22 - 2 - 15	Visited STEENVOORDE in afternoon. There are 1547 cases in the Divisional Rest Station here now. Lieut B. TENNANT - R.A.M.C. (Terr. Bn.) reported his arrival and is posted to the 84th (2nd Lincoln) Field Ambulance pro. tem.	ASM
23 - 2 - 15	Visited 84th and 83rd Field Ambulances at YPRES. Arranges for evacuation of 228 sick to VLAMERTINGHE.	ASM
24 - 2 - 15	Visited acting A.D.M.S. Army.	
25 - 2 - 15	Visited 8.C. (Northumbrian) Field Ambulance. Following changes have recently taken place in composition of the 27th Division. 83 and 84th Brigades have been reduced by 9th & 12th B.N.s from 3rd 1st Division. The 1st & 13th B.S. Monmouthshire Regts. and 5th K.O. Royal Lancs. have also joined the Division; all these units are complete in Field Amb. establishment.	ASM
26 - 2 - 15.	Inspected new Lake water supply just erected at OUDERDOM for troops in the rest camp area.	AR
27 - 2 - 15.	Went to STEENVOORDE to inspect the Convalescent Rest Station, and arrange for water supply. At present the only available water is from a shallow well too.	ASM

Army Form C. 2118.

WAR DIARY
or
INTELLIGENCE SUMMARY
(Erase heading not required.)

Instructions regarding War Diaries and Intelligence Summaries are contained in F. S. Regs., Part II. and the Staff Manual respectively. Title pages will be prepared in manuscript.

Hour, Date, Place	Summary of Events and Information	Remarks and References to Appendices
POPERINGHE 27-2-15	There is a firm supply which is present to be made from N.E.C. & expective machinery; decided negotiations with Civil authorities twenty-three men as may use the free water and baths. The Field Committee reported during the month have been 4801, sick, 1 which 2756 have been cases of "Chilled feet" and 1828 wounded.	HQ
POPERINGHE 28.2.15	Visited the two Field Ambulances & water supply at YPRES and the baths at BRANDHOEK.	HQ
1-3-15	Inspected Field Ambulance at YPRES. and arranged that the regular Officer temporarily attached (Major Clement & Major Richards RAMC) rejoin their permanent Field Ambulance Command.	HQ
2.3.15	Acting D.M.S. 2d Army visited & , this morning Inspected Convalescent Rest Station at STEENWORDE; the baths there are now in working order.	HQ
3.3.15	Inspected site for new hutments near OUDERDOM - Selected buildings & hospital for YPRES and on the commencing work indication More Appendix 18.	A.6.

(9 26 6) W 257 -976 100,000 4/12 H W V 79/3298

WAR DIARY
or
INTELLIGENCE SUMMARY
(Erase heading not required.)

Army Form C. 2118.

Instructions regarding War Diaries and Intelligence Summaries are contained in F. S. Regs., Part II. and the Staff Manual respectively. Title pages will be prepared in manuscript.

Hour, Date, Place	Summary of Events and Information	Remarks and References to Appendices
3-4-3-15. POPERINGHE	Inspected the Convalescent Rest Station STEENVOORDE, arranged for the use of the Steam Disinfector at the French Hospital Extraordinaire Manche for the Convalescent Station. (App 19.)	ASM
5-3-15 POPERINGHE	Prepared and rendered report for February on of working Bathing establishment express during February we bore men, the baths and the same number of sets of clothing were washed — The initial cost was of 13.15.0 and the weekly cost, including Coal, Civilian labour for sundry work, reserving soap to clean 800 men and their clothing is £14..0..6.0 approximately. E.i.e a mean rate of clothing — (App 20) Inspected the half male supply at YPRES.	ASM
6.3.15	Visited YPRES. A supply of water-tight paper mackers in the suppression of the will prevent the incidence of "chilled feet" and keep the men's feet and legs dry, arranged with brigades that the units going into the trenches tomorrow and three following days will enter these the M.O's of battalions rendering a report on the effect after their turn in the trenches. — Tonight they were issued to the Norfolk Regt. —	ASM

Army Form C. 2118.

WAR DIARY
or
INTELLIGENCE SUMMARY
(Erase heading not required.)

Instructions regarding War Diaries and Intelligence Summaries are contained in F. S. Regs., Part II, and the Staff Manual respectively. Title pages will be prepared in manuscript.

Hour, Date, Place	Summary of Events and Information	Remarks and References to Appendices
7.3.16. POPERINGHE.	Complaints have been made by some Medical Officers in charge of Battalions of the overcrowding of the New Poperinghe Water Cart. The Cage which supports the Sleeping Tubes is not strong enough to withstand the pressure of the water in the cylinder when a large of must is dependent on the Stove. Regimental Medical Officers cope with Brigade of Machine V Corps. he will arrange to take the matter and try to improve the condition. Examined several Regimental Medical Officers. Supplemented paper orders issued to R.M.O. each Regt. the Regimental gave out the Brooches today.	HQR
8.3.16. "	Inspected Convalescent Rest Station, STEENVOORDE; Adj. Wingate will have the Hut of the Presbyterian Field Ambulance. 86th Brigade upon which he will return this permanent hut. A Travelling Sanp Kitchen belonging to the Red Cross Society, was sent to the Division today, sent it to YPRES the attached to 2.3 London (Fd.) Field Ambulance.	HQR
9.3.16. "	Interviewed several Medical Officers in Charge of Units. Arranged with O.C. Cavalry Brigade for disinfection of New Hamlet after their bath. Inspected W.O.C. of Kingspot Section. Sent D.A.D.M.S. to inspect Water Reg. on 75 where new Divisional troops support a Paper Section.	HQR

(9 26 6) W 257-976 100,000 4/12 H W V 79/3298

Army Form C. 2118.

WAR DIARY
OF
INTELLIGENCE SUMMARY
(Erase heading not required.)

Instructions regarding War Diaries and Intelligence Summaries are contained in F. S. Regs., Part II. and the Staff Manual respectively. Title pages will be prepared in manuscript.

Hour, Date, Place	Summary of Events and Information	Remarks and References to Appendices
10. 3. 15. POPERINGHE	Visited YPRES. Inspected 14th Field Ambulance Rest. The number of sick reaching the Casualty Clearing Station is said to be large. Motors arranged that seventy beds are occupied in British Ambulances, with eight cases & 45 in P&I & 2 that in the division including Rest Station of 50% beds.	JHR
11. 3. 15.	Visited Field Ambulances at YPRES in morning — saw D.C. TURNBULL R.A.M.C. (T.C.) who was seriously wounded through the lung yesterday while attempting to rescue a wounded man of 1st Cheshire Regt. from the trenches. His gallant conduct was officially recognised today where by the O.C. 1st Cheshire Regt. — Inspected the latter of the regiment in support at ELVERDINGHE, arranged for post & Cavalry Station to undertake supervision & sanitation of billets	JHR
12. 3. 15.	Inspected Horses of the three Field Ambulances with R.A.V.S. as 2nd 2 2nd Army. has heard reports that they are in poor condition, found the horses most cared for but some inadequate transfer has received from a firm J. Chesler Kent was standing in mud. Submitted report (app. 21) to D.D.M.S. II Army. In afternoon visited STEENVOORDE Cept. representative of British Red Cross Society, arranged with them for supply of certain articles — photo- for hot drinks, what the Divisions were unable to obtain. —	JHR
13. 3. 15.	Inspected the billets of the brigade in the Reserve area with Col. the Hon'ble	JHR

WAR DIARY
or
INTELLIGENCE SUMMARY

(Erase heading not required.)

Army Form C. 2118.

Hour, Date, Place	Summary of Events and Information	Remarks and References to Appendices
12.3.15 POPERINGHE	Officers in charge of the Battalion - Inspected men of Duke of Wellington Regt. under the Osst in the Riverine Hospital for DofW L/C.	
14.3.15 POPERINGHE	M. D.C. TURNBULL died of wounds this Saturday morning.	HQR
14.3.15	Inspected billets & Divisional Ammunition Column and Divisional Train near Balie in charge. Received information from Gen. Staff that heavy Casualties might be expected this evening from Southern Sector of our Line. Arranged for evacuation of Ambulances 6th & 3rd Cavalry Cleary Station by 17th Motor Ambulance Convoy. Cav. Reserve Division Cav. Field Ambulance Inspre Evening Ret. (25 London) from 86 (Northumbrian) Field Ambulance. Maj W.T. McCarthy. R.A.M.C. (S.R.) M.O. 1st Norfolk Regt. killed in action this evening.	HQR
15.3.15	Inspected with D.M.S. 2nd Army. The Convalescent Rest Station, Hertainere & Watering establishment - The following officers arrived were posted units opposite their names - Lt. M. CRONIN. R.A.M.C. (T.C.) to 8/4 (2 London) Field Ambulance. Lt. J.M. FORSYTH " 1st Cheshire Regt. Lt. H.C. TURIANSKY. - 1st Norfolk Regt.	HQR
16.3.15	Inspected billets of 3rd and 146 Brig RFA and Surry Yeomanry. Two M.E.O's of 15 Sanitary Section Ranc T. was killed by shell this morning.	HQR
17.3.15	Inspected billet of 3rd and 8th Brig RFA. Submitted Recommendation for disposal of dead bodies in Trench area which cannot be buried. App 22

WAR DIARY
or
INTELLIGENCE SUMMARY

(Erase heading not required.)

Army Form C. 2118.

Instructions regarding War Diaries and Intelligence Summaries are contained in F. S. Regs., Part II. and the Staff Manual respectively. Title pages will be prepared in manuscript.

Hour, Date, Place	Summary of Events and Information	Remarks and References to Appendices
POPERINGHE 18. 3. 15.	29 N.C.O's and men arrived from their Reserve Units as reinforcement for the three Field Ambulances and Sanitary Section. Inspected Bart: 9 D.T. Hopes to 69 with Divisional Corps Commander. Submitted those Hospels report to Convalescent Rest Station A.D.M.S. 2 Army. app 23. Inspected Convalescent Rest Station with A.A.Q.M.G. 28 Division.	MGR
" 19. 3. 15.	Inspected site for Field Ambulance & the meeting area as it is possible that it may be necessary to take up QUDERDOM; found two farms which could be used as BASSEBOOM. Also inspected billet of Heavy Artillery Brigade. Went out to the Field Ambulances at YPRES in the afternoon.	MGR
" 20. 3. 15.	Visited the billets of the R.E. and Artillery in rear YPRES. Sent Lieut Brooke McCormack wheeled Stretchers to 85. (3 London) Field Ambulance for use between Regimental Aid posts & the point at which wounded are transferred to Motor Ambulance Cars, that will also be utilized for carrying rations to trenches. Divisional Commander inspected Convalescent Rest Station STEENVOORDE.	MGR
21. 3. 15.	Discussed Sanitation of Standing Camp area with D.M.S. 2nd Army, these camps (permanent) are becoming more or less permanent Rest Camps now and require a more permanent Sanitary Organisation to improve the State. Are engaged with Sanitary Officer	MGR

Army Form C. 2118.

Army Form C. 2118.

WAR DIARY
or
INTELLIGENCE SUMMARY.
(Erase heading not required.)

Instructions regarding War Diaries and Intelligence Summaries are contained in F. S. Regs., Part II. and the Staff Manual respectively. Title pages will be prepared in manuscript.

Hour, Date, Place	Summary of Events and Information	Remarks and references to Appendices
22. 3-15 POPERINGHE	Inspected Huts & hutments with Sanitary Officer arranged for deep trench latrines as a temporary measure.	ASR
23. 3.15	Visited Resting Camps of 6th & 4th Divisions with the A.D.M.S. of the Divisions & Sanitary Officer. They have a system of screened cess pits which would answer for this Division. Submitted Report on these to 2nd Division. App. 24.	ASR
24. 3.15	Five Cases of Enteric Fever having occurred in R.D. Battery RFA in ten days. Inspected the billets occupied by this unit. An investigation found cause of Enteric had occurred. Army Civilian occupying farm had been seen ill or cases of diarrhoea in the horses — Arranged for evacuation by the R.E.	ASR
25. 3.15	Accompanied D.G.M.S. at inspection of 63rd (2 London) Field Ambulance. Proposed site for small Convalescent Rest Station at convent &c. at STEENVOORDE in connection for the Midland Division or units.	ASR
26. 3.15	Chosen Sanitary Officer to render daily report to make supply of the Hospitals. Much is kept unsatisfactory — Interviewed D.M.S. Second Army.	ASR

Army Form C. 2118.

WAR DIARY
or
INTELLIGENCE SUMMARY.
(Erase heading not required.)

Instructions regarding War Diaries and Intelligence Summaries are contained in F.S. Regs., Part II. and the Staff Manual respectively. Title pages will be prepared in manuscript.

Hour, Date, Place	Summary of Events and Information	Remarks and references to Appendices
26.3.15. POPERINGHE	To meet the airplane & the maker Capper (Mr DICKEBUSCH Aerodome) Report APP 25 attached	AN
27.3.15.	Inspected the Hutments at VLAMERTINGHE – OUDERDOM Road – Conveninent Rest Station at STEENVOORDE Closed	AN
28.3.15.	Sweer Convalescent Rest Station and CONVENT of BRABANT N of Poperinghe HOOGRAAF	
29.3.15.	Inspected Convalescent Rest Station, 27 patients remaining today	
30.3.15.	Visited Infantry Barracks YPRES was 14 O.M.E. and arrived to a new Carillon System as many tramway charges among the troops in Barracks. They are at present dirty and unsanitary. A permanent fatigue party under the sanitary section to be carried out and attitude detailed and stats help cleaning the whole place thoroughly	AN
31.3.15	Visited the Convalescent Rest Station. Investigated cases of Cerebro-Spinal meningitis among D.a.c Ammunition Column. Total Number of cases reported during the month. Sick 2447. Wounded 2181.	AN

[signatures]

A.D.M.S. 28th Division

April 1915.

A.D.M.S 28 Army Form C. 2118.
Division

WAR DIARY
or
INTELLIGENCE SUMMARY.
(Erase heading not required.)

Instructions regarding War Diaries and Intelligence Summaries are contained in F.S. Regs., Part II. and the Staff Manual respectively. Title pages will be prepared in manuscript.

Hour, Date, Place	Summary of Events and Information	Remarks and references to Appendices
April 1. 1915. POPERINGHE.	Inspected the whole of the Camps occupied by the Rowing League. Visited Convalescent Rest Station at HOOGGRAFF.	ADM
April 2. 1915. "	Accompanied D.M.S. 2nd Army over Sanitary Commission round premises POPERDOM — water supply YPRES — and bathing establishment BRANDHOEK.	ADM
April 3. 1915. "	Re military disposition of troops necessitates that the British take over artillery areas in VLAMERTINGHE, and YPRES (vide pp 27th 5th and Canadian Divisions) – Interviewed D.M.S. 2nd Army & discussed Sanitary arrangements for increased number of trops –	ADM
April 4. 1915 "	Arranged billets for 86 & 84 Field Ambulances – (5th Division formations) being to YPRES (find suitable plan for field Ambulances in our new area – Scheme for collection in this area ready about app 26.	ADM
April 5. 1915 "	Interviewed Col Nickers A.M.S. who arrived today to take over duties of D.D.M.S. 5th Army Corps. 84, 86 Field Ambulances were relieved by 14 & 15 Field Ambulances. Inspected Convalescent Rest Station – 84 & 7 Rifles were struck by shell last night. Two men being killed and ten wounded.	ADM
April 6. 1915. "	Went over French Hospital in Chateau VLAMERTINGHE with M.O. in Charge with a view of ascertaining how many beds he had unfit for cases received. The building will not be fit for handing over for 10 – 15 days as there are several structural & security repairs upon been carried in it.	ADM

WAR DIARY or INTELLIGENCE SUMMARY.

Army Form C. 2118.

(Erase heading not required.)

Instructions regarding War Diaries and Intelligence Summaries are contained in F.S. Regs., Part II. and the Staff Manual respectively. Title pages will be prepared in manuscript.

Hour, Date, Place	Summary of Events and Information	Remarks and references to Appendices
April 6. 1915. POPERINGHE -	Inspected the Institute of the Holy Family YPRES with the Officer Commanding the 11th Field Ambulance. This building is capable of accommodating 130 patients and the personnel of a Field Ambulance and will be taken over by 56th (Northumbrian) Field Amb.t tomorrow — Scheme of Collection Stations from Feb.y 2 & ends reversed.	J.F.R. App. 26.
April 7. 1915. "	Arranged to move 56 Field Ambulance to Institute of Holy Family YPRES today. The 84th and 85th Field Ambce Divns. to POPERINGHE and Bearer Divisions 85th Fd. Amb.e to Hazebrouck Station. Institute of Holy Family YPRES on 9th inst: (see Rzen E. 28 Divisional orders 96. and 97.	App. 26.
April 8. 1915.	84th Fd. Amb. H.Q. in Cavalry Barracks YPRES. Their Bearer Division in the Collection of their Casualties by Bearer Division 85.t F.Amb.e & Bearer Divn. to collect Station in Institute of Holy Family YPRES.	J.F.R.
April 9. 1915.	85th Field Ambulance — (2nd London) moved from YPRES to - The Boys school RUE de BASSIN to RUE DE BRASSERIE. Col. 85th Fd. Bearer Divn. moved to the School of the Convent of the Resident. 12 RUE DE BRUGES - POPERINGHE. Bearer Divn. 85th - moved to Institute of Holy Family YPRES.	J.F.R.
April 10. 1915.	Inspected the Ecole Lueile Melheur Rue EINGLE de THIERET. In this building in addition to accommodating a battalion of Infantry, a Field Ambulance, with room for 250 & 300 patients could be established -	J.F.R.

(73989) W4141—463. 400,000. 9/14. H.&J.Ltd. Forms/C. 2118/10.

Army Form C. 2118.

WAR DIARY
or
INTELLIGENCE SUMMARY.
(Erase heading not required.)

Instructions regarding War Diaries and Intelligence Summaries are contained in F. S. Regs., Part II. and the Staff Manual respectively. Title pages will be prepared in manuscript.

Hour, Date, Place	Summary of Events and Information	Remarks and references to Appendices
April 11. 1915 Poperinghe	Onwards scheme for evacuation prepared from hour area - App 27 & 28	App 27 — 28.
April 12. 1915.	Received D.M.S. 2nd Army request * met. The but ambulances B.S. (3 Linas) Gibson Army to the made available (See App. NOTES). Inspected new huts and temporary build: (?) B.F.A. Bivouac and Chateau at VLAMERTINGHE to be used as Divisional Rest Stations.	NOTES.
April 13. 1915	Submitted short report on the work done of the Division. Also have we done the work and time of the Campaigns. The ones here all see (one of E. Therouanne, Cleary, etc) a modification or Variation in Trainway, all as now well or has been. The pump is to procure to the Clarifying cylinders as per the unit cope supporting to Weiny clerk becomes or the refuse sinkers, the joints between the Clarifying Cylinders Tanks and its spirit not sting all are not not or the later. Nov 1 the under stand the utility of the pant covers road, tops, roofs, clerk.—	NOTES App 29.
April 14 1915.	Submitted Report on suggested reduction of the scale of rations. App. 29. Submitted Supervisor of drafts suggestion would means of practical wartage especially the institution of Corps Convalescent Rest Stations to be organized in connection with + Stationary Hospitals, this would have all the advantages of a Divisional resting station without considering a Field Ambulance unavailable for mass to carry out its proper functions —	NOTES

WAR DIARY
or
INTELLIGENCE SUMMARY.
(Erase heading not required.)

Army Form C. 2118.

Hour, Date, Place	Summary of Events and Information	Remarks and references to Appendices
April 16. POPERINGHE	Inspected the New Field Ambulance of the Division, all are now ready. Visits to Sick mounted too in YPRES sent one in POPERINGHE the others in addition. Visited in turn of the sick of the Division will carry out the duties of a Convalescent Rest Station.	JFR
8. A.M.	G.S. informed in view the attack upon the sector of the trenches held by this Division might be expected that not the complete Bearer Subdivisions from each Field Amb to YPRES. The remainder standing ready there. The Cars + as many bearers as they could carry to the Ambulances in POPERINGHE were by 9 am there as a Motor Ambce. I ascertained myself at Fd. Amb. Amb 9 and 10 and arranged that new Orders would come from the Sy. F.A. should it be necessary then.	
April 17.	Interviewed D.D.M.S. army RycCorps - Inspected billets of 3rd Bn RFA. and the advanced Dressing Station	
April 18.	Inspected billets and Wagon lines of 31st Bde and 8th Howitzer Bde RFA. One Officer killed and 2 wounded from Northern Battalion in our sector, this part of the line was only taken over from the Canadians Yesterday, It is impossible keep the Motor Ambulance Car within 3½ miles of the Regimental Aid post owing the bad	

Army Form C. 2118.

WAR DIARY
or
INTELLIGENCE SUMMARY.
(Erase heading not required.)

Instructions regarding War Diaries and Intelligence Summaries are contained in F.S. Regs., Part II. and the Staff Manual respectively. Title pages will be prepared in manuscript.

Hour, Date, Place	Summary of Events and Information	Remarks and references to Appendices
April 18. POPERINGHE.	Surface of the road, three miles of the distance between Cassel can be used by the horse Ambulances before the remaining distance will be covered by the field Ambulance bearers.	MSR
April. 19.	Inspected billets of 31st 5th RFA wagon lines and 8th Howitzer Brigade.	MSR
April 20	Inspected billets, wagon lines of 146th, 18th RFA. There was a good deal of shelling of YPRES today. Casualties relieved by men of 86 (Northumbrian) Field Ambulance remained.	MSR
April 21. POPERINGHE	G.O.C. – I Corps decided that this Ambulance should be moved from YPRES. 85 (3rd London) remained to convert of Brielen – POPERINGHE Range The road. 86 (Northumbrian) ordered to be moved about 1½ mile E of POPERINGHE and parked there. All wounded are now taken to the advanced dressing station at VERDRENHOEK from Chateau of ELVERDINGHE first.	MSR
VLAMERTINGHE.		
April 22. VLAMERTINGHE. 4 PM	Inspected new billets near VLAMERTINGHE with O.C. sanitary Section. Went I considered present on my left. The possibility of a return G.C.E. is such that Administrative staff should move to POPERINGHE –	MSR

(73989) W4141–463. 400,000. 9/14. H.&J.Ltd. Forms/C. 2118/10.

Army Form C. 2118.

WAR DIARY
or
INTELLIGENCE SUMMARY.
(Erase heading not required.)

Instructions regarding War Diaries and Intelligence Summaries are contained in F. S. Regs., Part II. and the Staff Manual respectively. Title pages will be prepared in manuscript.

Hour, Date, Place	Summary of Events and Information	Remarks and references to Appendices
April 22. VLAMERTINGHE.	Issued orders that Frontier Units the proposed attack at short notice. arranged that an enemy from 2nd Ambulance remained at 3rd echelon to Army orders.— Move to PEPERINGHE 6 A.M.	HQ
April 23. PEPERINGHE	Advanced dressing Station moved from VLAMERTINGHE to POTYZE during the day. Discussed O.C. 3rd Field Ambulance troops and arranged echelon for evacuation & intended the casualty to keep casualties all officers—Ranks. 1 Ambulance Car & all men will be retained. Submitted list of names of Officers NCOs ranks recommended for gallantry and work. (app. 30.) Lieut V.A. Wade (85 (Northumbrian Field Amb.)) and Lieut R.E. Barnsley left wounded the East Riding also one Sergeant 84. F. Amb. This second attempt has been ambulance ushered 626 tot 127.	app 30. HQ HQ
April 24.	Considerable fighting on all flank. That wounded evacuated by this division in this Field Ambulance 349. Our Ranks Private wounded—	HQ
April 25.	Wounded embarked 610— The NCO's men of 84. F. Amb. wounded, are two injured by accidental (rifle) report.	HQ

Army Form C. 2118.

WAR DIARY
or
INTELLIGENCE SUMMARY.
(Erase heading not required.)

Instructions regarding War Diaries and Intelligence Summaries are contained in F.S. Regs., Part II. and the Staff Manual respectively. Title pages will be prepared in manuscript.

Hour, Date, Place	Summary of Events and Information	Remarks and references to Appendices
POPERINGHE April 26.	Collecting Station was established at village of ST JEAN and POTYJZE. Buried received of 207th through this station 248.	JHCL
April 22 11.am POPERINGEN	Scott Parker (Administrator) Present Room POPERINGHE to Chateau MACEWAN at COATHOVE near PEUVEN. Number of Wounded Evacuated 220. Cars on the way to collected from Regimental aid Post suddenly seen at St JEAN (83rd Y 85 and Batty) and POTYJZE and have branched to WESTERTIMME. Ambulance Cars from 27 Division steadily on our Cars — Trucks were reported held in aid Post & 30 Re Bouillon M.W.F. ZOUGEBEGE) Have been not located what happens this morning so tried that he wouldn't stop	JHCL
April 26. Nov POPEREN.	Number of Wounded Evacuated from Church Militchy Station 250 New Pickler. The tucks mean & 3 Dentro spokes whiskey all returned for air Post and both beilies certain close at 4 am this morning.	JHR

(73989) W4141—463. 400,000. 9/14. H.&J.Ltd. Forms/C. 2118/10.

Army Form C. 2118.

WAR DIARY
or
INTELLIGENCE SUMMARY.
(Erase heading not required.)

Instructions regarding War Diaries and Intelligence Summaries are contained in F. S. Regs., Part II. and the Staff Manual respectively. Title pages will be prepared in manuscript.

Hour, Date, Place	Summary of Events and Information	Remarks and references to Appendices
April 29.1915 AM PROVEN	Interviewed D.D.M.S. V Corps and Officer Commanding Field Ambulance re evacuation this morning. — 115 cases received from Casualty Station during the night. From the trying nature of the work, apart of the Motor Ambulance Car drivers are feeling the strain, in order that they keep down the spare drivers are kept decreased, instead of two drivers being allowed for each car. four drivers are the allotted for each car in the evacuation of the wounded. In them having had access been taken ground is clear passage now with severe experience junior cars are thrown on longer services.	1/2 R
April 30. 1915	D.A.S. cars evacuated up to 6 a.m. this morning. ferrying the Canadian Hospital evacuees from VLAMERTINGHE to the after 3 a.m. all cars were sent to POPERINGHE (park being occupying) about 24 hours. All cars from French Station Evacuy Station, between Sta. dies Champs at POPERINGHE. 2.30 AM from Dressing Section of POPERINGHE. - 148 cases stated evacuated from the station. Returned D.M.S. V Corps O.C. Field Ambulance re carrying on duties -	1/2 R

May. 1915.

ADMS 28th Division.

28th Divn
May 1915

Army Form C. 2118.

WAR DIARY
or
INTELLIGENCE SUMMARY.
(Erase heading not required.)

Instructions regarding War Diaries and Intelligence Summaries are contained in F. S. Regs., Part II. and the Staff Manual respectively. Title pages will be prepared in manuscript.

Hour, Date, Place	Summary of Events and Information	Remarks and references to Appendices
MAY 1. PROVEN	Following Officers joined the Division from the Training Depots their names:	JTKR
	Lieut. A. CURRIE. (TC) 12. Heavy Brigade R.G.A.	
	" H.J. MOSS (TC) Company L.I. now with 35. Langon Company attached for G.A. 7 days.	
	" J.T. HEFFERNAN (TC) 2 Royal Fusiliers now Capt. VALENTINE Munro On Div. HQ 29.4.15.	
	" J.N. DOBBIE. (TC) 85. Field Ambce - vice M.R. BARNSLEY wounded 22-4-15.	
	" R.W. BROWNE. (S.R.) 86. Field Ambce now H M.R. WARD LS Wounded 22-4-15.	
	Revd. C. F. J. DANBURY. C.F.(4th) 84 F.Ambce. (lately Achieved for C.C.S.)	
	Inspected site for 85. Field Ambce with A.C. branch attached from A.D. from 142. Casy. Main Ambulance from Dressing Station 2.66.	
MAY 2. PROVEN	85. Field Ambulance moved to HOPPOUTRE. Inspected site for 85 Field Ambulance in 28 Div area - Ambulance moved forward.	JTKR
	No 15. Sanitary Section moved from BRAND HOEK to PLACE BERTIN BRENBERG. Collected from A.M. 20-5 1918-128.	
	Rejoined Sanitation Buyck 84. F.Amb. duty vayl.	

(73989) W4141—463. 400,000. 9/14. H.&J.Ltd. Forms/C. 2118/10.

Army Form C. 2118.

WAR DIARY
or
INTELLIGENCE SUMMARY.
(Erase heading not required.)

Instructions regarding War Diaries and Intelligence Summaries are contained in F.S. Regs., Part II. and the Staff Manual respectively. Title pages will be prepared in manuscript.

Hour, Date, Place	Summary of Events and Information	Remarks and references to Appendices
May 3. 1915 PRISEN.	Casualties are still considerable, as the distance between the collecting stations (ST JEAN and POTYJZE) and dressing station is approximately 9 miles and the roads are such the not 9 Colloby is ill/proper. Motor Camp by hand from the Regimental aid post to a point near VELORINGHER about 800 yds from POTYJZE where the ambulance car carry the cases the advance. From this point they are carried to POPERINGHE by ambulance car, a motor Kitchen being retained about half way which furnished patients with hot soup &c. Cases collected last night 150. Total at 84.7 amb. and evacuated 966.	J.T.M
May 4. 1915 PRISEN.	The Division took up a new line & trenches last night with three members occupied, the arrangement tha all aid posts retired in scheme at 1 a.m.— The stretcher and S.B.S. been with them officers were sent out for this Coy & all the Divisional motor ambulance cars with 50 cars by 10th ambulance cars were employed. 748 cases were collected between dark that am and 794 approximately 30 cases were not brought as to the PRISEN in charge he Section was placed by a Brigade Staff officer to clear FREZEHBERG ridge where the case were found the attached report app.32a)	app 32 - 32.a. J.T.M

Army Form C. 2118.

WAR DIARY
or
INTELLIGENCE SUMMARY.
(Erase heading not required.)

Instructions regarding War Diaries and Intelligence Summaries are contained in F.S. Regs., Part II. and the Staff Manual respectively. Title pages will be prepared in manuscript.

Hour, Date, Place	Summary of Events and Information	Remarks and references to Appendices
May 5 1915. PROVEN.	In the new position the Battery situated at POTYZE and ST JEAN has become untenable and an advanced dressing station has been opened in the bank SAAS CANAL near the Asylum, YPRES. There are excellent cellars in this building well adapted for an advanced dressing station. – The officers' mess PROVEN village tram. – Casualties collected last night 231. – Total prisoners 8 off. 2 camps 536. Collections were undertaken by 63 Fld Ambg with all Cars of the Division.	JFR
May 6. 1915.	Proposed report on Ramc. work during recent operations at request of A.Q.M.G. App. 32. Cases collected last night 126. – Total sick 611	App. 32. WRR
May 7. 1915.	Wounded collected last night 150. Sick 266. – Submitted report on field supplies (App. 33) The enemy since April 23 have been using a poisonous gas apparently chlorine, which has seriously affected the efficiency of our troops. The men come to hospital depressed with signs of bronchitis – (Bronchitis Acute Chronica M) in some cases. There is a risk of temperature or in the very severe cases – including sore throat	App 33 JFR

(73989) W4141—463. 400,000. 9/14. H.&J.Ltd. Forms/C. 2118/10.

WAR DIARY
or
INTELLIGENCE SUMMARY.
(Erase heading not required.)

Army Form C. 2118.

Instructions regarding War Diaries and Intelligence Summaries are contained in F.S. Regs., Part II. and the Staff Manual respectively. Title pages will be prepared in manuscript.

Hour, Date, Place	Summary of Events and Information	Remarks and references to Appendices
	Case with very rapid acute pneumonia.	
	As an antidote Nitrite of Amyl – citric acid soaked in Hyposulphite of Soda and an alkali are being used. For treatment the Cases receive the hypodermic & gentle inhalation of Oxygen. Also by Duof-Nichols – Who covers all the hot water Oxygen Bed in all cases. There is better in the open Man in a bed.	JSR
May 8. 1915. PROVEN	Wounded evacuated last night 176. Touched Guns in Brewery Station. The 84 F. Ambg. moved from PPPERINGHE home farm S.W. of the line where the Gnl. Griven will remain close to the poison. The training activities will now be found by 85 Fd Ambce at mattresses – partly in School building, partly under Canvas, extra tent being borrowed from F8 Fd. An application has been recommended by DDmS V Corps the Field Ambulance be increased with the full establishment of Cars for sick vig 36 per Field Ambulance in addition to the 12 Bell tent and these specially tents have carried by each unit, the extra tents will be carried in horse Ambulance wagons as, on the march the Ambulance Cars attend carry any sick accompanying the Division.	JSR
May 9. PROVEN	Last night heavy Casualties were exposed in the trenches. The heavy rain...	JSR

(73989) W4141—463. 400,000. 9/14. H.&J.Ltd. Forms/C. 2118/10.

Army Form C. 2118.

WAR DIARY
or
INTELLIGENCE SUMMARY.
(Erase heading not required.)

Instructions regarding War Diaries and Intelligence Summaries are contained in F. S. Regs., Part II. and the Staff Manual respectively. Title pages will be prepared in manuscript.

Hour, Date, Place	Summary of Events and Information	Remarks and references to Appendices
MAY 9. 1915. PROVEN	One Hundred Bearers, 17 Motor Ambulance Cars with Capt. RAWES 84 Field Amb. & one junior Officer were employed in clearing Regimental Aid Posts to be Shelter 70 bearers and 7 Cars presently at R.P. of 6th Br. 7 Brigade where they were met from by quite from Battalions. Several Regiments were very a Chateau nor H.Q. & an aid post & these were clearly a considerable number of wounded & all these aid posts being a proportion of bearer went forward from these points. Wounded were evacuated to the Lunatic Asylum at YPRES where a but subdivision of 86 F. Amb. had established an advanced dressing station in the cellars which are large and safe. From the Lunatic Asylum Cars were sent after being unloaded for K. sent to the Dressing Station formed by 85 (3 London) Field Amb. at HOOGRAAF — partly in Small School and partly under Canvas. The evacuation from YPRES was superintended by an Officer of 84 F. Amb. (Capt BICKERTON). The Ambulance Cars of the Division East made two journeys. Ten Cars of No 4. Motor Ambs. Convoy made two journeys. The Three Horse Ambulance Wagons of 85 (3 London) F. Amb. made one journey. The Bearer wagon of 28. Div. Train made one journey. The remaining slightly sitting up cases were carried in ordinary Regimental supply Carts. The Aid Posts were all cleared by 4.40 a.m. when the evacuation of YPRES commenced and all were cleared with equipment & ammunition &c at 9. am. Distance from aid posts to Asylum 2½ 3 miles. From Asylum to HOOGRAAF 8¼ miles.	YPR

Army Form C. 2118.

WAR DIARY
or
INTELLIGENCE SUMMARY.
(Erase heading not required.)

Instructions regarding War Diaries and Intelligence Summaries are contained in F.S. Regs., Part II. and the Staff Manual respectively. Title pages will be prepared in manuscript.

Hour, Date, Place	Summary of Events and Information	Remarks and references to Appendices
	Number of cases evacuated between 9 p.m. and 9 a.m. (night 8-9 Aug) 455 194 lying 261 sitting. —	ACR
	Following Officers wounded last night. —	
	Lieut. J.R. MAPLETON Ramc H/O. 1/2 Monmouth Regt.	
	" A.D. McLEAN " " 3rd " "	
	Following Officers arrived through posted transits opposite Rail names.	
	Lt. WOOTTON. R.A.M.C. (T.F.) to 85 (3 Lndn) Fd Ambce	
	Lt. COWAN " " T.C. to 1/2 Monmouth Regt	
	Lt. HACK " " " 3rd " "	
Aug. 10. PROVEN.	Cases evacuated last night 240. Advanced to Bevi Cl 240.	
	Capt R.G. ELVERY. R.A.M.C. att. 2. YORK, L.I. reported missing	ACR
	Sanitary Section are employed in breaking reoccupied the work as a	
	Preventive against asphyxiating gases attacks. There are made of cotton	
	hair soaked in gauze two sizes with permanganate potash and	
	soaked in a solution of hyposulphite soda :- H'sulph' potassium and	
	sodium hyposulphite 110 %, Soda Carb. 2.6% Glycerin 1 pair made (Allen)	

(73989) W4141—463. 400,000. 9/14. H.&J.Ltd. Forms/C. 2118/10.

WAR DIARY
or
INTELLIGENCE SUMMARY.

(Erase heading not required.)

Army Form C. 2118.

Hour, Date, Place	Summary of Events and Information	Remarks and references to Appendices
May 11, 1915. POPERINGHE	2250 Respirators arrived & brigade at 7 a.m. this morning	
	101. Rowland Coleman died after 146. Trained his Dressing Station 146.	
	LIEUT A.K. HOOPER, RAMC. reported Kowledem yesterday (10-5-15)	
	LIEUT J.C. McCONAGHEY. RAMC. reported his arrival and is	
	posted to 31st Bde R.F.A. in LIEUT WHITE — wounded	
	Satisfied report on RAMC work in Dieren from April 23 — May 9. app 34.	app 34.
	on 8 Div	
	The following men's names were forwarded to H.Q. 28 Divn. recommended for	
	award of a Decoration for valour presented by H.M. The Czar of Russia. —	
	84. F. Amb. No 567. Sgt. F.C. INGRAM. } These men's names have already	app 30.
	" 972 " H.C. & SELL. } been (illegible word)	
	85. F. Amb. No 23. Pte MATTHEWS. W.F.	
	" 76 " PIPER. A.C.H.	
	" 182 " STEPHENS. P.M.	
	The name of the undermentioned N.C.O. has also forwarded on 10th inst. for	
	Special gallantry until the Divrn. has been in action.	
	84. F. Amb. No. 022303. Serjt LLOYD J.F. A.S.C. attaches in	app 35.
	charge Motor Ambig Cars	
	Visited Advanced Dressing Station or Asylum YPRES.	

WAR DIARY
or
INTELLIGENCE SUMMARY.

(Erase heading not required.)

Army Form C. 2118.

Instructions regarding War Diaries and Intelligence Summaries are contained in F.S. Regs., Part II. and the Staff Manual respectively. Title pages will be prepared in manuscript.

Hour, Date, Place	Summary of Events and Information	Remarks and references to Appendices
May 12. PROVEN.	Visited Dressing Station at HOOGRAAF. " 85 Fd Amb.g. Casualties Collected last night 48. Enemy Attacked (Turco S.R. as ach 160 strong) including two "gas" cases.	NOR
May. 13. PROVEN.	Casualties Collected last night 64 - Treated in Dressing Station 75. The Division carries with "Army Reserve" today with exception of R.A.M.C units. Field Ambulances will be attached to Brigades when they move into positions. 4 CHARGER (SIR) BARROW (MRS) - Dressing Station from Kinnetic Warfare moved down to H.Q. g " it A Amb"	NOR
May. 14. PROVEN.	Nos 84 and 86 Field Ambulances moved into Resting Area today & Present positions are: 64 - on a farm S. g WINNEZEELE- (J.22.d) with one Section at J.16.a. 86 " " " " " " " (K.4.a) at WATOU 85 Remains at HOOGRAAF forming a dressing Station for a Composite Brigade which is in Army Support N̊ 9 WARMERHINQUE and is the next unit to be called, for the present rest g the Division are evacuated. Following Officers admitted for duty yesterday and are posted as follows: Lieut C.C. HARRISON. (T.C.) to 2 E. Yorks. and M. HOOPER wounded " L.T. WELLS " 1. K.O.Y.L.I. Capt ELLERY missing. " M. MURPHY " 2. BUFFS. Lt. A. FLEMING Sick " C.K. WHITE " 3. FUSILIERS. Pt HEFFERNAN wounded " C. HUNTER } 86 Field Amb. (Transport) " P. REID " R.V. STEELE.	NOR

Army Form C. 2118.

WAR DIARY
or
INTELLIGENCE SUMMARY.
(Erase heading not required.)

Instructions regarding War Diaries and Intelligence Summaries are contained in F.S. Regs., Part II. and the Staff Manual respectively. Title pages will be prepared in manuscript.

Hour, Date, Place	Summary of Events and Information	Remarks and references to Appendices
Aug. 15. PROVEN	Inspected Field Ambulances in their new billets. Recommended Ten Officers in Medical Charge Combatant Units for 5 days leave while Brigade out in Rest Area & arranged reliefs from Field Ambulances. Three officers from the two Field Ambulances with Cavalry Bde also granted 5 days Leave.	HER
Aug. 16. PROVEN.	Visited all three Field Ambulances. Arranged Baths at Cross Roads near area with O.C. 15 Sanitary Section and for the issue of "anti-poisonous gas" respirators to battalions before they return to the Trenches.	HER
Aug. 17. "	Following Officers Transferred to 1st Cavalry Division (D.G.M.S. G.H.Q. instruction.) Lieuts HUNTER – REID – WHITE. Forwarded report F.G.B. 28 Div Water Cart & Workshop Lorry with emergency remarks	HER appx 36. HER
Aug. 18 "	85. Field Troops from WATTEN to relieve Composite Regt Cameron. 84 & 85 returned via HERZEELE. 86. F.A. will move to HERZEELE. 85, movement via HOOGBUNE, hall the Remainder from 85–5"	"
Aug. 19. "	86. F. Ambce moved to HERZEELE. (D.17.C.7.2.) - Dr is temporarily taking sick of 18th not to attend hands of Casualty Clearing Hospital.	"
Aug. 20. "	Sent a Douaine are now all being sent to F.C.S. 2 Cavalry from the other two who are only keeping "absolutely detained" Cases. 85. F.A. had Col. Ramsay DDMS this morning	HER
Aug. 21.	Brigade are in Trenches Support tonight 20–71, 21–72, 1-23–24 Field Ambulance	HER

WAR DIARY
or
INTELLIGENCE SUMMARY.
(Erase heading not required.)

Army Form C. 2118.

Instructions regarding War Diaries and Intelligence Summaries are contained in F.S. Regs., Part II. and the Staff Manual respectively. Title pages will be prepared in manuscript.

Hour, Date, Place	Summary of Events and Information	Remarks and references to Appendices
Aug. 21. PROVEN	All Motor Lorries carried home S. y. POPERINGHE as the Brigade HQRS is opened. 6. Field Ambce in L.28.d. Conference of O.C. Units at Town Hall POPERINGHE for 2.0. this evening. Salt Remaining in 85. Field Ambce (143. 84. N.Z. 86 N.Z.	JHR
May. 22.	85. Bn. took over Trenches night 21 – 22. 83 Bn. Major 22 – 23 – Attended conference of A.D.M.S. Divisions M.D.M.S. Corps & 2nd Army with D.M.S. 2 Army Conference of O.C. Medical Units Division at Town Hall – 11.30 P.M. Arranged for Representative of all the Field Ambces (Two Officers, Two N.O.'s per men & Two Cars) to accompany the Field Ambces now clearing the area & Trenches being taken over by the Division so as to learn the position of Aid Posts Re–	JHR
May. 23.	Evacuating lines &c Side of 66. Ironwork 45. map 12 – 2.3. y Huts - 6 air and 10 the usual kind & the Division & this through form has may WIPPENHOEK Station	JHR
Aug 28	of Medical Unit of Division etc is. 84 } Parked in Two Farms near WIPPEHOEK - Square L 28 a. (Sheet 27). 86 } 85. HOOGRAAF Opens & with Cars in opening Farm. Sanitary Section ACE BERTIN POPERINGHE. Detachment from 1st Northumbrian Field Amb.6 & (50th Division) attached to the Division and has relieved Dressing Stations Ecole BIENFAISANCE Nouvin, Rose and smoke Asylum W.G. YPRES. Wounded & Sick Division are evacuated through these Advanced Stations lithograph	

Army Form C. 2118.

WAR DIARY
or
INTELLIGENCE SUMMARY.
(Erase heading not required.)

Instructions regarding War Diaries and Intelligence Summaries are contained in F. S. Regs., Part II and the Staff Manual respectively. Title pages will be prepared in manuscript.

Hour, Date, Place	Summary of Events and Information	Remarks and references to Appendices
May 24 PROVEN.	Enemy attacked Ypres this morning (2.30 – 7 am) using approximately 7000 cylinders of poison gas. Captn R. DWYER R.A.M.C. and Lieut JONES obtained report from H.Q. units during exposure into nature of gases employed. From evidence of Medical Officers in charge of Battalions and patients it appears that two gases are used, and almost certainly, they were administered from separate cylinders. One of the gases is apparently Chlorine, a mixture smell of Chlorine near the front trenches itself was very pronounced in initial cough, dyspnoea, pain, constriction of the chest, which in best cases is followed by symptoms of later there of acute pneumonia. The chief early symptoms produced by the second gas is irritation of the eyes with lacrymation. The more severe cases showed great dyspnoea + marked cardiac symptoms but no coughing. The general features of poison was that this gas was a Lachrymator + it contained had a distinctive odour of bitter almonds + that Shells containing these Gases of Nitrogen formalin or SO₂ were employed. The supposed 'Chlorine' cases were much suggestive of experiences in inhalation of Chlorine to M.O.'s in some cases whilst gas some relief to other cases improved under cardiac stimulants. The evidence of all witnesses was unanimously in favour of the hypothesis &	/J.W.

WAR DIARY
or
INTELLIGENCE SUMMARY.
(Erase heading not required.)

Army Form C. 2118.

Hour, Date, Place	Summary of Events and Information	Remarks and references to Appendices
May 24. PROVEN—	Supplies of Cotton respirators and Sponges told apart those without those of which have been impossible. No new situation respirators the former the Division was well supplied with both respirators and sprayers in some cases. The former were small when prepared locally some are little protection to the nose, the respirators however are if any little protection to the eyes. Number of cases collected in armoured Bearing Station last night 164.	JHR
May 25. "	Cases collected in per 24–25 – 664. 77 Officers and 592 ORs there in addition to the Motor Ambulance Cars of the Division. The hors Ambulance wagons, the cars of the M. Amb. Convoy and some empty returning lorries Cars were utilised to transport cases from the Lunatic Asylum to HOOGRAAF. It has appeared after all out from were cleared, unfortunately we have (upshamme ?) Knew not be got away, the Ambulance Car were (Rangers?) two killed and no dangerously wounded 32 Ofors at 1115 668 O.R. have been admitted to the Dressing Station. it is hoped 23–25 May 7 Offrs 226 (Gens.?) Gas Asphyxiation	JHR
May 26. "	Owing to the military situation some cases could not be collected in tyre	JHR

WAR DIARY or INTELLIGENCE SUMMARY

Army Form C. 2118.

Hour, Date, Place	Summary of Events and Information	Remarks and references to Appendices
May 26. PROVEN	May 24-25. A special party of Two Officers sixty bearers and five motor Ambulance Cars was employed helping in the men who could not be removed yesterday, when this party arrived the majority of the wounded had been collected by Regimental Stretcher bearers in dug-outs in & behind the trenches and were removed by Field Ambulance to Advanced Dressing Station YPRES. One horse AD Scout wounded in foot — Casualties collected at Advanced Dressing Station 261 of which 15 were gas cases. Treated in Dressing Station — HOOGSTADE — B. Officers 36.35. Other Ranks including 77 gas cases 9 there 247 (46 gas asphyxiation) Wopen to 28 Division.	JXR
May 27. PROVEN	Inspected Advanced Dressing Station in billets at YPRES, where I found an Officer performing an operation (trephine) in a case of head wound although I had previously issued instructions that any emergency operations should be undertaken in Field Ambulances: Issued further orders requiring a report from O.C. per Ambulance when any major operation was performed in one of the Ambulances and that, only, after consultation with the O.C. should such operation be undertaken. Interviewed ACDMS. 3 Division, who will relieve 28 ADM.S. — Representatives from 3 Div. Got from out post with air Service. Wounded collected last night 96. Off which 4 were gas cases. Admitted to Dressing Station: Officers 6. Other ranks 178. 9 there 106 km 28 Division of gas cases.	JXR
May 28. PROVEN	Travelled to Collector Aid Piper 116 mess up of 28 Sick 1, gas care & 67. wounded. Treated in Dressing Station: 2 Officers & 135. Other ranks, 9 these 72 were in 28 Div. included 3 "gas" cases —	JXR

WAR DIARY
or
INTELLIGENCE SUMMARY.

(Erase heading not required.)

Army Form C. 2118.

Hour, Date, Place	Summary of Events and Information	Remarks and references to Appendices
May 26. PROVEN.	The Division is returning to the resting area in the next few days prior to transferred from V to II Army Corps. Arranged for ambulance trains for Base Auxiliaries in WINNEZEELE and 85 Field and WIETJE H.A. A.D.M.S. 1st Canadian Division gave addresses for S.B. RIMBOATELE which will be transported by 24 B.M. Arranged with A.Q.M.G. III Dist. for the handing out of Divisional Centre at HAZEBRATE on Sunday 30. and advanced Divisional Centre YPRES tomorrow. Tonight representatives from Field Amb. & III Div. will be occupying our Collecting Posts viz. W. GILLESPIE. M.O. NORTH'D FUSILIERS reported missing	AFR
May 29. PROVEN.	Ambulance Collected last night 93. Treated in Dressing Station Officers 2. (who receive 104 of whom 20 knee-cut & 25 sick) (45) Have 28 Division to get case — Informed G.O.C. Division — also A.D.M.S. 3rd Division who are taking over our Line tonight	AFR
May 30. PROVEN.	84. Field Ambulance moved to WINNEZEELE where it ill be the school for instruction of sick and Temple Fahm J.22.d for personal transport. 56. F. Amb. marched to WATOU where it took over the hostel for sick & Farm in K.4.a for personal transport. Reviewed from WINIZENE III Division They will take over the dressing station at HOOGRAFFE from 83 Field Temporary. Admitted 6. Dressing Station yesterday 88. 9 which 18 were 28 Division.	AFR

WAR DIARY
or
INTELLIGENCE SUMMARY.
(Erase heading not required.)

Army Form C. 2118.

Hour, Date, Place	Summary of Events and Information	Remarks and references to Appendices
ROUEN. May 31- 1916	Head Quarters moved to WATDU today. E.S. Field Ambulance move from HOEGRAAF to MERZEELE, handing Colgn. ne to No.7. Field Ambulce Following changes in Medical Officers have recently occurred in the Division. May 25. LIEUT. S. ROWLAND Armed posted to 2/5 Div: Train via Lt MOREM TRANSFD. to HAVRE 25. " H. H. DAVIS " 1/2 Y/L. via Lt K. JYEO. to ROUEN. 25. " I. M. MCPHAIL " 2. E. SURREY. via Lt J. MCLAND " 27 " R.G.J. MCENTYRE " 2. N. Bⁿ R.F.A. Capt W. E. TINLEY. wounded 27 " R. R. KERR " 1st WELSH " Lt G.H. FENNELL - ROUEN 27 " J. A. QUIN " 3. B^{de} R.F.A. " P.T. CASSELL HAVRE 29 " J. M. MCLAGGAN " 64. F^d Ambce Capt RAVES sick 29 . E. W. GRIFFITH " 84. F^d Ambce. hospital establishment. 26 . B.S. BROWNE from 86 F^d Ambce to 2. CHESHIRES Capt O. R. MCEWEN. Sick 28 . J. COWAN from 1st MONMOUTH (a return) to 2. N.F. via Lt G. GILLESPIE. wounded 29. A.C.SMITH to 2. MON (a return) to 86, 7 Amb. via Lt S. BROWNE (CHESHIRES Na)	JHRC

Report of work performed by R.A.M.C., of the 28th Division from the 22nd April to the end of the withdrawal to the present position.

The Medical Units of the Division took over 3382 wounded from the regimental aid posts during the period. The bearers of all three Field Ambulances were employed on this duty which can only be performed at night. The 86th took the YPRES-ZONNEBEKE Road and established an advanced dressing station near VERLORENHOEK, and later, when this post was untenable, at POTIJZE. The 84th and 85th took all the rest of the area and formed collecting stations at ST JEAN or as near to ST JEAN as possible. Motor Ambulance Wagons were sent as far as ZONNEBEKE and WILTJE nightly, and a horsed ambulance collected from the portion of the road inaccessable to motors.

On the night of the 29th/30th the dressing station of the Canadian Field Ambulance which was taking in the wounded from our bearer divisions had to close and the 84th Field Ambulance opened a dressing station at POPERINGHE. This Field Ambulance has treated 2618 cases since it opened and continues to act as a clearing hospital to the forces- the two clearing hospitals which were established in that town having been withdrawn.

On the night of the 3rd/4th May 748 cases were evacuated from the old area, nearly all the bearers of the division with 8 officers were employed as the aid posts had to be cleared by midnight. 66 motor ambulance wagons (50 lent from Motor Ambulance Convoy) were in use and carried all the wounded direct to POPERINGHE.

The following casualties occurred in the period under review;

Officers.	5 wounded.(3 regimental)
Other Ranks.	6 killed.(including 1 motor driver)
	18 wounded.(including 6 motor drivers)
Motor Ambulance Wagons.	2 abandoned.
	2 badly damaged.(sent to Base)
Horsed Ambulance Wagon.	1 destroyed.(with two horses)

May 6th 1915.

Colonel., A.M.S.,
A.D.M.S., 28th Division.

REPORT OF WORK PERFORMED BY THE R.A.M.C., OF THE 28th DIVISION
FROM THE 22nd APRIL TO THE 10th MAY.

(1) Regimental Aid Posts.

(a) Sick and wounded were transported from the trenches to Aid Posts under regimental arrangements. In some very exceptional cases the bearers of the Field Ambulances assisted.

(b)
(1) The Medical Units of the Division took over 4987 wounded from the regimental aid posts during the period. The bearers of all three Field Ambulances were employed on this duty which can only be performed at night. The 85th took the YPRES-ZONNEBEKE Road and established an advanced dressing station near VERLORENHOEK, and later, when this post was untenable, at POTIJZE. The 84th and 86th took all the rest of the area, and formed collecting stations at ST JEAN or as near to ST JEAN as possible. Motor Ambulance Wagons were sent as far as ZONNEBEKE and WILTJZE nightly, and a horsed ambulance collected from the portion of the road inaccessable to motors.

(2) On the night of the 3rd/4th May 748 cases were evacuated from the old area, nearly all the bearers of the Division with 8 Officers were employed, as the aid posts had to be cleared by midnight. 66 Motor Ambulance Wagons (50 lent from Motor Ambulance Convoy) were in use and carried all the wounded direct to POPERINGHE.

(3) On the night of the 8th/9th May 548 cases were transferred from the advanced dressing station in the cellars of the Lunatic Asylum, West OF YPRES, to the main dressing station at HOOFGRAFF. All the available motor and horsed ambulances were supplemented by the limber wagons of the 1st Line Transport and the 24 wagons of the Train for this duty, as the Motor Convoy cars available were not sufficient to evacuate this post with the necessary rapidity.

(2) <u>Work at Dressing Stations.</u>

(1) On the night of the 29th/30th the dressing station of the Canadian Field Ambulance, which was taking in the wounded from our bearer division had to close, and the 84th Field Ambulance opened a dressing station at POPERINGHE. This Field Ambulance has treated 3494 cases since it opened, and continued to act as a Clearing Hospital to the forces until the 8th instant, as the two Clearing Hospitals which were established in that town were withdrawn.

(2) On the 8th instant the 85th Field Ambulance opened a dressing station at HOOFGRAFF and has treated 582 cases up to date.

(3) <u>Evacuation of Dressing Stations.</u>

This duty was performed under arrangements made by the D.D.M.S., 5th Corps.

(4) <u>Any other points of Special Interest.</u>

(1) A Motor Soup Kitchen was in use during the period, sometimes on the road, sometimes at the dressing station, and proved to be of the greatest use.

(2) The strain on the drivers of the Motor Ambulance Wagons was very great as they had to be at work every night and were often under heavy shell fire. The roads were very bad and no lights were allowed. Seven had to go sick from severe neurasthenia and four were sent to the Base. To try and spare the drivers, four were allotted to every three cars instead of two to each, but this was not a success. A reserve of drivers is an urgent need in every Field Ambulance with Motor Transport, as many of the accidents to the cars would have been avoided were the drivers in a less exhausted condition.

Any other points of Special Interest. Cont'd.

(3)   The supply of dressings was adequate, but on several occasions it was necessary to provide blankets and stretchers outside the authorised number. This was rendered possible by using the equipment of the late Convalescent Rest Station.

(4)   The following casualties occurred in the period under review:-

Officers.	1 Missing. (Regimental)
	7 wounded. (6 Regimental)
Other Ranks.	7 killed. (including 1 Motor Driver)
	18 wounded. (including 6 Motor Drivers
Motor Ambulances.	1 abandoned.
	4 badly damaged. (Sent to Base)
	33 damaged and repaired by Motor Ambulance Workshop Unit.
Horses.	2 killed.

Nicholas Ferguson

Colonel., A.M.S.,
A.D.M.S., 28th Division.

May 11th 1915.

84th Field Ambulance. (2nd London T)

Nominal Roll of Officers, N.C.O's and Men killed and wounded in action from January 18th to July 18th 1915, inclusive.

Reg'tl No.	Rank	and Name.	Casualty.	Date.
71	Private	H. Ward.	Wounded.	Feb 19th.
415	do	W.T. Goldsmith.	do	Feb 20th.
89	do	W. Budden.	do	Feb 26th.
551	Sergeant	F.C. Ingram.	do	March 3rd.
374	Private	H. Angell.	do	March 4th.
409	do	C.N. Attwater.	do	March 5th.
230	do	C. Windebank.	do	March 18th.
20	Corporal	E.H. Thompson.	do	March 20th.
63	Private	F. Tomes.	Died of Wounds.	April 4th.
135	do	W.J. Robins.	Wounded.	do
972	do	H.C. Sell.	do	do
136	do	W.E. Round.	do	do
234	do	A.J. Finlayson.	Died of Wounds.	do
111	do	C. Turner.	do	do
319	do	H. Doughty.	Wounded.	do
288	do	N.A. Pester.	do	do
72	do	L.A. Brooks.	do	do
132	do	C.E. Knight.	Killed.	do
191	do	G.L. Boyes.	do	do
032463	Driver	T. Wittaker.	Wounded.	April 25th.
934	Sergeant	S.A. Bird.	do	do
353	Private	W.D. Vernon.	do	April 26th.
322	do	J.A. Mead.	do	do
277	do	J. Howes.	do	do
67	do	G.K. Froud.	do	do
211	do	D. Burbridge.	do	do
99	do	J. Reville.	do	April 29th.
149	do	L. Curtis.	do	do
314	do	J.N. Hawkin.	do	May 26th.
M.2/033547	Driver	F. Kay.	do	June 19th.

85th Field Ambulance. (3rd London T)

Nominal Roll of Officers, N.C.O's and Men killed and wounded in action from January 18th to July 18th 1915.

Officers.

Lieutenant   R.E. Barnsley.   Wounded.   April 22nd.

Other Ranks.

Regt'l No.	Rank and Name.		Casualty.	Date.
219	Private	A.E. Edward.	Wounded.	March 27th.
25	do	H. Salter.	do	April 19th.
61	do	W.T. Emery.	do	do 22nd.
1223	Driver	D.R. Newcastle.	Died of Wounds.	do 24th.
M.2021532	do	L.T. Washer.	Wounded.	do do
M.2032730	do	W.T. Harris.	do	do do
440	Private	W.A. Sollas.	do	do 25th.
172	Lc/Cpl	E.F. Smith.	do	do 29th.
204	Private	B.W. Wisternoff.	do	do do
168	do	A.F. Goodfellow.	Died of Wounds.	May 7th.
279	S/Sergt	J.C. Caswell.(Slight)	Wound.	May 26th.
M.2032634	Driver	A.R. Tree.	Wounded.	June 30th.

86th Field Ambulance (2nd North'bn T)

Nominal Roll of Officers, N.C.O's and Men killed and wounded in action from January 18th to July 18th 1915 inclusive.

Officers.

Lieutenant V.H. Wardle.   Wounded.   April 23rd.

Other Ranks.

Regt'l No.	Rank and Name.	Casualty.	Date.
1432	Private E. Spark.	Wounded.	April 23rd.
1389	Sergt T. Bell.	do	do
1509	Pte J. Lawther.	do	do 24th.
1323	do A. Ridley.	do	do 19th.
1398	do W.B. Cooper.	Died of Wounds.	do 19th.
1548	do E.J. Fothergill.	Killed.	do 26th.
1468	do J.J. Tomlinson.	do	do do
1513	do F. Hall.	do	do do
1450	do A. Falls.	Wounded.	do do
1541	do J. Pratt.	Missing.	do do
1906	do J. Corrigan.	Wounded.	do do
032073	Driver W. Drabble.	do	do do
1358	Private W.J. Cooper.	do	May 1st.
1423	do G.H. Cornick.	do	do
903	do J. Layfield.	Died of Wounds.	May 4th.
1588	do J.W. Mitchell.	Wounded.	May 10th.
1689	do J. Murphy.	do	do
1383	do T.E. Davey.	Killed.	May 25th.
1573	do W. Woodcock.	Wounded.	do

No 15 Sanitary Section.

No 944.   Lc/Corpl F.J. Bonding.   Died of Wounds.   Mar 15th.
No 246   Private   S.G.D. Froment.   do   do

28th Divisional Motor Ambulance Workshop Unit.

No 5889   S/Sergt F. Jackson.   Died of Wounds.   April 24th.

Casualties among Officers R.A.M.C., in Medical Charge of Combatant Units of the 28th Division.

Date.	Rank and Name.	Unit to which attached.	Casualty.
February 17th 1915.	Lieut D. Campbell. T.C.	2nd East Yorks Regt.	Killed in Action.
March 14th 1915.	Lieut D.C. Turnbull. T.C.	2nd Cheshire Regt.	Died of Wounds.
March 14th 1915.	Lieut W.T. McCurry. S.R.	1st Norfolk Regt.	Killed in Action.
May 4th 1915.	Lieut R.C. Neil. T.C.	8th Middlesex Regt.	Wounded.
May 5th 1915.	Lieut H.P. White. T.C.	31st Brigade R.F.A.	do
May 5th 1915.	Lieut J.T. Heffernan. T.C.	3rd Royal Fusiliers.	do
May 9th 1915.	Lieut G.D. McLean. T.C.	3rd Monmouth Regt.	do
May 9th 1915.	Lieut J.R. Marrack. T.C.	1st Monmouth Regt.	do
May 10th 1915.	Captain P.G.M. Elvery. Reg	1st K.O.Y.L. Infantry.	do and Prisoner.
May 25th 1915.	Captain W.E.F. Tinley. T.F.	2nd North'bn Bde R.F.A.	Wounded.
May 24th 1915.	Lieut J.M. Gillespie. T.C.	2nd North'd Fusiliers.	Prisoner.
June 18th 1915.	Lieut J. Cowen. S.R.	2nd North'd Fusiliers.	Wounded.

HONOURS AND REWARDS

Administrative Staff.

Colonel   N.C. Ferguson., C.M.G., Mentioned in Despatches.   June 23rd.

84th Field Ambulance. (2nd London T)

Lieut-Colonel	W.S. Sharpe.	Mentioned in Despatches.	June 23rd.
Captain	R.E. Bickerton.	do	do
Sergeant	F.C. Ingram. No551.	Distinguished Conduct Medal.	June 12. ~~do~~
Private	H.C. Sell. No972.	Mentioned in Despatches.	~~June~~ do 23

85th Field Ambulance. (3rd London T)

Lieut-Col	J.R. Whait.	Mentioned in Despatches.	June 23rd.
Major	E.B. Waggett.	do	do
Captain	H.A.T. Fairbank.	do	do
No 66. S/Sergt	J.T. Boyes.	do	do
No 679 do	J.C. Caswell.	do	do

86th Field Ambulance. (2nd North'bn T)

Lieut-Colonel	D.A. Cameron.	Mentioned in Despatches.	June 23rd
Major	D.L. Fisher.	do	do
Lieut	V.H. Wardle.	do	do
No S/Sergt	J.J. Webster.	do	do

Officers in Medical Charge of Combatant Units.

Lieutenant	J.M. Gillespie.	"The Military Cross"	June 28th.
Lieutenant	J.M. McNicholl.	"The Military Cross"	June 28th.
Lieutenant	D.C. Turnbull.	Mentioned in Despatches.	June 23rd.

(6414) Wt. W3900/P1607 2,500,000 7/18 McA & W Ltd (E 3591) Forms W3091/4. Army Form W.3091.

Cover for Documents.

Nature of Enclosures.

A.D.M.S. 28th Division

Notes, or Letters written.

June 1915.

WAR DIARY
or
INTELLIGENCE SUMMARY.
(Erase heading not required.)

Army Form C. 2118.

28th Div. June 1915

Instructions regarding War Diaries and Intelligence Summaries are contained in F.S. Regs., Part II and the Staff Manual respectively. Title pages will be prepared in manuscript.

Hour, Date, Place		Summary of Events and Information	Remarks and references to Appendices
WATOU	June 1. 1915.	The Three Field Ambulances are now established at:- 84. WINNEZEELE 85. HERZEELE 86. WATOU. Each has a Hulidur (School) for accommodation of sick and is occupying bivouacs in farms. Inspected Field Ambulance at WATOU. Interviewed O.C.'s each Field Ambulance & arranged that the O.C.'s choose among the Instruction of the new Indian Officers who have recently taken over Battalions	ADM
WATOU	June 2. 1915	FIVE Cases of Sickness, to which I have been referred in other days from:- 146. 8th R.F.A. 10. Pte LOW, TOWER, CARTWRIGHT, PALMER, NEVEL. Visited the R/S with the C. Recruits' Section, 4th Horse Batts.; Returned 6/6. Today, Dec. 6606. — On Investigation, it was ascertained that the other cases - RAMSBOW, BARROW and HAMMOND had also occurred in the R/B during May and that his suspicions cases were admitted Estaples today. — Allen and MITCHELL. — It was found that all these men belonged to the Ammunition Column. 2. Tyler looked after Sub-Section - a "short 3s" abody. 3. Only to break down of a water cart, water was obtained from a monofrot source for a short time Early in May. No cases of sickness has occurred among civilians at the billets recently occupied by the Ammunition Column; no doubt & villages among the troops.	ADM

Army Form C. 2118.

WAR DIARY
or
INTELLIGENCE SUMMARY.
(Erase heading not required.)

Instructions regarding War Diaries and Intelligence Summaries are contained in F.S. Regs., Part II and the Staff Manual respectively. Title pages will be prepared in manuscript.

Hour, Date, Place	Summary of Events and Information	Remarks and references to Appendices
WATTU. June 3, 1915.	Lt. McNee, O.C. Mobile Laboratory — BAILEUL came to assist in tracing cause of outbreak of enteric among 1st & 85 R.F.A. Ammn. Colm. Arrangd for specimens of urine from the men those men not on duty & the enteric and from the cooks & the men in bacteriological examination. Following precautions taken to prevent spread of disease: NCOs & 3 men of Flanders section to have charge of sanitary arrangements of camp (1) Have latrines into trenches emptying Bresol Naphthol Cresol daily + " Sobelia " Chlorinated Lime " (2) Faeces (3) Basin with cresol solution provided at latrine & cook house. Special precaution as to proper sanitation of Cook-house + prevention of flies + prevention and removal of manure &c. Inspected farm occupied by Lsection from May 4 — 24. Camp had been left in a filthy condition — increased latrine accomm. to back of barn, thorin horse-pond filled in & cliffs of pond filled which was being used to allow pole near water.	JHR
WATOU. June 4, 1915.	Lsection C.O.S. 14 Div to be Orlette Thrieve & Wells removed from 85 R.A. Batgallery attached to 14 Div. They will be attached no. to 42 2 Cavy 14 P. Inspected the three Field Ambulances. The 85/R.F. at Watou and Houtkerque were very good, clean the patients were comfortable. 6th at Winnezeele Anothre Case of enteric = 7461 Gr Hartley reported Today in 1/6 6th Amm. Col. W. 1/6 6th Amm. Col.	JHR

(73989) W4141–463. 400,000. 9/14. H.&J.Ltd. Forms/C. 2118/10.

Army Form C. 2118.

WAR DIARY
or
INTELLIGENCE SUMMARY.
(Erase heading not required.)

Instructions regarding War Diaries and Intelligence Summaries are contained in F.S. Regs., Part II and the Staff Manual respectively. Title pages will be prepared in manuscript.

Hour, Date, Place	Summary of Events and Information	Remarks and references to Appendices
June 4. 1915. WATOU.	LIEUT R.E. BARNSLEY rejoined 85 Field Ambce from Hospital (Hounslow 23-4-15)	
June 5. 1915	Inspected the three Field Ambulances and leading establishments in HOUTKERK during the Resting period. The Sanitary Section to Reinforce as follows.	
	1 N.C.O. and 3 Pte pushed to each of the four B2e group areas, first to assist Regimental Medical Officers who are all inexperienced, quite inexperienced in Camp work. Temporary latrines with bay trees explosion in Camp work in erection & arrangements for disposal of refuse &c.	
	1 N.C.O. and one Private at each bathing establishment. The additional men required will be provided from the Field Ambulances in the area.	
	1 N.C.O. and two Privates at the Disinfector Station POPERINGHE	
	1 Pte N.C.O. Everist Cavalry kept @ 146.B2 in special precautions being taken in their lines until cases of outbreak of illness at 82203 Pt KINCH. This man also belongs H.Q. Sect. Army Column.	
	Another case of Enteric reported in 146 B2 at 82203 Pt KINCH. This man also belongs H.Q. Sect. Army Column.	
	Field Ambulances have been drawn the higher scale of tents and now each has their opening tents and 48 Bell tents. With these wastage from slight illnesses should be reduced to a minimum and their admits generally be more healthy than formerly into ill ventilated farm shelters &c	
	To prevent accumulation of flies stamps are being made for men to eat at central messes while	

(73989) W.4141—463. 400,000. 9/14. H.&J.Ltd. Forms/C. 2118/10.

Army Form C.-2118.

WAR DIARY
or
INTELLIGENCE SUMMARY.
(Erase heading not required.)

Instructions regarding War Diaries and Intelligence Summaries are contained in F.S. Regs., Part II. and the Staff Manual respectively. Title pages will be prepared in manuscript.

Hour, Date, Place	Summary of Events and Information	Remarks and references to Appendices
June 5. 1915. WATOU	No matters are indeed of in their progress.	JSL
June 6. 1915. WATOU	Accompanied A.D.C. Division in inspection of the Three Field Ambulances. The Ambulances were clean, spacious, comfortable and well looked after but the cooking arrangements left much to be desired. Circulated a Confidential letter to O.C.'s Field Ambulances on this subject. (attached) In view of the outbreak of enteric fever in the 146 Bde R.F.A. Amm Column, I issued special Confidential letter to all Commanding Officers re my suggestion as to the vital importance of perfect "sanic" management during the hot weather (attached) and noted a guard on the pales per diem before. There were cases of sudden in 146 Bde reported viz ALLEN, WHITE, FORD.	Appendix 37. App. 38. JSR
June 7. 1915. WATOU	Inspected 146 Bde R.F.A. Ammunition Column with A.D.C. 8 S.B.E. action to HOUTKERQUE sent over from 146 Division tomorrow, arranged to Ambulance wagon accompanying them in the march. Arranged with ordering for a systematised issue and supply of respirators and Chemicals through U.S.E. Ordnance also in adequate reserves are well. The rotation will be prepared by Sanitary Section Corporal held to (1) The Bath (2) Royals. (3) Bde Engineers of Train in an "emergency" reserve by 2nd M.G.Q. Inspected men who have been temporarily unfit for duty with their Batteries and attached Sanitary Section, arranged for return of those fit ___ remainder to have: 8 Genere: 15 to Duty.	JSR

Army Form C. 2118.

WAR DIARY
or
INTELLIGENCE SUMMARY.
(Erase heading not required.)

Instructions regarding War Diaries and Intelligence Summaries are contained in F.S. Regs., Part II and the Staff Manual respectively. Title pages will be prepared in manuscript.

Hour, Date. Place	Summary of Events and Information	Remarks and references to Appendices
JUNE. 8. 1915 WATOU	No 19549 Pt. MITCHELL. A Cubicular. 146 Bde Amn. Colum. diagnosed enteric; this is the 15th case since 23-5-15. Going the Bde Amn. Colum. and of these seven were RTA instructors & the suspected possible carriers, is men with a history of past enteric. so far have all given negative results in attempts to cultivate B.T.A. from faeces and urine.	JSR
June 9. 1915	Inspected 86 Field Ambulance and saw myself all cases recommended for evacuation to Casualty Clearing Station. Lt. Col. BEVERIDGE A.D.M.S. (S.A.) and Lt. Col. WEBB D.D.M.S. (S.A.) came from G.H.Q. to assist in investigation of the outbreak of enteric among the 46 Bd Div. Exp., they wished Re- change throughout. apt. Called for a report on water carts of Division. Issued Confidential Circular memo on Camp Sanitation.	App 39. JSR
June 10. 1915	Two more cases of ENTERIC in 146 Bde Amn. Col. viz 15th in A Subsection. No 14172 Pte BERRY and 81304 FQ BOWDEN. Inspected the 146 Bd. Amn. Col. again with Lieut BOYD of Mobile Laboratory, who took specimens from all men of A subsection for cultures of B.T.A. Sent out Confidential Circular No 10. to M.O.'s of Division.	App 40.
June 11. 1915	Interviewed M.O.'s 85 Bde. These are all young officers - Temporary Lieutenants - with little or no Military experience. Briefed out the importance of Conservation under present conditions and generally instructed them in their chief duties and how to get on the possible difficulties on Regimental Medical Officers. Lieut. DEIGHTON, R.A.M.C. asked to relieve Lt. GEORGE, M.O. 5th W.O.R Longer probably. To No 18. General Hospital.	JSR

WAR DIARY
or
INTELLIGENCE SUMMARY

(Erase heading not required.)

Army Form C. 2118

Instructions regarding War Diaries and Intelligence Summaries are contained in F.S. Regs., Part II. and the Staff Manual respectively. Title Pages will be prepared in manuscript.

Place	Date	Hour	Summary of Events and Information	Remarks and references to Appendices
WATOU.	12/5/15		Inspected Army Convalescent Rest Station at MONT DES CATS. 200 beds are reserved here for this Division. Cpl. COPELANDS no 146 B.A. R.F.A. Requires further into Eutonie McMack as, so far, no carrier has been discovered. It appeared the men no 87318 SI. FORD who had suffered from diarrhoea about 14 days before their cases appeared. This man will be sent to No. 10. Cas. Clearing Sta. HAZEBROUCK for further investigation as none of the men sharing his bivouac have been dysenteric before.	HSR
"	13.5.15		Arranged details of move tomorrow. The 83rd Brigade marches to area near DICKEBUSCH. The Brigade will be accompanied by five Motor Ambulance Cars. The 84 and 85 Field Ambulances will march respectively to LA CLYTTE and WEST OUTRE and are not from Field Ambs. of 14th Division. The 86 Field Ambulance will remain at WATOU where it will take charge of 85th B.A. and Divisional R.A. 84 & 85 F. Ambs. will each take one Tent Subdivision. The Motor Ambulance Conv. & one unit cars now under their care. 62nd Field Ambulance attached the Tent Sub-division to take over Officers Convalescent Rest Station at MONT NOIR. This is a splendid château and consists of a site about 2 miles from WEST OUTRE with accommodation for 24 Officers almost one a considerable amount of "bracket", etc. here.	HSR
WEST OUTRE	14.5.15	2 pm	Head Quarters moved to WEST OUTRE today. Park no. this area from 14th Division. Enquired into evacuation of wounded tonight by 85 Field Ambulance. There is no convenient aid post at a large cellar about 1800 yds from PoperRie. The Ambulance Cars will take here at night, from this Cellar, all cases to LA CLYTTE. Whence by motor Amb. Convoy they are taken to BAILLEUL.	HSR

Army Form C. 2118

WAR DIARY
or
INTELLIGENCE SUMMARY
(Erase heading not required.)

Instructions regarding War Diaries and Intelligence Summaries are contained in F. S. Regs., Part II. and the Staff Manual respectively. Title Pages will be prepared in manuscript.

Place	Date	Hour	Summary of Events and Information	Remarks and references to Appendices
WEST OUTRE	15/6/15		Inspected 85th Field Ambulance at WEST OUTRE and the Officers Convalescent Rest Station near DES CATS. Visited S.A. Aust.s at LA CLYTTE and the hut for baths there. Hut to DICKEBUSCH with R.E. party and C.R.E. re water supply. There is a large supply at DICKEBUSCH and R.A.P. here in good, kits will be used by the troops. The huts in WEST OUTRE drain into POPR. BAILLEUL.	V.S.R.
WEST OUTRE	16/6/15		Two mile causeway of Soldiers reported in 146 Bde R.F.A. to A. RUPROLEN and the latter lived with a detachment for some time. Arranged for battery establishments personal used by L. Division, as DICKEBUSCH and WEST OUTRE the Taken over by our Sanitary Section for the Division and also in the new zone lines a week of the L. Division baths at RENINGHELST. Discussed D.D.M.S. 2nd Corps and acting A.D.M.S. 2nd Army.	V.S.R.
WEST OUTRE	17.6.		Inspected the Field Ambulance at LA CLYTTE - yesterday the Divisional Commander visited the unit and was kept waiting over a quarter by an army medic keep to send on the D.M.S. Enquired into this arranged for C.M.O. always the present in all visits to the Division. Arranged for inspection by Sanitary arrangements in trenches, in supply of drinks and pure supply of blankets to units - 1st a day for DIVISION - as some of the trenches have been made through wet ground and there is an accumulation of filth. Lt. MCMITCHELL. M.O. Suffolk Regt wounded & Capt. CLARRY Staff - officers mentioned. MONT P. FUSILIERS. wounded - shell wound arm. Lt. J. COWAN " "	V.S.R.
WEST OUTRE	18 - 6		Assistant Actg D.M.S. 2nd Army, Inspected site for 86 Field Ambulance near BERTHEN. O.C. held Laboratory again visited 146 Bde RFA arranged Horse enquired Canine to BAILLEUL for further investigation. The mule cases reported yesterday Bull. Entered.	V.S.R.

1875 Wt. W593/826 1,000,000 4/15 J.B.C. & A. A.D.S.S./Forms/C. 2118.

Army Form C. 2118

WAR DIARY
or
INTELLIGENCE SUMMARY
(Erase heading not required.)

Instructions regarding War Diaries and Intelligence Summaries are contained in F. S. Regs., Part II. and the Staff Manual respectively. Title Pages will be prepared in manuscript.

Place	Date	Hour	Summary of Events and Information	Remarks and references to Appendices
WEST OUTRE	19/6/15		Inspected billet at LA CLYTTE. Interviewed A.D.M.S. N.Midland Division, re: part of white cross we take over Tournai, visited his rest station at LOCRE. R. DONL. hth Amb. Camp visited the Divnl Hd quarters this afternoon. the delay in sending up spare parts appears the a difficult very different however – he pointed out the importance spare cars and spare drivers when there is a rush of wounded and it necessary three cars by day and night. Re had works mobile steel first — The DDMS. 2nd A. Corps interviewed in afternoon.	AER
"	20.		Visited billet of 84 Field Ambce and arranged for inspection of all R.A. civic with A.D.M.S. N.Midland Division visited will be take at 9am him, also Regimental aid posts + Communication trenches. Visited 3. N.Midland Rest Stn BAILLEUL. For Case of Private Sheldon reported in E spoke to Lieut 10. A.S.C. there in the Company, the man P.C. SHELDON in his company is reported as having suffered from dentine in 1914 than been employed as cook, seen him by BAILLEUL Specialist Hospital for investigation by O.C. N.M.D. latterly as a proving cashier. 8th Field Ambulance saw the tent subdivision marched from watou to farm between BENTINGH + BUSSENEBE (R 156) inspected there. H. H.B. TAYLOR. arrived packed to 2 Northumberland Fusiliers by cycle.	AER
"	21.		Inspected Camp of 5th Field Ambce – visited aid party St. Ann + trenches of Reserve Battalion – Arranged for establishment of a day Collecting post at Dickebusch, by the present Case be moved by day from the trenches, if necessary via CLYTTE	AER

Army Form C. 2118

WAR DIARY
or
INTELLIGENCE SUMMARY
(Erase heading not required.)

Instructions regarding War Diaries and Intelligence Summaries are contained in F. S. Regs., Part II. and the Staff Manual respectively. Title Pages will be prepared in manuscript.

Place	Date	Hour	Summary of Events and Information	Remarks and references to Appendices
WEST OUTRE	22		Inspected 84th Field Ambulance – Found it still not satisfactory, although little done for the comfort of the patients, arranged that the "Hospital" should be taken over by Major Montgomery Smith (2nd in command) with his section (the Sergeant Major (Australian) to be an independent unit under the Officer responsible for it &c, with his new duties, it appears likely to meet for the time being. Inspected Wilts & Buffs and E. Surrey Regts. Trenches occupied by Welsh & Cheshire Regts. inspected in afternoon. Lt. J. Mowat arrived – Posted to 1st Suffolk Regt. for duty.	HRR
WEST OUTRE	23		Visited 86 Field Ambce. and arranged for one Section under (Bailleul) take over Convalescent Rest Section from 3. N. Midland Field Ambulance tomorrow. Rode round camps of R.A. Wagon Lines. Inspected 146.(B. R.F.A. lines carefully.	HRR
WEST OUTRE	24		Visited the Army Rest Station at MONT DES CATS in the morning and arranged that some of the men there be utilized. Knew it for French duty be attached to the Sanitary Section for duty. Inspected the "Hospital" formed by 84 Field Ambce. No. Section 86 Field Ambulance moved to BAILLEUL & take over Convalescent Rest Station there.	HRR
WEST OUTRE	25		Inspected 85. Field Ambce. in morning and 86 in afternoon.	HRR
"	26		Inspected 84 Field Ambce. and camps at La Clytte – Reninghelst and Scherpenberg huts. Selected with O.C. 15. Sanitary Section sites for Hospital Washhouses – Issued Circular Memo. Re. Inoculation for Enteric after six men in six months.	App. 41.

Army Form C. 2118

WAR DIARY
or
INTELLIGENCE SUMMARY
(Erase heading not required.)

Instructions regarding War Diaries and Intelligence Summaries are contained in F. S. Regs., Part II. and the Staff Manual respectively. Title Pages will be prepared in manuscript.

Place	Date	Hour	Summary of Events and Information	Remarks and references to Appendices
WEST OUTRE	27/6/15		Accompanied D.D.M.S. 2nd Army on inspection of the Three Field Ambulances of the Division.	HTR
WEST OUTRE	28/6 -		Interviewed D.M.S. 2nd Army and D.D.M.S. G.H.Q. Inspected new site for 83 Field Ambulance and arranged for that unit to move tomorrow. Trenches inspected, arranged for supply of creosol, cresol petroleum oil syringes for destruction of flies, as well	HTR
WEST OUTRE	29 -		As regards inspection by Medical Sanitary Section. Inspected Rest Station at BAILLEUL. Visited proposed site for new hutment with representative R.E. and A.Staff.	HTR
WEST OUTRE	30 -		Interviewed medicine Inspector of Recruits. There are a large number of men now suffering from minor ailment but sufficient render them unfit for the trenches coming [?] the Division, derived [?] men of making most use of these men as L.of C. without "draining" the Division or allowing men really fit from finding their way down country.	HTR

Nichols known Col
H.Maj Gen of Ing [?]

1875. Wt. W593/826 1,000,000 4/15 J.B.C. & A. A.D.S.S./Forms/C. 2118.

28th Division

121/6443

Confidential

War Diary
of
A.D.M.S. 28th Division.

from July 1st 1915. to July 31st 1915.

Vol I. (previous months were sent direct to this Office)

121/6443

July '15

Perused but not copied
Dec. 1917.

Map has been detached from
July Diary & attached to
 Summary.

Army Form C. 2118

WAR DIARY
or
INTELLIGENCE SUMMARY
(Erase heading not required.)

Instructions regarding War Diaries and Intelligence Summaries are contained in F. S. Regs., Part II. and the Staff Manual respectively. Title Pages will be prepared in manuscript.

Place	Date	Hour	Summary of Events and Information	Remarks and references to Appendices
WEST OUTRE	July 1.		Inspected the Transport and Combatant Rest Station of 86. Field Ambulance. The Transport especially the Motor Ambulance Cars were clean and in good condition - horses looked well, harness good, motors clean. Patients seemed to be well cared for.	A.F.R.
	July 2		Inspected 84 & 85. Field Ambulances. Transport & horses was excellent, latter appeared much the thinner. The hospital arrangements of both these Ambulances are much better, but there is still room for improvement. Visited Section of F. Amb. at BAILLEUL, everything in the rest station there was in a very satisfactory condition, the patients were well cared for and general arrangements very good.	A.F.R.
	July 3		Visited all the hutment beds T.A. of G.H.Q. New washing places, cook houses, latrine accommodation &c are in process of erection at all these places, but they are slow in building them.	A.F.R.
	July 4.		Inspected hutments. The ventilation in these huts is very bad. Submitted a recommendation for its improvement of the ventilation by putting large doors at the closed ends of the huts. Men living are too few per square yard at night to be seconds of ground. Repairs to roof (slates) and to house 86 Field Amb. E.	A.F.R.
	July 5.		Went to 84. Field Ambs and visited Officers' rest station MONT NOIR	A.F.R.

WAR DIARY
or
INTELLIGENCE SUMMARY

Army Form C. 2118

Place	Date	Hour	Summary of Events and Information	Remarks and references to Appendices
WEST OUTRE	July 6.		Went round lines with O.C. 15 Sanitary Section; work is proceeding very slowly.	ASR
	July 7.		Informed D.M.S. 2nd Army. It has been decided by 2nd Army that no case is to remain in a Divisional Rest Station for more than 7 days, with an extra 7 days at most per case — every Rest Station in a Division is to be limited to 200 beds and that no case is to remain in a Field Ambulance more than 3 days — This must lead to a considerable increase in "wastage" — Any large number of minor cases were kept in the Division who must now go home — Any arranged for closing of Section Field Amb in Bailleul. Arranged for closing railway Ambulance work —	
	July 8.		Went round the collecting and dressing stations of D Dwin with ADMS & Div ordinance reports in positions. Likes the badly shelled in case of an attack so that it necessary reserve alternate places and collecting points which can be utilised without sending the cars along DICKEBUSCH & VIERSTRAAT road, R.F.A. of which are an exposed to rifle fire fire.	ASR
	July 9.		Visited aid posts now used by this Division. They are situated in farms. One of the Brigades, as a temporary dug out on KEMMEL VIERSTRAAT ROAD about ¼ mile N of VIERSTRAAT, the position is not good being at cross roads. The accommodation is good but limited — the large cellars — one dug out will have to be used by the M.O.s of four Battalions, travelled are collected on stretchers at night by cases which come up the road by day.	

WAR DIARY or INTELLIGENCE SUMMARY

Army Form C. 2118

(Erase heading not required.)

Instructions regarding War Diaries and Intelligence Summaries are contained in F. S. Regs., Part II. and the Staff Manual respectively. Title Pages will be prepared in manuscript.

Place	Date	Hour	Summary of Events and Information	Remarks and references to Appendices
WOUTRE	9/7/15		They are taken in Hutted stretchers one East to DICKEBUSCH where a permanent post is situated at the Dairy. The second Regimental Aid Post is situated in a divisional dairy about 3/4 mile S. of VIERSTRAAT on the KEMMEL—YPRES Road & a third in a Cottage ½ mile E. of this. These are for men of 83 Brigade. Cars clear these at night. They take Cases and carried KEMMEL STReet by car on to PLACHUTE. Ngres the V Divsn have an aid post at VORMEZEELE and 2 the L. Divsn one in KEMMEL.	JSR
	10/7/15		Visited the neighbourhood West of our present trenches and found suitable positions for advanced Dressing Stations the ground if necessary and farms in which bearers can bivouac the permanency near the Road they will clear in case of severe fighting.	JSR
	11/7/15		With A.D.M.S. selected farms to be occupied by Section 9 of 54, 86 Fd Ambulances taken positions to advanced pos for Kearns. These units will man the positions temporary. 85. Fd Ambulance advanced pos chosen, its position for a dressing station for the moment will remain WEST OUTRE. Capt BRERETON RAMC. called re Burial of the dead.	JSR
	12/7/15		Visited BAILLEUL and attended an exhibition of simple Sanitary appliances made from materials always at hand in camps, bivouacs.	JSR

WAR DIARY or INTELLIGENCE SUMMARY

Army Form C. 2118

(Erase heading not required.)

Place	Date	Hour	Summary of Events and Information	Remarks and references to Appendices
WEST OUTRE	13.7/15		Inspected Officers' Rest Station - MONTNOIR. The Home is now full of patients (25 officers) & is most admirably managed by Capt. VICK - 85 (London) Field Amb's assisted by Fr. ROSSANS. The D.D.M.S. 2nd Corps inspected Sir John Ardill at WEST OUTRE. Noted the advanced posts formed by the 15.6 F.Amb's. There are no cases that cases can be evacuated to LA CLYTTE without using the M.S. DICKEBUSCH & KEMMEL Roads.	HSM
"	14/7/15		Several of the Medicos of the Territorial F.A. Ambces of this Division are members of the Staff of London Hospitals for instance Capt FAIRBANK is a Surgeon at St MARY'S, Major WHAGGETT is a thoracic specialist surgeon at Charing Cross, Capt VICK is on the Staff at St BARTHOLOMEWS as an assistant Surgeon, Ltd BARNSLEY and TAYLOR-TAYLOR are also on the junior staff at "BARTS"; none of these Medicos have been offered posts as Surgeons or by Civilian Senior Consulting Surgeons making their position difficult, if they left their field units the latter could not possibly carry out their work as efficiently as at present. I visited A.H.Q. stay with O.C. 66 (London) Fld Ambce this eve. the S.O.Q. M.O. as the subject received a ruling that Medicos should not be moved from T.Force Ambulances. R.J.C. units —	HSM
"	15.7/15		The 28 Division is taking up a line of trenches Sg our present line. The V Division place 9-18 from the Canadian South, the L Division North on our South are moving down to replace them the Front the Ambulances of the L Division who are relieve themselves the Medical	HSM

1875 Wt. W593/826 1,000,000 4/15 J.B.C. & A. A.D.S.S./Forms/C. 2118.

Army Form C. 2118

WAR DIARY
or
INTELLIGENCE SUMMARY
(Erase heading not required.)

Instructions regarding War Diaries and Intelligence Summaries are contained in F.S. Regs., Part II. and the Staff Manual respectively. Title Pages will be prepared in manuscript.

Place	Date	Hour	Summary of Events and Information	Remarks and references to Appendices
			Into in water.	
			84 – Combined Rest Station from 86's with no Sector at DRANOUTRE	
			85 – WEST OUTRE – D. LOCRE and Officers Rest Station MONT NOIR.	
WEST OUTRE	16/7/15		86 LA CLYTTE with an advanced post in farm at M.I.C.	HSR
			84 and 86 Field Ambulances changed places. 84 now LA CLYTTE relieves 86 as Corps Rest Station. BOESCHEPE	HSR
			86 " " LA CLYTTE &	
			86 " BOESCHEPE "	
			Officer from 84 & 86 accompanied me & 2/L Northumbrian F.A. to collect from New Area – our Division	
WEST OUTRE	17/7/15		taking over from the 50 (Northumbrian Division) tomorrow –	HSR
			Attended Conference & No of A.D.M.S. II Corps at BAILLEUL this morning.	HSR
			Visited Officers Rest Station MONT NOIR afternoon.	
			84 & 86 Field Ambulances took over each post and dressing Stations from Northumbrian Division –	HSR
WEST OUTRE	18.7.15		Inspected 86 & 84 Field Ambulances. The Division has been in France 6 months today – also the Cavalry. Cases admitted to Field Ambulances, Casualties, army Rank. Horses received for 6 months	HSR
WEST OUTRE	19.7.–		Investigated the late question of rationing in Field Ambulances. Senior Orderly with Ambulance of C.C.S. Horse Route + Water accumulator of Stores at the same time attempt for private medical "make & patterns	App 4 3-4 & HSR

Army Form C 2118.

WAR DIARY
or
INTELLIGENCE SUMMARY
(Erase heading not required).

Instructions regarding War Diaries and Intelligence Summaries are contained in F.S. Regs., Part II and the Staff Manual respectively. Title Pages will be prepared in manuscript.

Place.	Date	Hour	Summary of Events and Information.	Remarks and references to Appendices
WEST OUTRE	July 20		Inspected billets and village of LOCRE. The sanitary condition of the village is very bad indeed and the billets are very poor. Arranged with Sanitary Officer & Divisional MO. — Inspected Divisional Station of 86.166 Field Ambulances in 6th Division. Seemed roomy. All men their in shelters in their clothes with no attempts made to take advantage of the barns as billets — explained my views on the same to the OCs very plainly. The officers responsible — PL KERR — a motor ambulance driver was involved in fatal accident in car.	ATR
"	July 21		Visited the Aid Posts occupied by 1 Battalion & 84 Brigade in KEMMEL, the arrangements in the ecellulein of wounded appear to work satisfactorily. Inspected Dressing Station of 84 F Ambly arranged arrangements of the building is their & their 25 beds cases can be retained here for three days.	ATR
"	July 22		West wind Kinsale occupied by 84 Bde Sanitation good.	
"	July 23		86 Field Ambulances moved from LA CLYTTE to WEST OUTRE leaving a small post at KEMMEL and an Office at LACLYTTE. The 17th F Division (Kitchener army) move into LA CLYTTE & Field Ambulance being to take Schief from us.	ATR
"	July 24		86 Field Ambulance relieved A Section 85 at LOCRE and collected from the Bn Bde and A Section reports HQ 85 F Amb, at DRANOUTRE, this Unit now clears 63 855 area (West Outre)	ATR

Stationery Services Press, X 8. 5,000 7/15

Army Form C 2118.

WAR DIARY
or
INTELLIGENCE SUMMARY
(Erase heading not required).

Instructions regarding War Diaries and Intelligence Summaries are contained in F.S. Regs., Part II and the Staff Manual respectively. Title Pages will be prepared in manuscript.

Place.	Date	Hour	Summary of Events and Information.	Remarks and references to Appendices
WEST OUTRE	July 25		Attended a meeting at BOULOGNE at which a discussion opened by Sir Kenneth Lenfit was led on the treatment of wounds. The Chief points were the almost failure of any antiseptics, importance of free opening and lymph draining assisted by hypertonic salt solution (Chic Acid 5%)	HER
"	July 26		D.D.M.S. 2nd Army visited 85 Field Ambulance, patients were comfortable and sick clean.	HER
	July 27		Inspected LOCRE and DRANOUTRE with Sanitary Officer, events disposal very unsatisfactory, steps were requested from hostile systems without delay.	HER
	July 28		Inspected 86 Field Ambulance HEORE, condition on the whole unsatisfactory, for the present has been so crowded was by troops that it is impossible to do more than shelter system & storage of improved treatment. Proposed to Field Amb. & Advanced Station DRANOUTRE must the nearest step wards getting evacuated etc. D.D.M.S. II Corps visited Area in evening.	
	July 29		Inspected hills and sanitary arrangements at LOCRE. The ultimate disposal of sewage in a difficult which must have to big vast dangers, attempts at Kemp made them all except Hospital divisions to the purpose but are not satisfactory. Arrangements are being made to have improved receptacles in the ...	

Stationery Services Press, X 8, 5,000 7/15

Army Form C 2118.

Instructions regarding War Diaries and Intelligence Summaries are contained in F.S. Regs., Part II and the Staff Manual respectively. Title Pages will be prepared in manuscript.

WAR DIARY
or
INTELLIGENCE SUMMARY
(Erase heading not required).

Place.	Date	Hour	Summary of Events and Information.	Remarks and references to Appendices
LUTRE	31/7/16		Investigated the milk supply of the Division area with C.O. 3rd Mobile Vety (Capt Myles Copeland). The present supply is inadequate and uncertain, and is kept going from milk sent by the Battalion harbours, the requisitioning of loose milk and remnants, my arrangements and direct purchase and the sale in front of them, and although the brokers be maintained by pro them this seems as much to slip to intermittent supply than the supply required is maintained. Suggested a Divisional reserve put up by the Divisions, the rest as a base supply to Divisions, on this requisitions the rate was strongly personal Authority sent to M.P.P. Delivery in arrange the supply from imported at the Chateau at La Dase base based on a base additional milk in which milk from the source is wanted, to not more than feasible to appointed sent him to Divisl Supplying Coy in the base to administration and analyses. Where requisitions received a suspicion - samples sent to analysis.	WFB

Stationery Services Press, X 8, 5,000 7/15

APPENDICES FOR JULY.

42.   Map showing Aid Posts June 15th --- July 15th.

43.   Total Casualties in Division in 6 months.

44.   Total Admissions in Field Ambulances.

45.   Roll of Casualties R.A.M.C., in 6 months.

46.   Honours and Rewards.

28th Division Expeditionary Force.

Casualties in Six Months:- January 18th to July 18th 1915.

	Sick.	Wounded.	Killed.	Missing.	Totals.
Officers.	196	469	163	99	927
Other Ranks.	7,273	10,554	2,647	7,016	27,490
Totals.	7,469	11,023	2,810	7,115	28,417

Cases treated in Field Ambulances, January to 18th July 1915.

		Officers.	Other Ranks.	Totals.
84th Field Ambulance.	Admissions.	358	13073	13431
(2nd London T)	Transfers.	-	231	231
	Total.	358	13304	13662
85th Field Ambulance.	Admissions.	428	10847	11275
(3rd London T)	Transfers.	-	118	118
	Total.	428	10965	11393
86th Field Ambulance.	Admissions.	85	3288	3373
(2nd North'bn T)	Transfers.	-	2038	2038
	Total	85	5326	5411
	Grand Total.	871	29,595	30,466.

HONOURS AND REWARDS.

Administrative Staff.

Colonel N.C. Ferguson., C.M.G.   Mentioned in Despatches.   June 23rd 1...

84th Field Ambulance. (2nd London T)

Lieut-Col W. Salisbury Sharpe.	Mentioned in Despatches.	June 23rd.
Captain R.E. Bickerton.	Mentioned in Despatches.	June 23rd.
Sergeant F.C. Ingram. No 551.	Distinguished Conduct Medal.	June 23rd.
Private H.C. Sell. No 972.	Mentioned in Despatches.	June 23rd.

85th Field Ambulance. (3rd London T)

Lieut-Colonel J.R. Whait.	Mentioned in Despatches.	June 23rd.
Major E.B. Waggett.	Mentioned in Despatches.	June 23rd.
Captain H.A.T. Fairbank.	Mentioned in Despatches.	June 23rd.
S/Sergeant J.T. Boyes. No 66.	Mentioned in Despatches.	June 23rd.
S/Sergeant J.C. Caswell. No679.	Mentioned in Despatches.	June 23rd.

86th Field Ambulance. (2nd North'bn T)

Lieut-Colonel D.A. Cameron.	Mentioned in Despatches.	June 23rd.
Major D.L. Fisher.	Mentioned in Despatches.	June 23rd.
Lieutenant V.H. Wardle.	Mentioned in Despatches.	June 23rd.
S/Sergeant J.J. Webster. No	Mentioned in Despatches.	June 23rd.

Officers in Medical Charge of Units.

Lieutenant J.M. Gillespie.	" The Military Cross".	June 28th.
Lieutenant J.M. McNicholl.	" The Military Cross."	June 28th.

121/6787

28th Aroroun

A.D.M.S. 28th Division

Vol II

August 15

Summarised LG not copied

August 1915

S1

Army Form C. 2118.

WAR DIARY
or
INTELLIGENCE SUMMARY
(Erase heading not required.)

Instructions regarding War Diaries and Intelligence Summaries are contained in F. S. Regs., Part II. and the Staff Manual respectively. Title pages will be prepared in manuscript.

Hour, Date, Place	Summary of Events and Information	Remarks and References to Appendices
	Confidential. War Diary of Adm.S. 28 Division from August 1st. – August 31st 1915.	

Army Form C 2118.

WAR DIARY
or
INTELLIGENCE SUMMARY
(Erase heading not required).

Instructions regarding War Diaries and Intelligence Summaries are contained in F.S. Regs., Part II and the Staff Manual respectively. Title Pages will be prepared in manuscript.

Place.	Date	Hour	Summary of Events and Information.	Remarks and references to Appendices
WEST OUTRE	Aug. 1st 1915		The Division is now holding trenches extending from about a mile N. of KEMMEL village to about 500 yds S. of WULVERGHEM, (N.15.50 & 20 E. of KEMMEL.) The Brigades are posted from N.E.S. 83 – 84 – 85. One Batt. Battalion 83 is attached to 85 in trench. The 16th of 26th Division to the III Brigade which is attached to the XIV "K" Division for our South are the Canadians. The Field Ambulances are as under: 84. Trinity Divisional Convalescent Rest Station nr BOESCHEPE with its own Section primary & Surgery Station at DRANOUTRE. 85. Group Station & "Apostle" incl. Canvas at WEST OUTRE with one Section primary an Officers Convalescent Rest Station at the Chateau MONT NOIR. 86. Group Station and Temporary Hospital at ABEELE Convent.	Atta
"	Aug 2		Hospital 85 Field Ambulance – both now completed & ready – respected DRANOUTRE area the trench of fever duties – ready to admit. The most cases of sickness are now being sent...	
"	Aug 3.		Inspected Convalescent Rest Station at Sr J. Camp BOESCHEPE. The arrangements & for the station... cooking scenery, ward rooms &... were all good. For Shop Empire Inc.	

Army Form C 2118.

WAR DIARY
or
INTELLIGENCE SUMMARY
(Erase heading not required).

Instructions regarding War Diaries and Intelligence Summaries are contained in F.S. Regs., Part II and the Staff Manual respectively. Title Pages will be prepared in manuscript.

Place.	Date	Hour	Summary of Events and Information.	Remarks and references to Appendices
WEST OUTRE	Aug 4		Inspected Nurses & of 86 Fd Amb Co — The scheme for feeding patients is good but experience to see that it is thoroughly carried out was not sufficient — Went over SS. Field Ambulance cart — ration tins complete. The medical part of the Territorial Medical Unit is the natural care of sick men requiring medical treatment for short stays. Field work including carrying of wounded & patient "orderly work" is best but their training must train them how to take off sick men — perhaps sometime before the time when this particular packed work alone — orderly partaken attendants (in its largest sense) & full alone can hope to make even passing good male nurses.	ATR
"	Aug 5		Attended before "E" Corp he asking how these certain men recently sent to the Battalions of the Division sick except. Quite a large number of cases of Rheumatism have recently occurred among the Troops — 23 cases over the amount of abdominal and large — 40% — Sick — Cases & losses are not recently present & the men complain of headache & suffer from severe depression slight fever. The patients recover completely in a comparatively short time — a History of previous kidney trouble to act as CF etc — Blood cultures are not present. In a certain proportion of cases but in the majority there is no obvious predisposing cause.	ATR

Stationery Services Press, X 8, 5,000 7/15

WAR DIARY
or
INTELLIGENCE SUMMARY
(Erase heading not required).

Army Form C 2118.

Instructions regarding War Diaries and Intelligence Summaries are contained in F.S. Regs., Part II and the Staff Manual respectively. Title Pages will be prepared in manuscript.

Place.	Date	Hour	Summary of Events and Information.	Remarks and references to Appendices
WEST OUTRE	Aug. 6		Inspected huts at LOCRE and BRANDTHOEK and approved too patterns of incinerator built by men of the Sanitary Section. The Hospital pattern supplied for camps is not a success, takes men to hunt in the will with careful supervision, at least to burn very slowly and some form of box is necessary in which the material used as fuel – horse manure – burn to keep dry. In the patterns built by our Sanitary Section there is a space between the fire place in which the material is put to dry before it is brought into close contact with the flames. Frozen meat not in the delivery.	/app
	Aug. 7		Attended conference at BAILLEUL presided over by D.D.M.S. 2nd Corps. Major R.R.B. (San) G.H.Q. was present. Re question of preventing an outbreak of para typhoid amongst the troops was discussed. Major ADDERLEY R.A.M.C. D.A.D.M.S. 27 Division joined for instruction.	/app
	Aug. 8		Visited the three Field Ambulances. Arranged for an advanced position for the Regimental Aid post in WINCHESTER Road in a dug out at R.E. Farm. The present aid post will be taken over by an advanced Reir aid post.	/app
	Aug. 10		In absence of Major ACKLEY accompanied D.A.D.Q & my A.S.C. Serjt & S.S.M.S. field ambulance. Went over LOCRE Camp, saw incinerators there. Met Major Maclare officers etc attached by Q.M. & Hotel Rep. Re: again, the Sanitary Reg the men Maclare...	/app

Army Form C 2118.

WAR DIARY
or
INTELLIGENCE SUMMARY
(Erase heading not required).

Instructions regarding War Diaries and Intelligence Summaries are contained in F.S. Regs., Part II and the Staff Manual respectively. Title Pages will be prepared in manuscript.

Place.	Date	Hour	Summary of Events and Information.	Remarks and references to Appendices
WEST OUTRE	Aug 10.		"Gideon Fare" & spraying of appeared rank & water & wind, this can be moved to keep it put up. Inexpensive appears to be efficient. — Trenches occupied by 1/2 and 1/6 West Rid: visited. Have had Daunatan 7/1/1/8's Road 1/6. bad. Inspected Seven men of 1/6 KOYLI recommended for duty in 67E. Major ADDERLEY informed this Division this evening.	MSR
"	Aug 11		Four Battalions from the 3) Division have been attached R.W.M. Division or withnessed — Group the 6 7 & 8 Yorks, 6 Leicester Res — Inspected all the billets, saw the medical Officers arranged for these instruction in trench work with M.O.'s of the Battalions in this Division. Four men 1/20 West Yorks have Red acute's 37 Division have been attached to 49 Division this morning from Aug 10 - Aug 14. The party has been divided into two half attached to the new stretcher bearer half Rth. Dressing Station at DICKEBUSCHE.	MSR
"	Aug 12		Inspected Regimental Aid Post at THE LAITERIE — NIGHTINGALE WOOD and at KEMMEL village. Reviewed Brigades 84 + 85 Brigade. Inspected advanced H.Q.S a 8 & 7 zubs at LYDENHOEK and 3 Sect. 20 at 204th BKR. Visited H.Q. 8 3+ Bde RFA, and 148 A.F. RFA, also Ammunition Column line & Ammr. sub Party Supply Arms Chateau at La Chaux entry necessary Rays —	MSR

Stationery Services Press, X 8. 5,000 7/15

Army Form C 2118.

WAR DIARY
or
INTELLIGENCE SUMMARY
(Erase heading not required).

Instructions regarding War Diaries and Intelligence Summaries are contained in F.S. Regs., Part II and the Staff Manual respectively. Title Pages will be prepared in manuscript.

Place.	Date	Hour	Summary of Events and Information.	Remarks and references to Appendices
WEST OUTRE	3/8/15		The 110 (LEICESTER) Brigade, a Company of R.E. and half Battalion back from 6 (Warwicks) & East Yorks Lancs. Regt. have been attached from 37th (Kitchener) Division. The 28th Division for instruction and for digging. Inspected the line of Warwick (East Lancs.) Composite Battalion. They have been a large epidemic of Diarrhoea among them, not apparently due to "shell" or "infect". Arranged Field part of one Sanitary Section keep in engagement of Rest Lines — There is no marked increase among any other troops in Division. The R.O. and O.C. Men of 37 Division Sanitary Section are attached (29 O.R. Sau. Sect. for instruction. Visited Water Station near Station ment hut.	AAA
	10/8/15		Attended Conference of ADMSS at BAILLEUL. For April 3, Division terms Corps & May Division attached AAA, 28th Div.	AAA
	15/8/15		Visited Chumberland Rest Station and arranged for Provision of fifteen Complements. Not yet for Rest Sta. AAA. The parties to the Divisional guard in H.Q. fatigues. They will be inspected weekly and a KY, they known fit for full duty will be replaced by discharges from Hospital a.	
	16.8.15		Inspected the wagon lines of all the batteries and the accommodation between of 312 By R.F.A. and The 56 Bot. Ammn. Attended Mr Statesman Representative of British Red Cross Society and arranged with him for supply of mosquito Curtains for 63 Ambulance score and for half line in a case for pusters in Whew Rest Station about 2000	AAA

Stationery Services Press, X 8, 5,000 7/15

WAR DIARY
or
INTELLIGENCE SUMMARY
(Erase heading not required).

Army Form C 2118.

Instructions regarding War Diaries and Intelligence Summaries are contained in F.S. Regs., Part II and the Staff Manual respectively. Title Pages will be prepared in manuscript.

Place.	Date	Hour	Summary of Events and Information.	Remarks and references to Appendices
WEST OUTRE	17/8/15		Went with LOCKE and Sanitary Officer. The trench is being turned satisfactorily in the village and arrangements are being made for its extra disposal at Mont de Cats Camp. The water supply from the upper pond at the Château is in good working order. The supply is ample. The arrangements for keeping the carts work satisfactory and the rate fairly good in Quality. At Mont Q. killed a cart overhead. 23 Carts were unloaded. A Sergeant of the Sanitary Company is posted at the Empty and Experimental. The Chairmaster of the Carts on the spot keeps the carts save the supply.	MSR
	18/8/15		Inspected Major Reid and Ammunition Column of 2nd Bn RFA. Kitchen in the battery are unmanned. Give training here in Early Form Game arranged to be required.	MSR
	19/8/15		Accompanied RIMF. II Corps around FLETRE at DRANOUTRE and LOCRE and touch the 86 Field Ambce.	MSR
	20/8/15		Inspected Info. Brit. Ammunition Column & 4 148 Bg RFA	MSR
	21/8/15		Attended Conference of A.D.M.S. at BAILLEUL. Inspected Rest Station Mont NOIR	MSR
	22/8/15		Visited ADMS (?) Division. This Division is now on our left.	MSR
	23/8/15		Inspected the Companies of the Divisional Train.	MSR
	24/8/15		Inspected the Divisional Ammunition Column and 8th Field Ambulance Dressing Station DRANOUTRE.	MSR
	25/8/15		Inspected the Lines of all R.E. units with A.A.Q.M.G. One company was in an insanitary and unreported condition. Visited the Sanitary Office. Visited BATTERIES BETWEEN BAILLEUL.	
	26/8/15		Visited LOCRE and DRANOUTRE with A.Q.M.G. and Sanitary Offer. Arranged new billet for Ambulances. Visited Advanced Pst. Posts by WULVERGHEM & NEUVE ÉGLISE. Rode at night.	MSR

Stationery Services Press. X 8. 5,000 7/15

WAR DIARY
or
INTELLIGENCE SUMMARY
(Erase heading not required).

Army Form C 2118.

Place.	Date	Hour	Summary of Events and Information.	Remarks and references to Appendices
WEST OUTRE	27/8/15		Prayed for the Reserve at Caurieux Port WYN BECK & the a day out with Adjutant of R.E. and Principal learn at "RE Farm" the used as a Regimental Aid Post the present Infantry Aid Post from the Trenches. Inspected camps at SCHERPENBERG Huts and Baths at LOORE.	JS872
	28/8/15		Attended meeting of A.D's M.S. at BAILLEUL and heard Secretary Solutions Read, there is a collection of appliances for hut in camps made from materials always available. Tea takes hospital Huts wire, Refuse tin lies &c v &. The exhibition is available against a most interests collection of most ingenious appliances. In the STORE of Corps + & a most network collection of most ingenious appliances. Visited St Paid Amb at LOORE and Advance Station at DRANOUTRE both doing fit Cops.	JS872
	29/8/15		Three Medical Officers from the Division - Major Sharpe, Lt Col Cameron for Parts Johnson an exhibition of Splints Surgical appliances referred to the nurses of Expenses during the War, at the Australian Hospital WIMEREAUX. The question of an interchange of Medical Officers so that the Reid and Officers could see the Condition in which Cases arrived at the Base & the officers at Remand Hospitals could appreciate the condition under which field Ambulance work in the Front was Discussed. It was generally agreed that such temporary exchange would be of very great benefit both consuned.	JS872

Army Form C 2118.

WAR DIARY
or
INTELLIGENCE SUMMARY
(Erase heading not required).

Instructions regarding War Diaries and Intelligence Summaries are contained in F.S. Regs., Part II and the Staff Manual respectively. Title Pages will be prepared in manuscript.

Place.	Date	Hour	Summary of Events and Information.	Remarks and references to Appendices
WEST OUTRE	Aug 30		BnONE II Capt. M°C Davies visited 85. Field Amb= at WEST OUTRE — Arranged with A.D.S. for supply of tetanus inocul. for females, the contact have must be tried in respect necessity, a high percentage than usual — In the majority of the group who exposed to hairy horse. In <s>the</s> afternoon visited officers rest station Mont NOIR	[JMcR?]
	Aug 31		Conference of officers commanding the Nine Field Ambulances. Visited aid posts & collecting posts. Had an opportunity with 2d & 3d Cand Fd ambs Held our initial return of sound with C.O. 85 Fd amb 9 amb 9 minly dressed a transaction...	[JMcR?]
			Health of division during month "Excellent" Average sick evacuation "0.53 %" Admitted "0.57 %" Total number of cases of scabies 2/5. Pediculosis 3/5.	

Stationery Services Press, X 8, 5,000 7/15

121/7551

Sep 1915

A.D.M.S. 28th Div.
Sep 1915
Vol II

51

Summarised & not copied
Dec 1924

War Diary.

A.D.M.S. 28th Division.

Period 1st to 30th September 1915.

Volume No 9.

Army Form C 2118.

WAR DIARY
or
INTELLIGENCE SUMMARY
(Erase heading not required).

Instructions regarding War Diaries and Intelligence
Summaries are contained in F.S. Regs., Part II
and the Staff Manual respectively. Title Pages
will be prepared in manuscript.

Place.	Date	Hour	Summary of Events and Information.	Remarks and references to Appendices
WEST OUTRE	Sept 1st		Position of Medical Units:-	
			B4 Field Ambce. Two Tent & One Bearer subdivisions near BEESCHEPE forming a divisional Rest Station with Camps.	
			No Tent and Two Bearer subdivisions forming Dressing Station at DRANOUTRE, an advanced Post in station on NEUVE EGLISE – YPRES Road with walking wounded to clear aid post by day & the higher point posts from aid post by night.	
			S5 J Ambce at WEST OUTRE. forming a Dressing Station at the huts close and a Hospital under canvas, with an advanced post in LA CLYTE – DICKEBUSCH Road. One Section forming Officers Rest Station MONT NOIR.	
			S6 7 Ambce at LOCRE. forming Dressing station in convent there with advanced post in Aug a.s S. O. RUMMEL HILL.	
			Health of Division Excellent. Average Strength 1st August 21107.	
			Sick rate .05%	
			Daily wounded .36%	
			Number of Infections Cases since 2 Aug. stood 3 Paratyphoid 3 Aonte 1 – 6 (cases)	
			Toilet and Pris ave transit to S.S. A.O. They were in good sanitary condition	

Stationery Services Press, X 8, 5,000 7/15

Army Form C 2118.

WAR DIARY
or
INTELLIGENCE SUMMARY
(Erase heading not required).

Instructions regarding War Diaries and Intelligence Summaries are contained in F.S. Regs., Part II and the Staff Manual respectively. Title Pages will be prepared in manuscript.

Place.	Date	Hour	Summary of Events and Information.	Remarks and references to Appendices
WEST OUTRE	Sept. 2, 1915		Attended Brigade DRUMHEAD in morning. – In afternoon examined the officers, Major THOMAS (P.M.) and Major MORGAN of 16th Welsh Regt. from a former suffering from NEURASTHENIA and latter from chronic emphysema with cardiac enlargement and left 684 F. Amb for evacuation. Visited 86 F. Amb at LOCRE.	MR
WEST OUTRE	Sept. 3.		F.C.M.E. T Corps being on 7 days leave, admr. RE Division assumed duties of DDMS Corps in addition to own Division. Visited all three Casualty Clearing Stations. Busy with work all day.	MR
WEST OUTRE	4.		Inspected Camps at LOCRE and DRANOUTRE with aar9mf – The position of trichter Kersing of the troops will soon have the faced they are now made in trener Station.	MR
"	5.		Inspected S.A. Ros Aux y at meeting station BOESCHEPE with aar9mf	
"	6.		Inspected Camps at SCHERPENBERG and KEMMEL with aar9mf	
"	7.		Inspected Divisional Ammunition Column, D.L.E. Train 13th RDD Ammunition Column with aar9mf	MR

WAR DIARY
or
INTELLIGENCE SUMMARY
(Erase heading not required).

Army Form C 2118.

Place	Date	Hour	Summary of Events and Information.	Remarks and references to Appendices
WEST OUTRE	Sept 7	3 P.M	Inspect 86 Field Amb-ce at OUTRE. Inspected site for hut near KEMMEL with Col. DARLING R.E. The first cases of "Trench feet" were reported yesterday. This after-noon cases seen in "The Buffs"	JHR
"	Sep 8	—	Accompanied by the D's the three Brig. Auchlaceds, inspected sites & finally selected troops to be used as Aid Posts when the VIERSTRAAT SWITCH, WULFERGHEM SWITCH and GITZ ENC. are occupied by our Troops —	JHR
"	Sep 9	—	Inspected Officers' Rest Station near MUIR and their Ambulances Rest Station at G. SEVEN.	HCR
"	10.	"	Inspected accommodation at BEDFORD EST for Ambulances Rest Station with Col. (?)LIP, there is nothing suitable in the village. Col. Jerguson received news concerning 2 RS corps as D.D.M.S. Col. TYACKE being medi-cally unfit to retain him in France.	HFR
"	11	"	Meet "G.A.Q. to interview Capt. J. DEIGHTON RAMC (S.R) to the D.G.M.S. This office is a Candidate for a permanent commission R.A.M.C.	JHR
"	12.	"	Captain Johnson on Eastern slope of KEMMEL HILL were opposite the dry steep ambulance there. Inspected, they are in a good site but on a close clay soil and in a wood so that after wet weather the soil is very difficult tang. Arranged that Coy Brown should be out	JHR

Stationery Services Press, X 8, 5,000 7/15

Army Form C 2118.

WAR DIARY
or
INTELLIGENCE SUMMARY
(Erase heading not required).

Instructions regarding War Diaries and Intelligence Summaries are contained in F.S. Regs., Part II and the Staff Manual respectively. Title Pages will be prepared in manuscript.

Place.	Date	Hour	Summary of Events and Information.	Remarks and references to Appendices
WEST OUTRE	17/9/15		and paths made between the huts. The will improve the condition but will not bring normally up. The site is a bad one and there is no that it is an important military position it would be convenient to Louvain grounds.	JTR
"	13		Went to G.H.Q. Entrance of H.C. FOODING R.A.M.C. (T.Res.) a Candidate for a Regular Commission to the Director General A.M.S. Lt. Col. Tempney Colonel M. TYACKE sent on extension [illegible] in the General Field pending his duties as A.D.M.S. from No. 3 General Hospital took over duties of A.D.M.S. from Col. M. TYACKE. A.M.S. Col. M. FERGUSON appointed D.D.M.S. XII Corps. Removed K.O.T.C. II amb. Inspected 86 Field Ambs Loads and bathing establishment there.	JTR
"	14			
"	15		Inspected 84 Field Amb's dressing Station at DRANOUTRE, a Rest Station at BOESCHEPE, also 85 Field Amb's WEST OUTRE Bathing establishment as DRANOUTRE & WEST OUTRE	JTR
"	16	"	Inspected Advanced & Aidpoints at KEMMEL, hired Aid post at the LAITERIE, NIGHTINGALE WOOD, KEMMEL. Inspected Camps at SCHERPENBERG. Visited Green Rest Station MONT NOIR Leaving	JTR
"	17	"	Advanced dressing and field equipment and dispensary & C.C's field ambulances to arrange details of disposal of surplus equipment & in case of a move.	JTR

Army Form C 2118.

WAR DIARY
or
INTELLIGENCE SUMMARY
(Erase heading not required).

Instructions regarding War Diaries and Intelligence Summaries are contained in F.S. Regs., Part II and the Staff Manual respectively. Title Pages will be prepared in manuscript.

Place.	Date	Hour	Summary of Events and Information.	Remarks and references to Appendices
WEST OUTRE	10/9/15		Attended meeting of A.D.M.S. II Corp. presided over by D.D.M.S. Reserve Canadian Division has now been formed and is to take over this ___ area next week.	
			Visited the Casualty Division with Bailleul and inspected the incidents of the dumping ground there. A convoy informed A.D.M.S. 2 Canadian Division and D.D.M.S. Canadian Corps relating to the handing over of the RCH ambulances & ____.	MSR
			Wires sent [?] ___ returned to the Dominion of Red Cross surplus equipment, all will be taken on & the morning ambulance on receipt.	
	19/9/15		Visited all Dressing Stations, Amalgamated Rest Stations to with R.A.M.C. II Canadian Division. These two and Motor Ambulances accompanied on their tour had been temporarily been attached from Ambulances. Duties for Pater — D.A.I. I Army visited office in arrangement for move.	MSR
	20/9/15		Conference of Officers Commanding Reserve units to move. The Division begins move from this area tomorrow and is being relieved by the 2nd Canadian Division. The areas being moved on-- Sept 31 — 84 & Bde with 85 F amb a move to PRADELLES — BORRE area " 22 — 85 " " " 86 " " " MERRIS — STRADEELE. " 23 — 83 " " " 84 " " " OUDERSTEENE — BAILLEUL "	
			A afternoon inspected new Divisional Area.	

Army Form C 2118.

WAR DIARY
or
INTELLIGENCE SUMMARY
(Erase heading not required).

Instructions regarding War Diaries and Intelligence Summaries are contained in F.S. Regs., Part II and the Staff Manual respectively. Title Pages will be prepared in manuscript.

Place.	Date	Hour	Summary of Events and Information.	Remarks and references to Appendices
WEST OUTRE	21/8/15	—	85 Field Ambce marched to PRADELLES, being relieved by IV Canadian F.A. The Section now at MONT NOIR retained HQ last night. Lorries and 2 Canadian San Sec. continued to hand in baths & camps.	JBR
"	22/8/15		86 FIELD AMBCE with 85 86 marched to STRAZEELE – MERRIS area, (the Ambulance at MERRIS) being handed over to No 5. Canadian Field Ambce. Visited the New Divisional Billetting area – BORRE – BAILLEUL (Farms). The accommodation for about 6 bar[?] at BORRE & PRADELLE Rd. F.A. are in the Rural quarters. At MERRIS 86 will be in the small hotel. No room in Gd field for bath. The 84 will be accommodated in a Fm[?] Farm S.E. of OUTERSTEENE – The Farm they originally occupied in January – Canadian 6th[?] Div. all baths & camps both in Sanitary section.	JBR
MERRIS.	23/8/15		84 Field Ambce marched to 83 B.B. area – OUTERSTEENE. Head Quarters moved to MERRIS. Returned D.M.S. & Army. Visited all three Field Ambulances in new billets. Arrived here 6.30pm to the 1000 Division.	JBR
"	24/8/15		Discussed Medical arrangements that have been made in case of a sudden move by two wth. G. Staff., Conference with O.C. the three Field Ambulances at 3 PM. Point out details. The Military arrangements will be made of [?]ownh (1) A.D.M.O. accompanied G.S. motor Cyclist will be wth. Advce Staff to have passing Station (2) The Adm Ambce cars will accompany Tack. Rn. Hellen with material for a Regt aid Post. (3) Remaining N Cars follow convoy with Moving Station parts & Ambce Cars toward station guides to motor Section.	JBR

Stationery Services Press, X. 8. 5,000 7/15

Army Form C 2118.

WAR DIARY
or
INTELLIGENCE SUMMARY
(Erase heading not required).

Instructions regarding War Diaries and Intelligence Summaries are contained in F.S. Regs., Part II and the Staff Manual respectively. Title Pages will be prepared in manuscript.

Place.	Date	Hour	Summary of Events and Information.	Remarks and references to Appendices
MERRIS.	Sep. 25		Interviewed D.M.S. 2nd Army re medical arrangements in case of a sudden move. Proposed 80 Fd Amb attached to Sanitary Section reformed an many as possible tonight. (recommended) transport alone. Horses for duty at base only. Heavy rain all day. Orders the ready to move at 2 hours notice.	VFR
MERRIS — MERVILLE — BETHUNE.	Sep. 26		The Division Marched South & Billets near BETHUNE and came under orders of 1st Corps 12 noon. Field Ambulances marched with the Brigade area as under. 84 FA with 83 Bde in area round ROBECQ 86 " " 84 " " " PARADIS 85 " " 85 " " " BETHUNE. Sits: H.Q. BETHUNE. Sick remaining in Ambulances were evacuated to BAILLEUL and HAZEBROUCK (controlled by mules) & sent to clearing Station — 2nd Corps Rly Station. The sick were by but had few had been left over & returned to Sanitas H.Q O.C. clearing Station. Thence evacuated to N.Z. Cas. Clearing Sta MERVILLE. Also 2d F.Amb: BETHUNE & HINGES.	
BETHUNE	Sep 27		Division moved R.E. tools were occupied to Orders Sart 2nd Inf. of Inf. division as g shown but were of 95 Brigade headlt to bivouac near AMEQUIN or BETHUNE — LA BASSÉE Road. In support of IX Corps 83 and 84 Brigades moved in three forces to area near NOYELLE to support 7th Division and latter to SAUVY LA BOURSE where they become Corps Reserve Troops.	

Army Form C 2118.

WAR DIARY
or
INTELLIGENCE SUMMARY
(Erase heading not required).

Instructions regarding War Diaries and Intelligence Summaries are contained in F.S. Regs., Part II and the Staff Manual respectively. Title Pages will be prepared in manuscript.

Place	Date	Hour	Summary of Events and Information.	Remarks and references to Appendices
BETHUNE	Sep 27		Sit Rep Quit R parked at VERQUIGNEUL. 83 and 86 at SAILLY LABOURSE. Charged Relats of Billing over Brewery Station to with A.DMS IR Division and water parts of MENS ypres. The ranks from 83 1ER Field Amby, kept with troops of 29 Fg Amby. Fought in new area —	
SAILLY LABOURSE	Sep 28		Divisional advanced Head Quarters moved from LABOURSE, along with moved from also 85 Field Amb & arrived 28 Field Ambs to SAILLY LABOURSE and at Station VERMELLES — The 85 BM taking on trucks for a hybrid of 9th Division. 86 Field Amb2 took the advanced Dressing Station, advanced pack and tigtly horsed station from 29 Field Ambs at CAMBRIN. The scheme for collecting wounded at the line is divided with a Motor Ambulance Loading by the AMERICAN branch of the SAILOR-LES BASSES-VERMELLES Railway. The advanced Dressing Station to be on the railway line in the LABOURSE village. Cars are collected here & going to the Railway Station from this point right on for a company of which a unit standard an motor than by field hrs on the back of the portion where the branch of the underbrush signed (by) the line been abandoned. Going for the drive on the water is a level of through main communication trench. The Riflemen we the people which are carried on support trenches from CAMBRIN back man an other to CAMBRIN will ambulances as they enter the line be an excellent road. The little Beaver trench is 6 miles.	

Stationery Services Press, X 8, 5,000 7/15

Army Form C 2118.

WAR DIARY
or
INTELLIGENCE SUMMARY
(Erase heading not required).

Instructions regarding War Diaries and Intelligence Summaries are contained in F.S. Regs., Part II and the Staff Manual respectively. Title Pages will be prepared in manuscript.

Place	Date	Hour	Summary of Events and Information	Remarks and references to Appendices
SAILLY LABOURSE	Sep 28		The Southern sector has the advanced dressing station in the cellars of the brewery at VERMELLES. Its main dressing station at SAILLY LABOURSE, and can go to VERMELLES night & day from A.D.S. if the situation might keep a hole there. The horse line is a second A.D.S. not advanced dressing station known as BARTS FARM. This is BARTS ANNEX, close to the aerial communication trench in which the appointed aid posts are situate. The 88 Field Ambulance has the N.W.R. frong from VERMELLES north on SOUTH of GUYS. The last division holds the dressing station at CALEVY LABOURSE. The forward aid post were killed in action today. M. BAG. Lt. GOODYEAR, K.C. KRANNICKE R.S. J. of the personnel were reported missing. M 17.9. Pt. MARRIOTT VC.	? Baek
SAILLY LABOURSE	Sep 29		4 officers & 240 other ranks were evacuated through N° 1 CORPS rest depôt. (290 7 K.D.m + 215 Pt.B.H.) So sick purchases left per advanced dressing station at le CHATEAU VERMELLES from 88th F Amb (7.30). 88 Field Ambs Feel Demais took over FERME JULES FERRY from 29 F. Amb (9.15 a.m.) Feel Cartel Took Demais for the 83. F.A. who relieve the 89 F.A. in trenches tonight. Personnel R.A.G. to K.K.N. C.O. retained A.D.M.S. 7th Division in orders, to relieve 9th ambulances also acting strong points. Nickel additional dressing stations at VERMELLES and "BARTS" also for use of Y ZONE.	

Stationery Services Press, X 8, 5,000 7/15

Army Form C 2118

WAR DIARY
or
INTELLIGENCE SUMMARY
(Erase heading not required).

Instructions regarding War Diaries and Intelligence Summaries are contained in F.S. Regs., Part II and the Staff Manual respectively. Title Pages will be prepared in manuscript.

Place.	Date	Hour	Summary of Events and Information.	Remarks and references to Appendices
SAILLY LABOURSE	Sept 30		Been under fire since 12 open and 5.30 oClock tonight (356 wounded & 64 killed) wounds chiefly shrapnel and head wounds, in addition to 9/10th Divisions were Bearer by own F. Amts. Inspected main dressing station of 8th Div Staff or ECOLE DES JEUNES FILLS and ST. PAUL at ECOLE FERY. A daily conference of Officers commanding the Field Ambulances has been instituted in our Place in Contact Truck with the Force under AdMS met each of F. Amt at 4 pm. Evening attack yesterday afternoon note on mortified by Letter orders. Inspected EDSS & CCP — in coming heard considerable shooting taken the man Pt. F. Amts none of our wounded yesterday —	

N. Nicolls
Colonel AMS
ADMS 28th Division

Stationery Services Press, X 8, 5,000 7/15

A. D. M. S. 28th Division

Volume 10

Army Form C 2118.

WAR DIARY
or
INTELLIGENCE SUMMARY
(Erase heading not required).

Instructions regarding War Diaries and Intelligence Summaries are contained in F.S. Regs., Part II and the Staff Manual respectively. Title Pages will be prepared in manuscript.

Place.	Date	Hour	Summary of Events and Information.	Remarks and references to Appendices
SAILLY LABOURSE	1915 Feb 14.1		Order received through B. Amb'ce Workshop — Officers 7 Other Ranks to give O.R. 180 horses to 57 vehicles & 28 bicycles and 7 other ORs. Received J.O.N.R. 4th Corps Proposed B3. Field Amb'ce dressing station. Proposed connection between Aid Posts, Advanced Posts & Advanced Dressing Station & Collecting Zone. 8.3. Infantry Brigade handed over to 65th Infantry Brigade (2nd Division) this evening. Accompanied 84 F. Amb'ce O.C. Rourke, who will take on aid posts tomorrow. Bde found today at ANNEQUIN (tr Neuf) Noeal (RE dispatches) in Mine buildings. Position of Dressing Station R: 84 F. Amb'ce Advr Dressing Stn. VERMELLES Chateau. Main Dressing Station. ECOLE JULES FILLES BETHUNE SAILLY LABOURSE VERMELLES Brewery. ECOLE JULES FERY BETHUNE CAMBRIN (near Church) 85 " " " " " " " " " 86 The aid Posts Evacuating to 85 FA are situated near Central Keep and at this Battalion at "The Quarry" " 86 " " " " " In front of VERMELLES to a further advanced dressing Station situated near B.H.Q. Central BARTS. Consists of Communication areas cold GUYS In front of CAMBRIN " " "	

Stationery Services Press, X 8, 5,000 7/15

Army Form C 2118.

WAR DIARY
or
INTELLIGENCE SUMMARY
(Erase heading not required).

Instructions regarding War Diaries and Intelligence Summaries are contained in F.S. Regs., Part II and the Staff Manual respectively. Title Pages will be prepared in manuscript.

Place.	Date	Hour	Summary of Events and Information.	Remarks and references to Appendices
DILLY CABOURG	Oct 2.	19.00	85 Field Amb⁹ Tent Division moved to the School at VENDIN leaving Sally LABOURSE w/ to No 6. F. Amb of 2ᵈ Division. 85 Bearer Division returning at BERMELLES between CAMBRIN and VERMELLES, No 16th Company to FOSSE 3 VALES FERY. Advanced dressing stations at BETHUNE and advanced F.S. at VERMELLES, CAMBRIN. Casualties admitted yesterday Officers wounded 7. Other ranks wounded 250 Rat 59 That 314. 9 There are the Officers and 264 men 2ᵈ Division —. The F.A. has killed the Advanced F St. Field Ambᶜ last night —	
"	Oct 3.	—	Visited the three Field Ambulances. Went over the 85 Ambulance at VENDIN with a view to possibly expanding it of using them for light Cases — all our F.A.S were kicked fairly frantically them with knocking ↓ aCen. employed. Coming to very heavy ↓ especially in their Rastor at the Knocks are having the out their Rolay to very stopped after a little rain others one so too hard, the ground very sharp — Casualties Yesterday Officers wounded 4. Other ranks 196. Sick Ax. ranks 42 = 172. 9 There are the Officers and 145 OR here 85 F.A	
"	Oct 4	—	Inspected 85 F.A. Units arrived 12 open three R take in wounded from VERMELLES, Ban. Ambed with Bt. Col of Oʳ Supply Column for use of Lorries in slight evacuations to rear of a week. Visited 16 FA at FOSSE VALES FERY.	

Stationery Services Press, X 8, 5,000 7/15

WAR DIARY
or
INTELLIGENCE SUMMARY
(Erase heading not required).

Army Form C 2118.

Place.	Date	Hour	Summary of Events and Information.	Remarks and references to Appendices
SAILLY LABOURSE	Oct. 4		Casualties: Military Officer wounded 13. Other ranks Wounded 240. Sick 49. Total 302.	
			9 More all the Officers and 212 wounded, and 48 sick returned to 28 Division.	
	Oct. 5		Casualties admitted Military Officers wounded 4. Sick 170. Other ranks Wounded 150 Sick 68. 9 These all the Officers and 74 wounded 186 sick were of 28 Division.	
			The 28th Division handed over to GUARDS Division today, and details of relief with 82nd Guards Division. The Division marches N.W. through own Bussnes area arrived march when __ and marked BUSNES (See possible position for Ambulances, the M.G. Clearing Station.	
BUSNES	Oct. 6		28 Division marched to our area N.W. of BETHUNE to rest and "refitting".	
			84 Field Amb. marched to 83 Bde area, to billets at GONNEHEM.	
			85. LE CORNET-BOURDOIS in 84 Bde area.	
			86. F. Amb. marched with 85 to BUSNES in 85 Bde area.	
			2 Bde 84 own Field Ambulances are arranging for a reception room, they will collect cases from the Medical Inspection rooms sending them 83 FA or VENDIN, which will act as the "Divisional Hospital"—Casualties last night Wounded Officer 1. O.R. 87 Sick O.R. 46 g Mess the Officer 81 O.R. wounded x 41 Sick were of 28 Div.	
	Oct 7		Conference at 11 AM. with D.S. of the Three Ambulances to arrange a programme of Training which to Commence. Special steps will be taken concerning the men to undergo ... in ...	

WAR DIARY
or
INTELLIGENCE SUMMARY
(Erase heading not required).

Army Form C 2118.

Instructions regarding War Diaries and Intelligence Summaries are contained in F.S. Regs., Part II and the Staff Manual respectively. Title Pages will be prepared in manuscript.

Place	Date	Hour	Summary of Events and Information	Remarks and references to Appendices
BUSNES	Oct 7.		Visited Divnl Field Trenches also in digging "slug ot" aid posts and dressing stations in trenches. The amount necessary of a field cooker in a field Ambulance has been again demonstrated in the recent operations. The want being of the greatest use not for the personnel on the march and for wounded as absolute rest for a many of those men come in exhausted suffering from shock and exposure a hot meal is a most essential part of their treatment. In not making this now not proving stews & cooking pt. 6 but in many positions where this cannot be made for feeding reasons a Field Cooker would be invaluable.	
	Oct 8		Inspected 85. Field Amb^{ce} at VENDIN. The accommodation is limited, it being ??? and attacked in Hill ?? Wassan ???. Knuckle Military Asylum. FOSSE JULES FERRY. BETHUNE. Inspected 86 Field Ambce at BUSNETTES and Training ??? 785 7.R. & LA CACHET BOURSCIS. The minute of Casualties passing through this Ambulance between Sept 29 & Oct 5 was. Officers 60 O.R 1720 of these 52 officers + 1588 other ranks belonged to 28 Division. Both were quiet in their Brigade area viz. 83rd B^{de} at AUCHEL-HEM. 84 R.M. FRUGESORE 85 Bde at L'ECLEME	
	Oct 9		Visited Ambulances En bloke bunt, 83. 186 field Ambs. 85.186 field Ambces arranged plans in Ambulance bus and new men, hill hom air "dump" at LOCRE for use at VENDIN	

Army Form C 2118.

WAR DIARY
or
INTELLIGENCE SUMMARY
(Erase heading not required).

Instructions regarding War Diaries and Intelligence Summaries are contained in F.S. Regs., Part II and the Staff Manual respectively. Title Pages will be prepared in manuscript.

Place.	Date	Hour	Summary of Events and Information.	Remarks and references to Appendices
BUSNES.	10/10/16		Inspected 85 Brig Aunts with D.D.M.S. V Corps.	
			Interviewed the OC's these Field Aunts and after consultation with them submitted following Officers names for promotion:—	JFR
			S4 + Rank Capt R.E. BICKERTON promoted Major from April 1st to complete establishment.	
			85 " " " Capt H.J. FAIRBANK " " " "	
			S6 " " " Capt A.R. ELLIS " " " "	
			" Temporary Major, June 20 "	
11-10			Inspected Billets of SUFFOLK Regt. Conferred & all Battalion Medical Officers & arrangements	JFR
			for their rapid evacuation if wounded.	
			Visited No 6 Casualty Clearing Station re evacuation & Capt McCOY	
			Gaunt BUTLIN for on sick list that Feby suffering from very severe migraine, he will be evacuated from no.	
			as experience & medical officers has again brought out in future in this division a Medical officer	
			that ambulance wagons will be attached back to their Casualty Clearing Station he holds his Medical officer	
			for on ambulance will be attached Casr to holding Medical officer	
			to fix up the squad christly he has ordered his aid post —	
14:12			Inspected the bandsmen units of 63 & 85 Brigade, ambulance extensively.	

Stationery Services Press, X 8. 5,000 7/15

Army Form C 2118.

WAR DIARY
or
INTELLIGENCE SUMMARY
(Erase heading not required).

Instructions regarding War Diaries and Intelligence Summaries are contained in F.S. Regs., Part II and the Staff Manual respectively. Title Pages will be prepared in manuscript.

Place.	Date	Hour	Summary of Events and Information.	Remarks and references to Appendices
Oct 13. 15 BUSNES			Inspected 85 Field Amb'ce made arrangements for extension of accomo'dation at VENDINS —	AAR
			Inspected Chronic cases of 2nd Middlesex detachment now being "reclass'." rendered very fair	
			help for staff at the Base.	
			Visited 86 Field Amb'ce interviewed D.D.M.S. I Corps.	
BUSNES Oct 14			Inspected Chronic cases now employed at SALVAGE Depôt accommodation there for huts as Base —	MAR
			Interviewed New A.D.C. Divsion Maj. Gen. C. J. BRIGGS — C.B.	
			Visited 84 Field Amb'y.	
	Oct 15		Inspected Billets of 2 Cheshire Reg't. & 6th held	
			83, 84, 85 Fd. Ambs. marched there near BETHUNE filling in from 21 Inf. Bde.	
			arranged for necessary Medical arrangements for the march and for the relief of Field Amb'c's of VIIth Divsion by	
			Ambulances of this Division. Reliefs will be carried out as follows:—	
			84 F Amb. marched to Bient Mulitaire hospitale BETHUNE in relief of 21st F Amb. Oct 16.	
			85 " " 2 Sect both Give the Garison 22 " " 18	
			(Sur 23 " " 17.	
			at ANNEZIN " " 16.	
			86 " " marches to FROGE VILELE FERY. BETHUNE	
	Oct 16.		84 field Amb'ce marched in relief of 6 Am. L.BETHANE 86. at 2 P.M.	AAR
			Visited 82 D.A at new billet arranged for Am's Dsp'm's also Motor Lorry transport will paul R. M. 72 Issue	
			Three Add para ACM to Bde are F & Auto Tromspor	

Stationery Services Press, X 8, 5,000 7/15

Army Form C. 2118.

WAR DIARY
or
INTELLIGENCE SUMMARY.
(Erase heading not required.)

Instructions regarding War Diaries and Intelligence Summaries are contained in F.S. Regs., Part II. and the Staff Manual respectively. Title pages will be prepared in manuscript.

Hour, Date, Place	Summary of Events and Information	Remarks and references to Appendices
Oct. 17. BETHUNE	83rd Bde. Arrived RE and VTC Moved to area ESSARS - LE QUESNOY - 83. Bdl. on Trench from 21st Bde. The 8.4.t Took over and 22 advanced dressing Station HARLEY STREET with "aid post" CONNAUGHT and CAMBRIDGE from 21 F. Amb. Visited D.M.S. Meerut. at AIRE.	ASR
Oct. 18. BETHUNE	Inspected billets of E. Yorks Rgt. 6th KO.R. Lancs The BUFFS at ST QUESNOY and LA PLEOLES - Trenches, aid post advanced dressing Station occupied by 83 Bde. inspected midwife & collection ground organised. met H.Q. MEERUT Division and arranged to take over aid Posts from his Division tomorrow morning by 86 Field Amb.	KTR
Oct. 19. BETHUNE	86 Field Amb. handed over ECOLE JULES FERRY to 11th Corps and sent Bearer Subdivision. Take over aid Post at LONE FARM near GUINCHY & LE2 LA BASSEE from the MEERUT Division. Adv. Hdm. arr. 83 Bde. an Canal school. Strd. about 100 yds. 83 Field Amb. moved their unit to ANNEZIN, being relieved at ECOLE LIGNE as GARDIN'S by 88 F. Amb. Visited aid post advanced dressing _____ station of 65. Bde. taking on the morning from MEERUT Division & arranged for disinfection of blankets khaki clothing at civil Hospital.	ASR

(73989) W4141—463. 400,000. 9/14. H.&J.Ltd. Forms/C. 2118/10.

Army Form C. 2118.

WAR DIARY
or
INTELLIGENCE SUMMARY.
(Erase heading not required.)

Instructions regarding War Diaries and Intelligence Summaries are contained in F.S. Regs., Part II and the Staff Manual respectively. Title pages will be prepared in manuscript.

Hour, Date, Place	Summary of Events and Information	Remarks and references to Appendices
3.45P.M. OCT. 19. BETHUNE.	Message that our Division would be relieved from TOUCHE GUINCHY & hold Divisional entraining at LILLERS and CHOCQUES on 21st	ADMS.
OCT. 20. BETHUNE	83 Field Ambce handed over to 23rd Amb of 7th Divn. and replaced their Field Ambce with WOLSELEYS, the unit moving to horses near HINGES. 84 Field Amb. handed over advanced dressing station to 57 F.A. of 2nd Divn., and exchanged all their Ambce Cars for SUNBEAMS. 85. F.A. remain at ANNEZIN, handing over Touraine 623 Fords. The VAUXHALL Cars will be exchanged for SUNBEAMS from 47th Divn. Also forthcoming received this evening	VRF ock. ADMS.
OCT. 21st LILLERS	Headquarters 2nd Division entrained at LILLERS at 6.07pm for MARSEILLES. Train actually departed 6pm. MAJOR P.H. HENDERSON R.A.M.C. joined Division as D.A.D.M.S. in relief of Lt. Col. H.S. ROCH who retired him as R.M.S.O. 8th Division. Authority — L.O.C. instructions issued under 1st Corps DAA+QMG No 2264/A d/20/10/15. F.A.'s to entrain as follows — 84th on 23rd — 83 + 56th on 24th. F.M. Hinderson Major Inspr KPDMS

Army Form W.3091.

Cover for Documents.

Nature of Enclosures.

Summary of Medical Operations of 28th Division, January – June 1915, together with Apps., Maps, etc.

Notes, or Letters written.

A.D.M.S
28th DIV.

Dec 1914 – Oct 1915.

Summary of Medical
Operations of 28th Div
Jan — 1 July 1915.
together with appendices, maps etc.
Forwarded by Lt Col H.S. Roch. Sept 1915.

Contains.

1. Summary.
2. Casualties 28th Div.
3.   "   treated by individual F.A⁰.
4.   "   of RAMC Officers & men
5.   "   of M.O⁵ Regiments
6. Mentions etc
      &c
7.   Maps.

The following appendices have been detached + attached to an extract of this report which has been made for the period of the 2nd Battle of Ypres for the use of the Editor-in-Chief.

No. 13.
No. 14
No. 28.
No. 32.
No. 34.
No. 36.
No. 36A.
No. 45.
No. 46.

J. Shea
11/10/1921.

28TH DIVISION.

SUMMARY

A. D. M. S.

SIX MONTHS

JANUARY ------ JULY

1915

SUMMARY.

Diary : A.D.M.S., 28th Division: January -- July 1915.

The 28th Division mobilized at Winchester under Major General E.S. Bulfin., C.B., between the latter end of December 1914 and the middle of January 1915.

It was composed of Regular Infantry and Artillery recently returned from India, Egypt and Hong Kong, and Territorial Cavalry and Administrative Troops.

The Medical Units were the 2nd and 3rd City of London and the 2nd Northumbrian Field Ambulances - renamed the 84th, 85th and 86th; originally mobilized on August 4th they had been working with their Territorial Divisions at CROWBOROUGH and GATESHEAD since the commencement of hostilities.

The Division was inspected by His Majesty the King on January 12th and arrived in France on January 15th where it comcentrated North of HAZEBROUCK in the villages of CAESTRE, PRADELLES and STRAZEELE. Here the establishment of Medical Units was completed by No 15 Section of the 1st London Sanitary Company, T.F., and a Divisional Motor Ambulance Workshop Unit, A.S.C.

Lieut-Colonel S.G. Allen was admitted to Hospital on January 24th and Lieut-Colonel N.C. Ferguson., C.M.G., was appointed A.D.M.S., on January 28th.

On February 2nd the 28th Division took over the trenches in front of YPRES from a French Division extending the British Line as far North as ZILLEBEKE. The 84th and 85th Field Ambulances opened Dressing Stations in YPRES, the former in the RUE DE LILLE at the HOSPICE - BELLE, ST ELIZABETH ORPHANAGE and HOSPICE ST JEAN, and the latter at the FEMALE/LUNATIC ASYLUM on the POPERINGHE Road.

Collecting Posts were established on the LILLE Road by the 84th Field Ambulance, who cleared the Aid Posts

Jan.-July 1915.

Map 26.

Posts of the Battalions in the Southern Sector of the trenches, and on the MENIN and HOLLEBEKE Roads by the 85th Field Ambulance who cleared the Aid Posts of the Northern Sector. The collection of wounded could be carried out only at night as there were no communication trenches, the area cleared by the 84th Field Ambulance was even then exposed to considerable rifle fire, one Officer and seven other ranks being wounded while at the work between the middle of February and the middle of March.

App. 20.

On February 9th a <u>Divisional Bathing Establishment</u> was opened at BRANDHOEK by No 15 Sanitary Section, local labour being employed for washing of clothing etc. At these baths, improvised from Tubs, Boilers, etc, obtained by local purchase, an average of 1,000 men received hot baths and clean under clothing daily, their uniforms were ironed and mended or if necessary replaced so that all men in the Resting Area were bathed and provided with clean clothing before returning to the trenches.

App. 23.

On February 12th a <u>Divisional Convalescent Rest Station</u> capable of accommodating 300 patients was opened at STEENVOORDE by a Section of the 86th Field Ambulance - this was found to afford a great saving of wastage from minor sickness. The remainder of the 86th Field Ambulance at this time was at OUDERDOM looking after the Brigade in the Resting Area.

Owing to the wet muddy condition of the trenches during February and March, a great many cases of "<u>Chilled Feet</u>" occurred among the Infantry, this condition was especially prevalent among the 27th Division and ourselves as both were composed of battalions recently returned from service in the tropics. Endeavours were made to prevent the condition by smearing the feet and legs with a grease

grease composed chiefly of whale oil and boric acid, greasing of boots and socks, the issue of a certain proportion of rubber boots and of water-proof paper waders, as well as avoidance of long marches, shortening the tour of duty in the trenches and provision of hot meals before going into them, but in spite of these precautions the wastage in the Division from this cause alone amounted to 2756 cases in February out of a total casualty list of 4801 including 1828 wounded.

Towards the end of February the Brigades changed trenches for one month with three more-seasoned Brigades, the 9th, 13th and 15th of the 3rd and 5th Divisions who came from drier trenches on our South near NEUVE EGLISE, the change was at once attended by a great diminuition in the number of cases of frost bite.

Evacuation of the Dressing Station at YPRES was carried out by No 4 Motor Ambulance Convoy, patients were taken to POPERINGHE where No 3 Casualty Clearing Station opened on February 5th 1915. From POPERINGHE they were at first transferred to HAZEBROUCK and BAILLEUL by Motor Ambulance Convoy but on February 10th No 12 Ambulance Train came up and from that date casualties were transferred to the Base daily by rail.

On taking over YPRES the importance of a safe water supply was immediately appreciated, one was established in the swimming bath of the town, water was derived from the YSER CANAL and after the Bath had been thoroughly cleaned it was possible to provide the Division with an ample supply of water rendered safe by natural precipitation and chlorination.

The town was indescribably filthy when the British first took over, heaps of rubbish were collected in all the streets, latrines were choked and filth existed everywhere. By employ-

Jan.-July 1915.

employing local labour this condition was remedied and YPRES put into a comparatively sanitary condition, rubbish was removed by carts from the town, burning being impossible as it ~~would~~ attracted the attention of the enemy causing the place to be shelled. The adjacant villages necessarily used for billeting were no cleaner than the town itself and gave the Sanitary Section plenty of work. On March 15th while employed on this duty at KRUISTRAAT, two men of the Unit were killed by shell fire.

On March 27th the Divisional Convalescent Rest Station moved to HOOGRAFF, on the POPERINGHE - WEST-OUTRE Road, STEENVOORDE being handed over to the 50th (Northumbrian Territorial) Division. The accommodation at HOOGRAFF was very much smaller than STEENVOORDE but was extended by the use of tents, the worst of the winter being over.

In the beginning of April the 28th Division was relieved by the 3rd and 27th Divisions and, moving to the North, took over the trenches in front of ZONNEBEKE from a French Corps from before FORTUIN on the North to the POLYGON-WOOD, South. The Canadians now separated us from a French Division on the left and the 27th Division were on our right.

The 86th Field Ambulance opened a Dressing Station in "The Institute of the Holy Family" in YPRES on April 7th capable of accommodating easily 130 cases. The 84th Field Ambulance took over "The Boy's School", RUE BASSIN, POPERINGHE, on the 9th April and the 85th Field Ambulance on April 13th established itself in "The Male Asylum", RUE DE THOROUT, YPRES, with an advanced Dresing Station (One Section) at the School near VELORENHOEK.

For purposes of the collection of wounded the area was divided into a Northern and Southern Section by the ZONNEBEKE Road, the 86th Field Ambulance collecting from the Northern and the 85th from the Southern Section. A collecting station

Jan.-July 1915.

station was established at a cottage about half a mile West
of ZONNEBEKE, on Main ZONNEBEKE - YPRES Road, where hot
soup was prepared. Cases were carried or brought by wheeled
stretchers to this post and sent on in Motor Ambulance Cars
to the Dressing Stations at YPRES or VELORENHOEK. At this
period there was a good deal of activity, attacks and counter
attacks were constantly being made by small parties, the
average number of wounded each evening being about 50, chiefly
bullet, hand grenade and trench mortar wounds. The distance
over which the wounded had to be carried was in some places
long, (from POLYGON WOOD 2,500 yards) and exposed to rifle
fire.

The shelling of YPRES was now becoming more constant
and on April 21st the G.O.C., V Corps decided that the Field
Ambulances should leave the town. The 85th was marched to
POPERINGHE and the 86th to a farm one and a half miles East
of that town on the VLAMERTINGHE Road where they parked and the
wounded were taken to the advanced Dressing Station at VERLOR-
ENHOEK.

On April 22nd the enemy used asphyxiating gas for the
first time against the French on our left and attacked very
vigourously, the Canadians and a Brigade made up of the
"Resting Troops" of the 28th Division under Colonel GEDDES,
The Buffs, were immediately sent up to reinforce, while other
Divisions were brought up in support. The YPRES Salient was
now constantly shelled. The School at VELORENHOEK was struck
on the 23rd April and the Dressing Station moved to POTIJZE
where it was established in several houses in the village and
soon degenerated into a collecting post. From April 22nd to
29th about 400 wounded made up of British, French, Indian and
Algerian Troops passed through this post daily. A similar
collecting post was established at ST JEAN on the following
day by the 86th Field Ambulance. Three Canadian Field

Jan.-July 1915.

Field Ambulances opened Dressing Stations at VLAMERTINGHE on the 23rd and 24th April and took in cases from the 28th Division.

On April 24th POPERINGHE was shelled and on the 28th the Casualty Clearing Station moved to BAILLEUL, and the Hospital Train stopped running so that the 84th Field Ambulance was acting as a Casualty Clearing Station; wounded being evacuated from it by Motor Ambulance Cars to HAZEBROUCK and BAILLEUL, slight cases going down on the Motor Buses returning empty after bringing up reinforcements.

On the night 29th/30th April, the Canadians were shelled out of VLAMERTINGHE and moved to farms on the POPERINGHE Road. The 84th Field Ambulance immediately opened a Dressing Station in "The Boy's School", RUE BASSIN, POPERINGHE, and cases were transferred from our collecting posts at POTIJZE and ST JEAN direct to it, a distance of approximately 8 miles. A Motor Soup Kitchen presented through the British Red Cross Society by Lady Wantage, was now mostbusefully employed, stationed near VLAMERTINGHE it provided every patient with hot soup, tea or cocoa when about half the journey to POPERINGHE was finished. Approximately 500 casualties were now admitted to the 84th Field Ambulance each day, the greatest number admitted on one day was 1015 on May 3rd. The majority of the cases were shell wounds but they included also a certain proportion of men suffering from Gas poisoning.

On May 2nd the 85th Field Ambulance opened a Dressing Station at bHOOGRAFF previously used as a Convalescent Rest Station, partly in the School buildings and partly under canvas, and the Sanitary Section moved from BRANDHOEK to POPERINGHE, the former being handed over to the 27th Division for a Dressing Station.

On night May 4th/5th, in order to shorten the Salient in front of YPRES the Division retired about 5,000 yards to a new line of trenches, and all Aid Posts had to be cleared by midnight.

Jan.–July 1915.

midnight. To carry this out and send casualties as far as POPERINGHE in the time available, 8 Officers, 150 bearers with 60 Motor Ambulance Cars (50 borrowed from No 4 Motor Ambulance Convoy) were employed. Altogether 994 cases were collected at the Dressing Station during the night from the Aid Posts in front of POTIJZE and ST JEAN.

On the following day, May 5th, the Field Ambulance posts at POTIJZE and ST JEAN became untenable and an advanced Dressing Station was opened in the cellars of "The Male Asylum" West of YPRES by the 86th Field Ambulance; the Regimental Aid Posts now were situated in "The White Chateau" at POTIJZE and in houses near ST JEAN village whence the Ambulance Cars brought them to the Asylum. The work of the Ambulance Car Drivers was particularly trying, they drove their cars night after night without lights and under shell fire on roads broken by shell holes, blocked by debris and congested with Ammunition and Supply carts, it is not surprising that the cars are constantly becoming damaged. The Workshop Unit was kept busy, besides repairing Ambulance Cars brought to the shop, it recovered, under fire, seven damaged by shell which otherwise must have been abandoned, only one car was lost, this was so hopelessly destroyed by shell at ST JEAN that it was not worth recovering; while employed in saving a broken car in YPRES on April 24th the Senior N.C.O., of the Workshop Unit was killed.

app 13
(map)

The casualties among the Field Ambulances personnel in April were 2 Officers ~~killed~~ wounded, 10 other ranks killed and 32 wounded.

On May 8th the 84th Field Ambulance moved from POPERINGHE to a farm South West of the town, this Unit having borne the brunt of the Dressing Station work in all the recent fighting, the 85th Field Ambulance at HOOGRAFF took in casualties from that date.

Jan.-July 1915.

On May 13th two Brigades moved into a "Resting Area" at WINNEZEELE, HERZEELE and WATOU, one remaining near VLAMERTINGHE as Brigade in support. The 84th and 86th Field Ambulances marched into the Resting Area, the 85th remaining at HOOGRAFF to take in casualties.

During this period the Sanitary Section in addition to opening baths at HERZEELE and WINNEZEELE, was employed preparing respirators and solution for use against asphyxiating gas, they supplied the troops with 50,000 in three weeks.

On May 22nd and 23rd the 83rd and 85th Brigades took over trenches South of our previous line, from the ROULERS Railway through HOOGE Wood to about 1,500 yards South of the MENIN Road, the 85th on the right and the 83rd on the left relieved part of the 27th Division and a Cavalry Division.

On May 24th the enemy attacked at 3 am, again using poisonous gases, these thay continued to use for about four hours. The effects of the gas were even felt in the Dressing Station at the Asylum.

The bearers of all three Field Ambulances were employed on the night May 24th/25th to collect casualties, the horse Ambulance wagons and 5 Motor Ambulance Cars borrowed from No 4 Motor Ambulance Convoy were used to assist in the moving the patients from the Asylum to the Dressing Station at HOOGRAFF. It was daylight before all Aid Posts could be evacuated and the bearers and cars were subjected to considerable shelling, one bearer was killed and two wounded during the morning and one car was temporarily put out of action by shrapnel.

On the following night parties from the Field Ambulances brought the casualties from the trenches of the 84th and 85th Brigades; the regimental stretcher bearers with their Medical Officers carried many men who could not be collected the previous evening from the ground between our trenches and those of the enemy. Lieut Gillespie was taken prisoner while

Jan.-July 1915.

while thus employed and both he and Lieut McNicholl were awarded the Military Cross for work performed on this night.

Altogether 40 Officers and 1570 other ranks including 226 cases of gas asphyxiation passed through the Dressing Station between the 23rd and 26th May.

On May 30th the Division again moved to the Resting Area, the 83rd Brigade to WINNEZEELE, the 84th to HERZEELE and the 85th to WATOU. The Field Ambulances established small hospitals in buildings of in each of the Brigade areas where cases of fever of short duration were treated in beds moved from shelled buildings in YPRES, the slighter cases and convalescents being accommodated under canvas. The Sanitary Section instituted baths in each area, drafts came out rapidly from home, short periods of leave were granted to a certain proportion of Officers and men, and the whole Division refitted.

In June a somewhat startling but very localized outbreak of Enteric Fever and para-typhoid occurred in the Ammunition Column of the 146th Brigade R.F.A., altogether 22 cases occurred in the Column of which 16 were in one subsection of 35 men, all attempts to discover the "carrier" failed but stringent sanitary precautions were taken to prevent the disease from spreading, and the outbreak subsided at the ned of June.

On June 2nd the 28th Division was transferred from the 5th to the 2nd Army Corps, and on June 15th returned to the trenches, taking over the line South of DICKEBUSCH from the 14th (Kitchener) and part of the 46th (North Midland Territorial) Divisions, the 5th Division were on the left, and the remainder of the 46th on the right separated the 28th Division from the Canadians. The 84th Field Ambulance

Jan.-July 1915.

Ambulance established a Dressing Station at the Schools in LA CLYTTE on June 14th. There is a Brewery on the YPRES-NEUVE-EGLISE Road due East of DICKEBUSCH and about 1,500 yards North of VIERSTRAAT with good cellars. This was used as a combined Aid Post by the 3 battalions of the 84th Brigade in the trenches, cases were evacuated from this post by Ambulance Cars to LA CLYTTE at night thence to the Clearing Hospitals at BAILLEUL by No 9 Motor Ambulance Convoy; during the day this aid post which is at the entrance of a Communication Trench about 1,800 yards from the fire trenches was cleared by hand carriage through DICKEBUSCH where an Ambulance Car and small parties from the 84th Field Ambulance were permanently posted to convey casualties to the Dressing Station. A second Aid Post occupied at this time by Units of the 83rd Brigade was situated on the same road near KEMMEL, this was also reach by the Ambulance Cars at night and evacuated to LA CLYTTE. The 85th Field Ambulance moved to WEST OUTRE on the 14th June where it equipped the School with beds etc for acute cases and opened a Camp for Convalescents and mild caess, one section took over the Chateau at MONT NOIR and converted it into a Convalescent Rest Station for 25 Officers.

On June 20th the 85th Brigade moved from WATOU to the trenches extending our line to the South and taking over from a Brigade of the 46th Division. The 86th Field Ambulance moved to a farm near BOESCHEPE where it opened a Convalescent Rest Station under canvas, sending one section into BAILLEUL to form a "hospital" for acute cases in a Private house in RUE DE MUSEE, previously occupied by an Ambulance of the North Midland Division. This was handed over to the

Map 42.

Jan.-July 1915.

the Northumbrian Division on July 7th and the 84th Field Ambulance changed places with the 86th on July 16th.

During July the Division slightly altered its position in the trenches, the 50th (Northumbrian) Division coming in on our South at one time; but at the end of the month our trench line extended from VIERSTRAAT-WYTSCHAETE Road, north, to the WULVERGHEN-MESSINES Road, South. The 3rd and 14th Divisions being on the left and the Canadians on the right.

LA CLYTTE and the "Brasserie" Aid Post were handed over to the 17th Division on July 23rd and on the following day the 86th Field Ambulance moved to LOCRE where it established a Dressing Station in the Convent and cleared Aid Posts at WYNDHOEK and KEMMEL used by 84th Brigade. The 84th Field Ambulance on the same day sent one section to form a Dressing Station at DRANOUTRE clearing the posts near WULVERGHEN used by the 85th Brigade, the 83rd Brigade casualties being brought to WEST OUTRE from the Aid Posts at KEMMEL and the Laiterie on KEMMEL-VIERSTRAAT Road by the 85th Field Ambulance.

The casualties at the time were very few in number, about ten wounded at night, all posts were cleared by day and night and patients evacuated to No's 2,3 or 8 Casualty Clearing Stations at BAILLEUL by No 9 Motor Ambulance Convoy.

Bathing establishments were opened at WEST OUTRE, LOCRE and DRANOUTRE, about 1,000 men being bathed daily.

The general health of the Division was excellent the average daily sick rate in July being 0.054%.

The total number of patients admitted to the Field Ambulances in the 6 months was, thirty thousand, four hundred and sixty six. This total does not include about two thousand men treated at advanced Dressing Stations and transferred

Jan.-July 1915.

transferred direct to the Casualty Clearing Stations.

app.43   The casualties occurring in the 28th Division were twenty eight thousand, four hundred and seventeen.

The battle casualties of the R.A.M.C., during the period were, Officers, killed, three, all in charge of Combatant Units, wounded, eleven, (eight Regimental and three Field
app.45   Ambulance)Officers), two Regimental Medical Officers were made prisoners of war, seventeen N.C.O's and men were killed or died of wounds and forty nine were wounded.

Two Medical Officers were awarded the "Military Cross". Sergt INGRAM, 84th Field Ambulance was granted the "Distinguished Conduct Medal" and the names of 9 Officers and 4 other
app.46   ranks of Medical Units, 28th Division, appeared in the Despatch from the Field-Marshall Commanding-in-Chief, published in the London Gazette of 23rd June for Distinguished Service in the Field during the six months.

28th Division Expeditionary Force.

Nominal Roll of Officers R.A.M.C.

July 18th 1915.

Headquarters Staff.

Colonel	N.C. Ferguson., C.M.G., A.M.S.	
Lieut-Col	H.S. Roch., R.A.M.C.	

84th Field Ambulance. (2nd London T)

Lieut-Col	W.S. Sharpe.	T.F.
Major	E.C. Montgomery Smith.	T.F.
Captain	R.E. Bickerton.	T.F.
Lieutenant	L.A. Harwood.	"
do	J.I. Lawson.	S.R.
do	W. Baxter.	T.C.
do	B.C. Tennent.	"
do	N.J. Cronin.	"
do	R.V. Steele.	"
do	A.W. Forrest.	"
Capt Qr Mr	A.J.H. Knights.	T.F.

85th Field Ambulance. (3rd London T)

Lieut-Col	J.R. Whait.	T.F.
Major	E.B. Waggett.	"
Captain	H.A.T. Fairbank.	"
do	B.E. Potter.	"
do	R.M. Vick.	"
Lieutenant	H. Robbins.	"
do	R.E. Barnsley.	"
do	K.V. Smith.	"
do	J. Taylor.	"
do	L.H. Wootton.	"
Hon Lieut Qr Mr	P.A. Baynes.	"

86th Field Ambulance. (2nd North'bn T)

Lieut-Col	D.A. Cameron.	T.F.
Major	D.L. Fisher.	"
Captain	G.R. Ellis.	"
Lieutenant	W.M. Wilson.	"
do	V.H. Wardle.	"
do	E.P. Swott.	T.C.
do	T.D. Inch.	S.R.
do	D.R. Roberts.	T.C.
Hon Lieut Qr Master.	E. Lyall.	T.F.
Hon Lieut Trans Off.	A. Ferens.	T.F.

No.15 Sanitary Section.

Lieutenant	C.N. Draycott.	T.F.

Divisional Motor Amb Workshop Unit.

2/Lieutenant	D.L. Hewitt.	A.S.C.

Officers in Medical Charge of Combatant Units.

83rd Infantry Brigade.

2nd King's Own Royal Lancs.	Lieut H.C. Godding. (T.C)
2nd East Yorks Regt.	Lieut C.C. Harrison. (T.C)
1st K.O.Y.L. Infantry.	Lieut L.T. Wells. (T.C)
1st Yorks and Lancs.	Lieut H.H. Davis. (T.C)
5th King's Own Royal Lancs.	Lieut J. Deighton. (S.R)

84th Infantry Brigade.

2nd North'd Fusiliers.	Lieut H.B. Taylor. (T.C)
1st Suffolk Regiment.	Lieut J. Mowat. (T.C)
2nd Cheshire Regiment.	Lieut B.S. Browne. (T.C)
1st Welch Regiment.	Lieut R.R. Kerr. (T.C)
Monmouth Regiments.	Lieut D. Haigh. (T.C)
1st/6th Welch Regiment.	Lieut W.A. Sneath. (T.C)

85th Infantry Brigade.

2nd The Buffs.(East Kent)	Lieut C.S.P. Hamilton. (T.C)
3rd Royal Fusiliers.	Lieut J.M. McLaggan. (T.C)
2nd East Surrey Regiment.	Lieut J.M. McPhail. (T.C)
3rd Middlesex Regiment.	Lieut J.M. Mithhell. (T.C)

Divisional Troops.

3rd Brigade R.F. Artillery.	Lieut J.N. Dobbie. (T.C)
31st do	Lieut E.W. Griffith. (T.C)
146th do	Lieut A.D. Vernon Taylor. (T.C)
Divisional Ammunition Col.	Lieut M.M. Cruikshank. (T.C)
Divisional Engineers.	Lieut T.E. Parker. (T.C)
Divisional Train A.S.C.	Lieut S. Rowland. (T.C)

CONFIDENTIAL.

CIRCULAR MEMORANDUM
on
CAMP SANITATION.

The onset of the hot weather with it's accompanying rapid decomposition of organic matter and presence of flies renders it imperative that the standard of Camp Sanitation be placed on a much higher level than has ever yet been reached by Units of this Division.

Defects of detail which, in the winter months, seemed to have no influence on the sick rate, will, in the summer indubitably lead sooner or later to epidemic disease.

Up to date the health of the Division has been most satisfactory but it cannot possibly remain so unless every Officer is as jealous of the sanitary efficiency of his Unit as he is of it's fighting efficiency.

To show that this is no exaggerated statement it must be remembered that in most wars for each man admitted to hospital wounded there were twenty-five admitted for some form of disease. The cause of this very high sick rate has always been the presence of Epidemics.

In no spirit of carping criticism but to help Officers to combat the ignorance, stupidity and prejudice that exists against every restriction the reason of which is not thoroughly understood, I have compiled the following notes.

The axioms of sanitary science which are to guide our efforts in Camp Sanitation are presumably known to all. The following are the principal:-

WATER SUPPLY.

If water be efficiently chlorinated the danger of an epidemic disease from this source is practically nil.

PRESENCE OF FLIES.

If all decomposing and decomposable organic matter, animal or vegetable, is immediately destroyed, flies cannot

TIME TABLE
Convoy Control Town Hall Poperinghe
Evacuation night 3-4. 5.15

Hour	Narrative	Report from	Dated	Subject	Action taken	Remarks
6.30 pm	Reported to ADMS					
7.45 pm	Instructions from DADMS				10 Cars depart with Bearers (100) Capt Fairbank Lieut Robbins.	To clear from Aid post to Collecting Stations ZONNEBECK Road.
8.10 pm					5 Cars (6-1) depart with 56 Bearers Capt Lawson Lt Inch	To clear FORTUN road aid post to WEILTJE or St JEAN
8.25 pm					12 Cars + 3 = 15. Lts Tennant & Roberts with Col Roch 4 = Ford Cars	"

Hour	Narrative	Report from	dated	Subject	Action taken	Remarks
8.35 pm	3 Cars of 6.10 Dep arrived with report (1) + 12L 12S.	Capt Scott (1)		Potijze for Evacn 10L 100S		
8 50	14 M.A.C. 6 Cars reported here					
9 30	20 Cars on ZONN Rd					
	10 " " FORTUN Rd					
10 15					A.D.M.S. 7 M.A.C. to WEILTZE 7 " VELDREN	These to evacuate direct to 94 FA
10 50	6 more M.A.C. report here					
11 30					5 M.A.C. Cars to P.O.T.	

Hour	Narrative	Report from	dated	Subject	Action taken	Remarks
11.50 pm		St Inch Verbal (2)	S.J.	Lt Col Roch is collecting at Cellar		
11.55		Capt Fairbank (3)	POT	ST. JEAN about 200 cases		
11.55		Capt SCOTT (4)	POT 10.50	25 L, 125 S. for Evac		
12.20	Major IRVINE Sending 15 MAC					
12.25	Lt Inch to S.J. Journeys are taking from 3 to 5 Hours					
2.7	POT. is now being cleared direct by St Cars & being piled by 17 Cars				Sent 15 M.A.C. to POTIJZE & one	

Hour	Narrative	Report from	dated	Subject	Action taken	Remarks
2 40 am	~~Lt Koch~~ 5	~~STEIN~~ Lt Col Koch	STEAN 12.50	70 L. 85 S. for Svac 80 Walkers 3/4 W		
3 30		Lt Col Koch (5) (6)	SJ 2.10	Asylum M L 82 S.		
3 40					Sent 11 M.A.C. POT	
3 50	C	Capt Fairbank (7)	POT 2.40	240 Sitting		
4 20					Sent 7 additional to POT	To go on to S.J. & to
4 30					Sent 6 to POT	Walkers ynot used at POT
5 10		Lt Col Koch (8)	S.J.	10 L. 51.S. 80 Walkers 65 Bearers		
		Sgt A ? Verbal	POT	80.S.		
5 50	S.J. Cleared	Lt Col Koch Verbal	S.J.	S.J. Cleared 30 bearers on road 80 walkers picked up by Red Cross		

Hour	Narrative	Report from	date	Subject	Action taken	Remarks
6.10 am		Capt Scott (9)	P.O.T.	95 sitting at POT	Sent 6 Cars POT	5 Cars on way to Pot = 11
6.11 "						" "
6.40		Verbal	POT 5.45	70 sitting at POT		
6.41 "	Evacuated 606 = 155 L. 451 S.					
8 "		Capt Scott 10	POT 7.15	"50 odd" still at POT		11. M.A.C. on way up
9.5	POT cleared	Off M.A.C. Verbal	POT	POTIJZE Cleared		Officers verbal report corroborated by the fact that he brought Bearers & Cars half empty = 66 Cars.
9.10	668 Evacuated (156 L 512 S)					136 journeys of those between aid posts & collecting Station
9.11	All cleared Control Pot Closed				sd E.B. Waggett. Major R.A.M.C	8 Cars put out of action

LIST OF APPENDICES, WAR DIARY, D.A.D.M.S., 28TH DIVISION.
----

16. Roll of Medical Officers who left England with 28th Division.
18. Report on Sanitary Condition, YPRES. March 3rd 1915.
20. Report on Bathing Establishment., BRANDHOEK, March 5th 1915.
21. Report on Horses, Field Ambulances.   March 13th 1915.
22. Sanitation Trench Area.   March 17th 1915.
23. Report on Convalescent Rest Station., STEENVOORDE.
24. Recommendation for disposal of Excreta. Camp Hutments. March 24th.
25. Report on Water Supply for OUDERDOM Huts. March 25th.
             (Sanitary Officer 2nd Army)
26. Map showing scheme for collecting wounded. February to April 1915.
27. Position of Dressing Stations, etc, April 11th 1915.
28. Map showing collection of wounded. April 11th 1915.
29. Report on suggested reduction of in Scale of Rations.
30. Names of Officers and Other Ranks recommended for rewards.
32. Report on R.A.M.C., work, 22nd April to May 5th 1915.
    32 (a) Report of Capt Fairbank, on work night May 24/25.
33. Water Supply of Division. May 7th 1915.
34. Report on Work of R.A.M.C., April 22nd to May 10th 1915.
36. Report on Motor Ambulance Cars.
37. Letter to Officers Commanding Field Ambulances re diets for
                                                        patients.
38. Confidential letter to all Officers Commanding on outbreak of
    Enteric in 146th Brigade R.F.A.
39. Circular Memo on Camp Sanitation. June 8th 1915.
40. Confidential Circular sent to all Regimental Medical Officers.
41. Letter calling for re-inoculation.

APPENDICES.

43. Total Casualties in the Division for 6 months.

44. Total Admissions to Field Ambulances.

45. Roll of Casualties R.A.M.C., in 6 months.

46. Honours and Rewards.

MAPS.

26. Position of Aid Posts etc.   February 1915.
28.   "   "   "   "   April 11th 1915.
12.   "   "   "   "   April 20th 1915.
13.   "   "   "   "   May 5th - 8th 1915.
14.   "   "   "   "   May 24th 1915.
42.   "   "   "   "   June 15th - July 15th 1915.
47.   "   "   "   "   July 31st 1915.

1. Original Nominal Roll of Officers R.A.M.C.

2. Nominal Roll of Officers R.A.M.C., serving with the 28th Division on the 18th July 1915.

(The numbers of Appendix refer also to the Appendix of the War Diary)

ORIGINAL

NOMINAL ROLL OF OFFICERS R.A.M.C., 28TH DIVISION.

Headquarters Staff.

Lieut-Colonel	S.G. Allen.,	R.A.M.C.
Major	H.S. Roch.,	R.A.M.C.

84th Field Ambulance.(2nd London T)

Lieut-Colonel	W.S. Sharpe.	T.F.
Major	E.C. Montgomery Smith.	T.F.
Captain	R.E. Bickerton.	T.F.
do	H.G.L. Haynes.	T.F.
do	L. Rawes.	T.F.
Lieutenant	L.A. Harwood.	T.F.
do	J.I. Lawson.	S.R.
do	F.S. Turner.	T.F.
do	L. Courtauld.	T.F.
Capt Qr Mr	A.J.H. Knights.	T.F.

85th Field Ambulance.(3rd London T)

Lieut-Colonel	J.R. Whait.	T.F.
Major	E.B. Waggett.	T.F.
Captain	H.A.T. Fairbank.	T.F.
do	B.E. Potter.	T.F.
do	R.M. Vick.	T.F.
Lieutenant	F.H. Robbins.	T.F.
do	R.E. Barnsley.	T.F.
do	K.V. Smith.	T.F.
do	J. Taylor.	T.F.
Lieut Qr Mr	P.A. Baynes.	T.F.

86th Field Ambulance.(2nd North'bn T)

Lieut-Colonel	D.A. Cameron.	T.F.	
Major	D.V. Haig.	T.F.	
do	D.L. Fisher.	T.F.	
Captain	G.R. Ellis.	T.F.	
Lieutenant	W.M. Wilson.	T.F.	
do	V.H. Wardle.	T.F.	
do	A.C.C. Lawrence.	T.F.	
do	E.P. Scott.	T.C.	
do Qr Mr	E. Lyall.	T.F.	
do T.O.	A. Ferens.	T.F.	(Non Medical)

No 15 Sanitary Section.

Lieutenant	C.N. Draycott.	T.F.

OFFICERS IN MEDICAL CHARGE OF COMBATANT UNITS.

83rd Infantry Brigade.

2nd Royal Lancs.	Lieut H.C. Godding. (T.C)
2nd East Yorks Regt.	Lieut D. Campbell. (T.C)
1st K.O.Y.L. Infantry.	Capt P.G.M. Elvery. (Regular)
1st Yorks and Lancs.	Lieut K.J. Yeo. (T.C)

84th Infantry Brigade.

2nd North'd Fuslrs.	Lieut J.M. Gillespie. (T.C)
1st Suffolk Regt.	Lieut J.M. McNichol. (T.C)
2nd Cheshire Regt.	Capt O.R. McEwen. (Regular)
1st Welsh Regt.	Lieut J. Davidson. (T.C)

85th Infantry Brigade.

2nd The Buffs.	Lieut C.S.P. Hamilton. (T.C)
3rd Royal Fusiliers.	Capt W.A. Valentine. (T.F)
2nd East Surrey Regt.	Lieut J.M. Land. (T.C)
3rd Middlesex Regt.	Lieut H.R. Knowles. (T.C)

Divisional Troops.

3rd Brigade R.F. Artillery.	Lieut P. Chissell. (T.C)
31st ditto	Lieut H.P. White. (T.C)
146th ditto	Lieut D. McVicker. (T.C)
Heavy Brigade R.G.A.	Capt C.J. Wyatt. (Regular)
Divisional Amm Column.	Lieut M.M. Cruikshank. (T.C)
Divisional Engineers.	Lieut T.E. Parker. (T.C)
Divisional Train A.S.C.	Lieut T.W. Morcom Harneis. (T.F)

Copy.

The D. M. S.,
   2nd Army.

I have the honour to report that, in my opinion, the Sanitary Service at YPRES is now sufficient, and is well and suitably carried out. All that is done is unquestionably necessary, and, in my opinion, the work is being carried on in as economical a manner as is consistent with efficiency.

On our arrival at YPRES on the first ultimo, the town was indescribably filthy, heaps of rubbish containing among other things, bones and putrid flesh, and usually surmounted by human excrement, were present in many of the streets.

Excrement was everywhere, all latrines were choked and filthy, and heaps of manure were in every corner, every barrack yard, and in every open space.

These accumulations have now been cleared away, adequate latrine accommodation has been provided, all cess-pits in buildings occupied by British Troops have been emptied, and are being emptied as often as necessary, all manure and other rubbish likely to cause a nuisance have been removed, and no accumulation is now permitted.

The daily removal of all rubbish from all barracks, and from the many buildings in which troops are of necessity located, involves a great amount of horse and manual labour.

It is impossible to burn this rubbish, as the smoke would attract the enemy, and cause the town to be shelled.

The responsible contractor has done his best, and has kept his word in doing, in the time stated, the work which he promised should be done.

March 3rd 1915.
                            (s) N.C. Ferguson.,
                                Colonel., A.M.S.,
                        A.D.M.S., 28th Division.

Copy.

STATEMENT OF EXPENSES
28TH DIVISIONAL BATHING ESTABLISHMENT.

(1) The initial outlay of the Bathing Establishment was approximately £13/18/0., as per detailed cost of items attached.

(2) The average daily expenditure to wash 800 men and their clothes, is fourteen pounds, eleven and eightpence. (£14/11/8.) = 4½ per man.

March 5th 1915.
                              (Sd) H.S. Roch.,
                                       Lieut-Col.,
                           D.A.D.M.S., for A.D.M.S.,
                               28th Division.

Copy.

DETAILED COST OF ITEMS.

                                          Francs.

Sponges............................ 16.05

Wood for making racks
for men to stand on............. 15.00

Baths and Tubs..................186.00

Heating Pans for boiling
water........................... 63.20

Brushes for baths and
clothes......................... 28.40

Washing Books................... 3.25

Repairs to Water
Tank............................ 1.10

Table...........................20.00

Flat Irons......................12.50

March 5th 1915.
                          (S-) H.S. Roch.,
                               Lieut-Colonel.
                       D.A.D.M.S., for A.D.M.S.
                             28th Division.

cannot exist.

CONTAMINATION OF FOOD. If the issuers, cooks and consumers of food disinfect by washing or otherwise their hands, use clean utensils and furthermore do not allow food to come into contact with soiled clothing, etc, no contamination can occur.

DISPOSAL OF EXCRETA. If all excreta is covered up with earth, the paper destroyed and the surrounding probably poluted ground covered with Chloride of Lime, no disease can be spread from this source.

WASHING PLACES. If washing places are concentrated, the disposal of soapy water causes no great difficulty.

Let us see now where the application of these principles is apt to fail in practice. I quote from my personal observations during the last five months in this Division.

WATER SUPPLY. Chloride of Lime is issued in $\frac{1}{4}$lb airtight tins for purposes of water purification. There is a measure in each tin and one measure full is sufficient for one water-cart. Such is the regulation in theory -- the practice is otherwise. Two quartermasters on one day complained to me that they could not obtain these tins at the Refilling Point. The Supply Officer proved beyond doubt that it had never been asked for.

One water cart orderly put the Chloride of Lime in by hand-fulls. Another thought it was best from a sack. Tobacco and even biscuit tins have been used for the purpose.

I have only once seen a regimental water-cart where it's Lime was so stored as to convince me it was being properly used. The impression left on my mind was that the Chloride of Lime was used " for inspection" only.

I have never seen any arrangement made for the storage and

and chlorination of water during the temporary absence of the Unit Water-cart -- and yet water-carts have frequently been absent from a Unit for weeks at a time. A barrel or even a tub fitted with a tap would have been quite efficient but nobody seemed to think of this.

PRESENCE OF FLIES.

Because on the line of march it is necessary to issue the daily ration in bulk to each man, the same system is continued in billets and bivouacs.

Every man eats his food where he likes and preserves the surplus jam, cheese, bacon and bread in his bivouac for the evening meal.

A better system for the prolific propagation of flies can hardly be imagined.

I have never seen an arrangement where men messed in groups, returning their unconsumed portion of ration into store, and incinerating the refuse in situ.

CONTAMINATION OF FOOD.

It may be that there are cooking places where the cooks have facilities for washing their hands — where rough smocks or aprons are used by storemen issuers and cooks, and where a place is set apart for the washing of cooking and messing utensils; but I have never been lucky enough to meet one on my various inspections.

DISPOSAL OF EXCRETA.

The failure of attention to detail in this connection has been so universal and fraught with such danger that special specific instructions have been issued on this subject.

WASHING PLACES.

The tendency to individualism is here very evident. Every man seems to wash where he likes and leave the soapy water where it falls hoping that it may be washed away by the rain.

Copy.

D. M. S.,
   2nd Army.

In compliance with your telegraphic instructions, accompanied by the Assistant Director of Veterinary Services, I investigated the condition of the horses in the Field Ambulances in this Division.

The general condition of the horses was excellent, and proved that the stable management left nothing to be desired.

A virulent form of cracked heel, due to standing in the mud, has broken out in the 85th Field Ambulance, which necessitated sending 13 horses to the Veterinary Hospital and placing 11 temporarily on the sick list.

The Military exigencies of the situation has, up to now, made it impossible to transfer horses of this Field Ambulance to better ground but the improvement in the weather and the Military situation has allowed arrangements to be made which, will I trust, obviate a recurrence of the disability.

March 13th 1915.

(S) N.C. Ferguson
Colonel A.M/S.,
28th Division.

Copy.

SANITATION OF THE TRENCH AREA.

The presence of decomposing animal matter in the vicinity of the trenches occupied by troops is liable to affect their health in two ways.

(1) The highly unpleasant gaseous emanations, by reducing their vitality, renders men more liable to attacks of disease bearing Microbes.

(2) The opportunities for the developement of flies which act as carriers of such Microbes are very much increased.

It is therefore highly desirable that all dead bodies should be buried as soon as possible, but when this is not practicable, they should be treated chemically. For this purpose the most reliable, most efficient and most economical substance is the so called Chloride of Lime. This substance is not a Salt of Lime, but a mechanical mixture of the powerful element, Chlorine Gas with Lime.

It acts in the following manner:- The free Chlorine masks the disagreeable odours and kills the flies in their embryonic state while the Lime hastens the process of disintegration of animal matter to the stage when it become innocuous.

It follows that to give the Chloride of Lime it's maximum efficiency, it should be kept in closed tins or boxes and as dry as possible, and that frequent sprinkling of small quantities will have a better effect than the single application of large masses.

The rules therefore should be:-

(1) All unburied or partially buried dead bodies should be permanantly kept under a thin covering of Chloride of Lime as long as they emit unpleasant odours.

(2) Chloride of Lime before use should be kept as dry and free from contact with air as practicable.

March 17th 1915.

(S) N.C. Ferguson.,
Colonel., A.M.S.
A.D.M.S., 28th Division.

ORIGINAL

NOMINAL ROLL OF OFFICERS R.A.M.C., 28th DIVISION.

Headquarters Staff.

Lieut-Colonel	S.G. Allen., R.A.M.C.	
Major	H.S. Roch., R.A.M.C.	

84th Field Ambulance. (2nd London T)

Lieut-Colonel	W.S. Sharpe.	T.F.
Major	E.C. Montgomery Smith.	T.F.
Captain	R.E. Bickerton.	T.F.
do	H.G.L. Haynes.	T.F.
do	L. Rawes.	T.F.
Lieutenant	L.A. Harwood.	T.F.
do	J.I. Lawson.	S.R.
do	F.S. Turner.	T.F.
do	L. Courtauld.	T.F.
Hon Capt Qr Master.	A.J.H. Knights.	T.F.

85th Field Ambulance. (3rd London T)

Lieut-Colonel	J.R. Whait.	T.F.
Major	E.B. Waggett.	T.F.
Captain	H.A.T. Fairbank.	T.F.
do	B.E. Potter.	T.F.
do	R.M. Vick.	T.F.
Lieutenant	H. Robbins.	T.F.
do	R.E. Barnsley.	T.F.
do	K.V. Smith.	T.F.
do	J. Taylor.	T.F.
Hon Lieut Qr Master.	P.A. Baynes.	T.F.

86th Field Ambulance. (2nd Northumbrian T)

Lieut-Colonel	D.A. Cameron.	T.F.
Major	D.V. Haig.	T.F.
do	D.L. Fisher.	T.F.
Captain	G.R. Ellis.	T.F.
Lieutenant	W.M. Wilson.	T.F.
do	V.H. Wardle.	T.F.
do	A.C.C. Lawrence.	T.F.
do	E.P. Scott.	T.C.
Hon Lieut Qr Master.	E. Lyall.	T.F.
Hon Lieut Trans Off.	A. Ferens.	T.F. (Non Medical)

No 15 Sanitary Section.

Lieutenant	C.N. Draycott.	T.F. (Joined in France)

Divisional Motor Ambulance Workshop Unit.

2/Lieutenant	D.L. Hewitt.	A.S.C.(Joined in France)

OFFICERS IN MEDICAL CHARGE OF COMBATANT UNITS.

83rd Infantry Brigade.

2nd K.O. Royal Lancs.	Lieut	H.C. Godding. (T.C)
2nd East Yorks Regiment.	Lieut	D. Campbell. (T.C)
1st K.O.Y.L. Infantry.	Capt	P.G.M. Elvery. (Reg)
1st Yorks and Lancs.	Lieut	K.J. Yeo. (T.C)

84th Infantry Brigade.

2nd North'd Fusiliers.	Lieut	J.M. Gillespie. (T.C)
1st Suffolk Regiment.	Lieut	J.M. McNicholl. (T.C)
2nd Cheshire Regiment.	Capt	O.R. McEwen. (Reg)
1st Welch Regiment.	Lieut	J. Davidson. (T.C)

85th Infantry Brigade.

2nd The Buffs.(East Kent.)	Lieut	C.S.P. Hamilton. (T.C)
3rd Royal Fusiliers.	Capt	W.A. Valentine. (T.F)
2nd East Surrey Regiment.	Lieut	J.M. Land. (T.C)
3rd Middlesex Regiment.	Lieut	H.R. Knowles. (T.C)

Divisional Troops.

3rd Brigade R.F. Artillery.	Lieut	P. Chissell. (T.C)
31st do do	Lieut	H.P. White. (T.C)
146th do do	Lieut	D. McVicker. (T.C)
Heavy Brigade R.G.A.	Capt	C.J. Wyatt. (Reg)
Divisional Ammunition Col.	Lieut	M.M. Cruikshank. (T.C)
Divisional Engineers.	Lieut	T.E. Parker. (T.C)
Divisional Train A.S.C.	Lieut	T.W. Morcom Harneis. (T.F)

COPY.

To:-
    The A. D. M. S., 28th Division.

Sir,

I have the honour to forward for your information copies of "Routine Standing Orders for Convalescents on Admission and Discharge, Standing Orders for Convalescents and Routine Standing Orders in case of Fire, together with a Report on the Convalescent Rest Station at STEENVOORDE.

Under instructions received from the A.D.M.S., 28th Division the building known as the SALLE DES FETES - which is a large oblong hall with a stage at one end capable of holding 70 men and some old disused School Buildings including one Hall with Stage at one end, capable of holding 50 men, situated behind the MAIRE, were taken over on the 11th February 1915 at STEENVOORDE and prepared as a Convalescent Rest Station for the 28th Division. Another Block of Buildings known as the ECOLE MUNICIPALE, capable of holding 180 men, situated about three hundred yards distant was taken over on the 14th February as up to that date this Building had been occupied as a Billet by a detachment of Belgian Infantry who were employed until that date on road duty in the STEENVOORDE District.

The Convalescent Rest Station is thus composed of two blocks of buildings known separately as (a) The MARIE BLOCK and (b) The SCHOOLS BLOCK.

The process of preparing these buildings, washing and cleaning up etc, was handicapped by the unavoidable delay in receiving Ordnance Stores, but with the help of the British Red Cross Society and local purchase of necessary articles the Convalescent Rest Station was able to cope with the first batch of 45 Convalescents which arrived on the 16th February at about 4 pm. Since when 689 Convalescents have been admitted up to date.

date.

The majority of Convalescents admitted, have been mild cases requiring minor treatment and a few days rest, such as Scabies, Debility, milder forms of frost bite and sore feet, colds and mild cases of Influenza; the more serious cases being those which appeared unlikely to recover quickly being transferred to the Casualty Clearing Stations first at HAZEBROUCK and since the 6th inst to No 3 Casualty Clearing Station, POPERINGHE by means of Motor Ambulance Wagons.

One horsed Ambulance Wagon and one Motor Ambulance Wagon are permanantly stationed at the Convalescent Rest Station for use in transferring cases and for any emergency arising, and have been most useful.

The Staff is comprised of 3 Medical Officers, with a Sergt/Major, a Quarter Master Sergt and the personnel of a tent sub-division at first, supplemented later by part of another Tent sub-division both of the 86th Field Ambulance.

The general scheme of the treatment of Convalescents at this Convalescent Rest Station is to give each Convalescent a hot bath, a clean change of raiment, treat their minor ailments, give them good nourishing food and discharge them to duty after a few days rest.

BATHING. The bathing arrangements for Convalescents are very satisfactory as the town of STEENVOORDE possesses Municipal Douch Baths capable of bathing 9 men at once, giving each a hot bath, and this is supplemented by tub baths in the Convalescent Rest Station Ablution Room at the Marie Block, with a separate set of tub baths for Convalescents suffering from Scabies, in the ward set apart for these Convalescents in the SCHOOLS BLOCK.

The water supply of the town is excellent and has been examined and found to be of pure quality. It is obtained from an Artesian Well and by means of a Gas Engine at the Pumping Station is distributed to different parts of the town where it is obtained by means of Stand Pipes. The Pumping Station supplies

supplies the water for the Douche Baths.

DISINFECTION OF CLOTHING. By arrangements made with the Authorities of the French Hospital here, the steam Disinfector is used on three days a week, (Monday, Wednesday and Friday) to clean blankets and dirty underclothing and this is done before they are sent to the wash. The clothes of the Scabies Convalescents are disinfected outside the Scabies Ward in a portable Field Disinfector set aside for these cases alone.

WASHING OF CLOTHES. Satisfactory arrangements have been made for washing of clothes by local washerwomen: This work has been well and efficiently carried out. The ironing of Service Jackets and Trousers has been delayed for want of Irons, but these have now been received and arrangements for dealing with this work are in hand.

DRINKING WATER. is obtained from the Artesian Well already described.

Water for drinking purposes is chlorinated and kept in a recepticle in the SCHOOLS BLOCK and in the Water Cart at the MAREE BLOCK.

FOOD. The food is excellent and meals are supplementary by Hospital Comforts. Stout is given to those whom the Medical Officers consider require it.

The milk which has been issued up to the present has all been tinned but there is an excellent Creamery in STEENVOORDE managed and conducted on scientific hygienic principals where butter is made and fresh milk can be supplied at Hospital Rates of 25 frcs per 100 litres per diem.

BEDDING The beds are composed of paliasses filled with straw which are periodically washed and refilled (there being sufficient paliasses surplus to carry this out without reducing the accommodation) each Convalescent has three blankets and more if he requires or desires them;.

Coal and Fuel are obtained from the Army Service Corps.

The total number of Convalescents admitted from the 16th Fenruary 1915 to date is	689
The average admission have been	33
The average daily discharged to duty have been	13
The average daily Transfers to Casualty Clearing Station have been	5 to 8 ø

ø This average is a flu/tuating one because cases have been transferred to other Casualty Clearing Stations because they belong to Units other than those composing the 28th Division.

In accordance with instructions I handed over the Command of this Convalescent Rest Station this morning to Lieut-Colonel D.A. Cameron., Officer Commanding 86th Field Ambulance.

I have the honour to be

Sir,

Your obedient Servant,

(Sd) B.F.Wingate.,
Major R.A.M.C.

STEENVOORDE.
9/3/15.

COPY.

ROUTINE STANDING ORDERS FOR CONVALESCENTS ON ADMISSION OR DISCHARGE.

Every Convalescent on arrival at the Convalescent Rest Station will be seen by the Medical Officer in charge of the Ward and the following will be the procedure:-

(1) Those Convalescents fit to do so will have a hot bath in the Ablution Room at the MARIE BLOCK or in the Douche Baths, and Convalescents suffering from Scabies will have their hot bath in the Scabies Ward.

(2) The Convalescents will take off their soiled linen and will be given a clean issue of corresponding garments., i.e., Shirts, Vests, Pants and Socks.

The Bath Attendant and an Orderly from the Linen Store will check the soiled linen of the Convalescent and obtain his signature for the same and the clean underclothing issued to him. The soiled clothes will then be taken to the Linen Store and checked.

The soiled articles will first be disinfected at the Frenxch Hospital for which arrangements have been made and then taken straight to the Washerwomen.

Convalescents suffering from Scabies will be issued with their clean underclothing in the Scabies Ward. The clothes of these Convalescents will be disinfected in the disinfector at the SCHOOLS BLOCK and then taken to the Linen Store where they will be checked and afetrwards sent to the wash.

(3) The clean clothes from the wash will be taken over by the N.C.O., in charge of the Linen Store and issued as required.

(4) The Wardmaster will be responsible that the articles are properly checked and the signature of the Convalescent in the book kept for the purpose.

(5) Great Coats will be brushed, neatly folded and placed at the head of the bed.

(s) B.F. Wingate.
Major R.A.M.C.

(6) <u>Boots,</u> will be kleaned and kept in the place appointed for them.

(7) A knife, fork and spoon will be issued to each Convalescent while at the Convalescent Rest Station, and Convalescents marked "Up" will be responsible that they are cleansed after each meal. Those unable to do so will have the same cleaned by the Orderlies in the Wards.

(8) When a Convalescent is transferred to the Casualty Clearing Station for further treatment, the Medical Officer who recommends his transfer will be responsible that such Convalescent has clean underclothing.

(9) Before being discharged each Convalescent will hand over to the Wardmaster any utensils which have been issued to him during his stay in the Convalescent Rest Station.

8/3/15.
           (Sgd) Wingate.
           Major R.A.M.C.
        O i/c Convalescent Rest Station
           STEENVOORDE.

STANDING ORDERS FOR CONVALESCENTS.

(1-) All Convalescents marked "Up" will be available for general duty in the Convalescent Rest Station.

(2) All Convalescents marked "Up B.D.", i,e, bed down; will be available for light duty in their ward.

(3) All Convalescents marked "BED" are to stay there and only to leave when necessary to go to the Latrine if allowed to do so.

(4) For Convalescents Reveille will be at 6-30 am, and Lights Out at 7-30 pm.

(5) The Convalescents must be washed, shaved, and wards cleaned up by 8-30 am daily.

(6) Smoking is Forbidden in the Wards unless special permission is given by the Medical Officer, but it is permitted in the Dining Hall and Recreation Rooms.

(7) All civilians and any unauthorised individual are forbidden to enter or be in the precincts of the Convalescent Rest Station.

(8) Convalescents are forbidden to leave the block of buildings in which their ward is situated and under no circumstances are they to visit the town of STEENVOORDE or enter any Estaminet, Shop or Civillian dwelling.

8/3/15.

(S-) B.F. Wingate.,
Major R.A.M.S.
O i/c Convalescent Rest Station.
STEENVOORDE.

Copy.

ROUTINE STANDING ORDERS IN CASE OF FIRE.

(1) The Alarm to be given by the person who first discovers the outbreak. If in a Ward all the Convalescents who are able to walk will assist the Orderlies to help out the Convalescents unable to walk and place them in:-

    (1) Marie Block. In the Courtyard.

    (2) The Schools. Quadrangle.

All Convalescents able to do so will assemble in the respective places.

(2) When an outbreak occurs at night:-

    (a) If in the Marie Block the Alarm is to be given and the Sergt/Major called at once.

    (b) If in the Schools Block the Medical Officer living there is to be called at once and all ranks must turn out.

In every case the Orderly Medical Officer and the Commanding Officer are to be invariably sent for.

(3) All R.A.M.C., personnel and those Convalescents able to do so are to use every effort to extinguish the flames.

(4) A recepticle which must be always kept full of water will be kept in each Ward.

8/3/15.

                         (s) B.F.Wingate.
                         Major R.A.M.C.,
          O i/c Convalescent Rest Station
                      STEENVOORDE.

Copy.

The most urgent need of the Hut Encampment of this Division is the suitable form of Latrine. The trench system at present in use has proved mostly unsatisfactory owing to the nature of the soil and large amount of ground required. As the time is fast approaching when there will be no more suitable ground available a more permanant arrangement is essential.

A similar difficulty has occurred in connection with the large factories and warehouses occupied as billets by the 4th and 6th Divisions where the ground for latrine trenches was limited. The difficulty was overcome by constructing a large cess-pit over which latrine seats were fitted. A roof protects the latrine from rain and arrangemnets are made for the periodical emptying of the cess-pit. The best form of this structure is to be seen at the Civil Hospital at ARMENTIERES.

It is strongly urged that immediate steps be taken to build similar structures in each of the hut encampments and that the question of the ultimate disposal of the excreta be considered later.

March 24th 1915.

(Sgd) N.C. Ferguson.,
Colonel., A.M.S.,
A.D.M.S., 28th Division.

Copy.

To:- A.D.M.S., 28th Division. (repeated D.M.S., 2nd Army.)

Water Supply Hutments;- VLAMERTINGHE-OUDERDOM Road.

I have already inspected the proposed source of supply in company with Captain Agg, Camp Commandant of Hutments, and I have personally examined samples of the water.

Both the streams suggested are extremely foul. Their bacteriological content is such that the water requires careful and quiescent storage for long periods before it can be efficiently treated by chlorination. These two surface streams drain a densly infected typhoid area, in which, in addition, the infantile mortality has been terribly high. This water supply should be avoided if humanly possible.

As to quantity, these particular streams are known to dry up even after a short period of dry weather. They cannot be depended upon as a constant source of supply. Deep Wells may prove more valuable, but a good well is a lucky strike, and much moving sand may be encountered in this neighbourhood. The deeper you dig in this Ypresian formation the greater the amount of salts of soda found in the water, which to those not habituated to their use are liable to give rise to diarrhoea and other bowel disturbance. This matter of salt content is one which has been the subject of special investigation in the Mobile Hygienic Laboratory.

A source of water which I find excellent in both quantity and quality is available at L'ETANG DE DICKEBUSCH. It is derived from MONT KEMMEL. It may be brought to the Hutment area by a pipe line 3,500 metres in length with the aid of intermediary reservoirs by gravity alone. 5,000 gallons daily of good drinking water requiring no further treatment would then be available.

I have already submitted an independent survey of the proposed pipe line and other data to the Brigadier General Petrie, R.E. 5th Corps.

Chateau Elizabeth,   (Sgd) M. Coplans., Capt R.A.M.C.,
POPERINGHE 25/3/15.   Sanitary Officer 2nd Army.

Copy.

POSITION OF AMBULANCES AND DRESSING STATIONS, 28TH DIVISION ON THE IITH APRIL, 1915.

(1) Ambulances for Resting Area.

    84th Field Ambulance.(2nd London T) "The Boy's School", RUE BASSIN, off RUE DE LA BALANCE, POPERINGHE.

    85th Field Ambulance.(3rd London T) "The School of the Convent of Penitents", 12 RUE DES BRUGES, POPERINGHE.

(2) Main Dressing Station. (86th Field Ambulance)

    "Institute of the Holy Family", RUE DE STUERS, YPRES.

(3) Advanced Dressing Station.

    School at I. 5 a 5. 7.

(4) Point to which Motor Ambulances are to go by day.

    Road junction at C. 30 c 7. 3.

(5) Position of Motor Ambulances at night.

    Road junction at D. 27 a 7. 5.

(6) Position of Divisional Collecting Station.

    Farm House at D. 27 a 7. 5.

(7) Position of Regimental Aid Posts, from the right.

    (1) Dug out at J. 10 a 8.9.

    (2) Cottage at J. 4 c 5.2.

    (3) Cottage at J. 4 b 1. 5.

    (4) House at D. 27 d 8. 2.

    (5) Last house in ZONNEBEKE at D. 22 c 9. 2. (Two Battalions)

YPRES 1; 40, 000.

(Sgd) N.C. Ferguson.,
Colonel, A.M.S.,
A.D.M.S., 28th Division.

COPY

Report on the suggested Reduction of Rations during the
Summer Months.

As it would appear that the Director of Supplies cannot
undertake:-

(1) The substitution of condensed milk or milk and
cocoa for part of the present ration;

(2) To arrange for relative underdrawals;

(3) The issue of two different scales of rations

I consider any reduction inadvisable.

I quite agree with the Assistant Director of Medical
Services, (San) that " we can afford to give diet in excess
but we cannot afford to risk deficiency in form", and consider that the present wastage is due to the fact that in
most cases the troops can, and do supplement their rations
by the purchase of more palatable food stuffs.

When local individual purchase of substitutes for plum
and apple jam, badly baked bread, tough recently killed meat
and uninviting cheese is not possible, not only is there no
wastage, but the A.D.M.S., and G.O.C., of the 1st Division
on the Aisne in September, reported that the rations issued
were not sufficiently rich in certain constituents.

(Sgd) N.C. Ferguson.,
Colonel., A.M.S.,
A. D. M. S., 28th Division Exp Force.

30.

Names of Officers and other ranks in medical units of 8th Division recommended for good service.

St. A/3rd London/Field Ambulance

Lieut Col. W. Salisbury-Sharpe — Officer Commanding. For especially good administrative work in commanding the unit, and for personal ability through which the sickness in the division has been kept at a low figure.

Captain R.E. Buckston — For his powers of organisation, surgical skill, thoroughness in his work, and thoughtfulness for his patients when in charge of a detached section at YPRES between February and April when the work of this section was exceptionally heavy.

No.551 Sergt Ingram F.C.
No.973 Pte Sell W.E.

For conspicuously good work in visiting the trenches and clearing them of wounded under heavy fire on nights of Feb 28th March 1st and March 4–5 respectively. Sergt Ingram was severely wounded on night March 3–4.

Names of Officers and other ranks in Medical units 58th Division
for good services

85th (3rd London) Field Ambulance

Lieut Col J. R. What — Officer Commanding. For especially good administrative work in commanding the unit, and professional ability through which the sickness in the division has been kept at a low figure.

Captain R. M. Vick — For skill and resource in the work of both his tent and division when on hospital duty, and his keenness when on evacuating regimental aid posts

Captain H.A.T. Fairbank — For skilful and careful work with the bearer thus preventing casualties amongst the personnel in evacuating over exposed ground.

Major E.A. Wagget — For devotion to duty in connection with the Hospital work

N°66 Staff Sergt F.T. Boyes — For unstinting and capable work in the receiving room and dispensary

N°679 Corp'l J.C. Caswell — For skill & resource in working with the bearers at night.

Names of Officers and other ranks in medical units 28th Division for good services.

86/2 Northumbrian Field Ambulance

Lieut Col D.A. Cameron — Officer Commanding. For especially good work in Commanding his unit and preserved ability through which the sickness in the Division has been kept at a low figure.

Major D.L. Fisher — For especially good work in connection with the Divisional Convalescent Rest Station between February and March 1915

Lieut V.H. Wardle — For exceptional coolness and bravery under fire when working with the bearer divs, infusing them with a spirit of confidence. Lieut Wardle was wounded in the night April 2–3.

No 136 Staff Sergt Webster S.J. — For steadiness and coolness when collecting wounded, and control of the young bearers when first under fire

(s) London Sanitary Company

Lieut C. N. Dray Cav¹.

In connection gave work in connection with the Sanitary duties of the Division especially in connection with the Divisional Bathing establishment

From
    O.C. 84th Field Ambulance
To
    A.D.M.S. 28th Division

    In supplement of the names given you in my report of yesterday as recommended for special notice or decoration. I should much like to add that of No. O. 22303 Sergeant Lloyd. J.F., A.S.C., who is in charge of my Motor Ambulance Cars. I have no special act of gallantry to relate of this N.C.O., but his coolness under high explosive, and shrapnel fire, his steady judgment, and unfailing presence of mind, total absence of all fear, and worry have been of more value than I can express, in keeping his drivers together and saving his cars & their freight of wounded on not one, but many occasions. I consider him worthy of the highest award that can be given for such high soldiery character, and consistant reliability

        (sd)
        W. Salisbury Sharpe
9.5.15.   Lieut Col

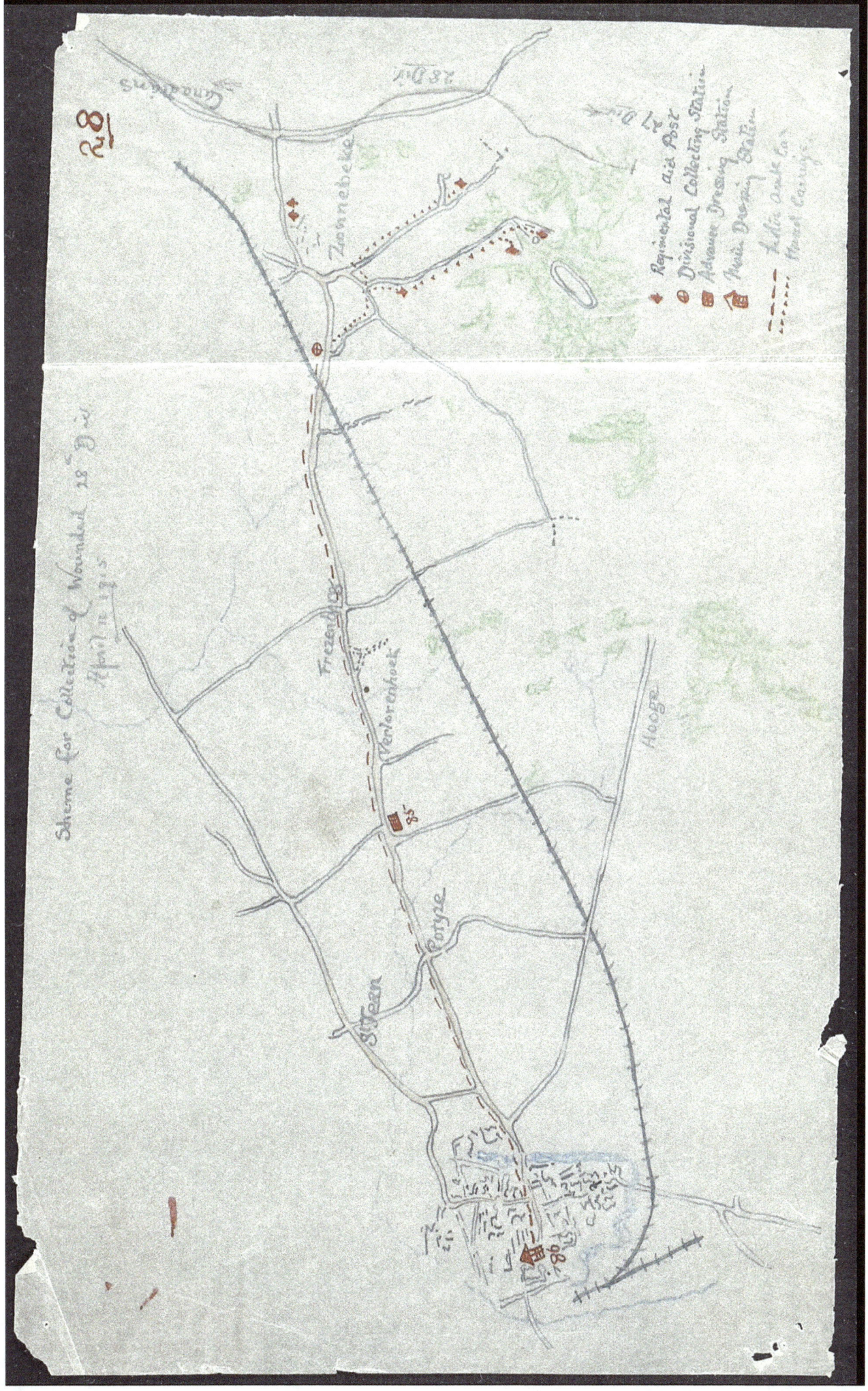

Scheme of Collecting Wounded 28 Division
June 15 – July 15. 1915.
1/40,000.

Copy.

To:-
    O.C., 85th (3rd London) Field Ambulance.

From:-
    Captain H.A.T. Fairbank.

I beg to report that I was able to clear the whole of the area around ZONNEBEKE and to the East of POTIJZE with the exception of one Regimental Aid Post. At this Aid Post to the north of the YPRES -ZONNEBEKE Road, 30 cases were left by a R.M.O., in charge of two stretcher bearers. The reason for this unfortunate state of affairs were, (1) Nothing could be done in daylight to empty this aid post, such as was done by every other R.M.O., in charge of an aid post. (2) No messenger was sent to warn me of the number of cases in any aid post. I had to send Officers and squads to every aid post that I could not myself visit and thus some unnecessary journeys were made. In spite of this 21 squads were sent in batches to this aid post which we were unable to completely evacuate before the hour at which the Brigade Major of the 85th Brigade said I must leave ZONNEBEKE. The cases left included men of the Hampshires, East Yorks and Royal Fusiliers.

Having cleared every other batch of wounded back to POTIJZE I superintended the despatch of all the lying down cases from the Dressing Station. A loading party of 1 Officer and 8 men of the Northumbrian Field Ambulance, having reported at the Dressing Station, and there being nothing further for us to do, I marched the men back to camp, calling myself at POPERINGHE to report to Major Waggett.

May 24th 1915.

(s) H.A.T. Fairbank.,
Captain R.A.M.C.(T)

Water Supply of the 28th Division on 7th May 1915.

Battalions in Trenches.

Drinking Water. From nearest pump, stored in biscuit tins and treated with Chloride of Lime.

Washing Water. Nil.

Bathing Water. Nil.

Battalions in Reserve.

Drinking Water. From selected local well, stored in Water Cart and treated with Chloride of Lime.

Washing Water. From nearest source.

Bathing Water. Nil.

Brigade in Reserve and Medical Units.

Drinking Water. From Laiterie on DUNKIRK Road when possible, otherwise from selected local well and treated with Chloride of Lime.

Washing Water. From nearest source.

Bathing Water. Hot baths are available at the College, PLACE BERTIN, POPERINGHE, water derived from local pump.

May 7th 1915.

Colonel., A.M.S.
A.D.M.S., 28th Division.

The G.O.C., at his inspection to-day considered that nothing had been done in the way of cooking to increase the well-being of the patients in the Field Ambulances.
Owing to the Military exigencies the men have recently been living on monotonous food, and liberal and varied regimen is essential to rapidly restore them to perfect vigour.

In order to improve the messing of the patients, Officers Commanding Field Ambulances will select an Officer who will be responsible for the feeding arrangements of all patients on ordinary diet.

There should be no difficulty in providing for these cases a roast joint with extra vegetables and a pudding for dinner each day. In addition to early morning cocoa a substantial supper should always be provided. "Extras" such as fowls, eggs, butter, milk and fruit can be obtained through the Brigade Requisitioning Officer, dishes for baking milk puddings etc, may be purchased through the imprest account or obtained from the Red Cross Society.

The Field Ovens are to be used only for the preparation of patients food, and the kitchen for the Hospital is to be distinct from that of the detachment or Sergeants Mess.

June 6th 1915.

Nicholas Ferguson.
Colonel., A.M.S.,
A.D.M.S., 28th Division.

CONFIDENTIAL.

A localized epidemic of Enteric Fever has broken out in the Division of the most startling intensity. In 16 days 10 cases have occurred in a sub-section of an Ammunition Column of 30 strong, in spite of the fact that every man had been inoculated.

The immediate cause of the epidemic may prove to be an Enteric Carrier, but the ultimate cause is the adoption of the system of disposal of human excreta which becomes a positive source of danger if the essential details are neglected.

We can render water safe by Chlorination, we can diminish flies by incineration of all waste food stuffs, but the carriers power of evil can only be broken by rigid and unfailing latrine supervision. It is therefore the interest of every Unit Commander to direct the best talent of his Unit in this direction.

A Unit Commander must guarantee that every latrine is supervised in such a way that;-

    (1) Dry earth always covers completely the fecal matter day and night.

    (2) All paper is burned after use.

    (3) The surroundings of the urine pit and latrine is kept constantly covered with Chloride of Lime.

To ensure these measures being carried out, a guard must be posted over each latrine, whose duty will be to throw earth in the trench and see that the excreta is always covered. If necessary the Battalion Police must be employed to supervise this duty.

In addition to the latrines, the greatest care must be given to the prevention of flies collecting about the Cooking places.

                                  R. HENVEY.
                                      Lieut-Colonel.,
                            A.A., and Q.M.G. 28th Division.

rain.

The result in a camp occupied for more than a few days in warm weather is often painfully obvious to the olfactory sense.

Carefully and constantly chlorinated water-- central and supervised messing places--scrupulously clean issuers, and cooks, and utensils-- perfect earth latrines-- and concentrated properly constructed washing places, may be a council of perfection but nothing less can ensure our immunity from epidemic diseases.

8th June.1915.

Colonel., A.M.S.,
A.D.M.S., 28th Division.

CONFIDENTIAL CIRCULAR
No 10.

SICK LEAVE. OFFICERS.

Officers will not be granted leave to England on Medical Certificates.

Officers serving at the front, who are incapacitated for duty on account of illness or wounds, are to be transferred sick to a Base in the usual way.

All cases in which leave to England on Medical grounds is considered necessary, will be dealt with at each port of embarkation by a Standing Medical Board which will not recommend leave for periods of less than three weeks.

The practice of recommending Non-Commissioned Officers and Men as fit for duty on the Lines of Communication only or unfit for Active Service should be restricted as much as possible The Assistant Director of Medical Services should be personally consulted by Regimental Medical Officers before such recommendations are forwarded to the Regimental Authorities. Defective Teeth in subjects who show no signs of emaciation are not to be considered as a disability.

Medical Officers are reminded that the premature diagnosis of Infectious or Contagious Diseases is apt to cause unnecessary alarm and despondency among the troops.

NICHOLAS FERGUSON.,
Colonel., A.M.S.
A.D.M.S., 28th Division Exp Force.

June 1915.

As it is necessary to take every possible precaution against an outbreak of enteric fever, it is proposed to reinoculate all men who only received one dose of the Vaccine last year.

Will you please arrange to have a list of such men sent to this office at your earliest convenience. The necessary information will be found in Army Book 6, entered thus,- "T.V. 13/10/14 A.D.H", which means Typhoid Vaccine on 13th October 1914 -initials of Medical Officer performing the inoculation. Men who have received more than one inoculation will have two dates in their pay books, or T.1/2 with one date; such men, and those who state that they received two inoculations within the last two years, need not be shown on the list.

25/6/1915.

Lieut Colonel.,
A.A.& Q.M.G. 25th Division.

28th Division Expeditionary Force.

Casualties in Six Months:- January 18th to July 18th 1915.

	Sick.	Wounded.	Killed.	Missing.	Totals.
Officers.	196	469	163	99	927
Other Ranks.	7,273	10,554	2,647	7,016	27,490
TOTALS.	7,469	11,023	2,810	7,115	28,417

Cases treated in Field Ambulances, January to 18th July 1915.

		Officers.	Other Ranks.	Totals.
84th Field Ambulance.	Admissions.	358	13,073	13,431
(2nd London T)	Transfers.	-	231	231
	Total.	358	13,304	13,662
85th Field Ambulance.	Admissions.	428	10,847	11,275
(3rd London T)	Transfers.	-	118	118
	Total.	428	10,965	11,393
86th Field Ambulance.	Admissions.	85	3,288	3,373
(2nd North'bn T)	Transfers.	-	2,038	2,038
	Total.	85	5,326	5,411
GRAND TOTAL.		871	29,595	30,466

moot/2270(2)

moot/2270(2)

28TH DIVISION
DIVL ENGINEERS

C. R. E.
DEC 1914 – OCT 1915

121/4610

H⁰ Qrs: R.E. 28th Division

Vol I. 18.12.14 — 28.2.15

Dec '14
Oct '15

Original.

Headquarters.
28th Divisional Engineers.

Army Form C. 2118.

WAR DIARY
or
INTELLIGENCE SUMMARY.

Instructions regarding War Diaries and Intelligence Summaries are contained in F.S. Regs., Part II. and the Staff Manual respectively. Title pages will be prepared in manuscript.

Hour, Date, Place		Summary of Events and Information	Remarks and references to Appendices
18-12-14 to 17-1-15.	Winchester.	Mobilizing, equipping, etc.	
18-1-15.		Proceeded from Winchester to Southampton and there embarked on S.S. Rhidau. Left at 6.30 p.m.	
19-1-15.	Havre.	Arrived at Havre. Delayed at tide for. from 8.0 a.m. till 12.0 noon on account of tide, then disembarked.	
20-1-15.	Havre.	Remained in shed in docks till 4.30 p.m.; entrained at left June. Finally, travelled via Rouen. Then all round north of Havre till we were within only 3 hours of Havre, and eventually arriving	
21-1-15.	Hazebrouck.	at Hazebrouck at about 5.0 p.m. in very heavy rain. Took 4½ hours getting out of station. Marched to Borre, where we were billeted in a cattle farm (R. Ordway).	
21-1-15.	Borre.		
21-1-15 to 31-1-15.	Borre.	Remained at Borre for 10 days. Companies had a start at making huts, fascines, hurdles, etc. Which work is required in the future war Vaurentinghe.	
1-2-15 to 5-2-15.	Vaurentinghe.	Moved by march route to Vaurentinghe on 1-2-15, where we were billeted. We went uncomfortably in a shed recently vacated by two calves. Companies billeted in neighbouring farms. Companies at work hut building — also collecting stores for use in the trenches and sending same to Port Lille, Ypres.	

WAR DIARY

INTELLIGENCE SUMMARY.

Army Form C. 2118.

Hour, Date, Place	Summary of Events and Information	Remarks and references to Appendices
6-2-15 to 19-2-15. Poperinghe.	Billetted at Poperinghe. There are moved on 6-2-15. The Assistance away from Ypres and Vlamertinghe greatly hindered administration, organization, supervision & the work of Companies, one of which (1st Northumbrian Field Co.) is even into Ypres during this period. They were employed in making/preparing shelters and materials for the trenches, and each Company had a section attached to a brigade, which it accompanied into the trenches.	
14.2.15	Captain C.F.J. Galloway. 3rd/First Company. R.M.R.E. (S.R.) wounded. (Company attached for work.)	
15.2.15.	Lieut. J.C. Keith G. Fearns. 1st Lancashire Field Co. R.E. was wounded.	
17.2.15	3rd Lndn Field Coy. R.E. was called to Ypres urgently to do trench work (digging) & attached to 149th Northumbrian Fd.Coy. (Sui. Clay Euystoye) on the night of 17/18-2-15, his Brig to task of guides. They did no work. They came into Ypres tomorrow. On the following day for work on the following night. Brig. to various delays took Start) Rd. during 18-2-15 Lieut. 149th Star. 3rd Lndn Fd.Coy. R.E. was killed & the early evening of	
18.2.15		
19.2.15	19.2.15 Major S.D. Sewell. Comdg. 3rd Lndn Fd. Coy. R.E. was killed, the same evening Lieut. W.C. Stroud, 1st Northumbrian FieldCoy. R.E. was command the Coy Company devolved on Captain W.S. Shelley. On the same evening Lieut. W.C. Stroud, 1st Northumbrian FieldCoy. R.E. was wounded, shot through both legs.	

Army Form C. 2118.

WAR DIARY
of
INTELLIGENCE SUMMARY.
(Erase heading not required.)

Instructions regarding War Diaries and Intelligence Summaries are contained in F.S. Regs., Part II. and the Staff Manual respectively. Title pages will be prepared in manuscript.

Hour, Date, Place	Summary of Events and Information	Remarks and references to Appendices
17.2.15	Line at Potinje 60 was blown up by Lieut. R.E. White (1st Northumbrian Fld Coy) Result - difficult to visualt; but probably not very large, especially as no arrangements were made for occupying up craters &c.	
20.2.15. Ypres.	Lord fox.	
22.2.15	Fortnight to Ypres, where we were billetted.	
25.2.15	Lieut: H.N. Davis, 3rd London Field Coy. R.E. died of wounds received at 20.2.15.	
	Party of "Clay-kickers" under Lieut. Hill, arrived. Their right to leave Gen. 26 of Plans, but about half were Tostry or Jerney. They arrived at 26.2.15. Party attacked to 1st Northumbrian Field Coy. R.E., for &c.	
26.2.15	Gatrick Coy is supervising all the mining belonging to the Division for Ypres. There "Clay-kickers" are to form part of Major Porter Griffith, as a matter of fact, as of some of them are Clay-kickers, the remainder being ordinary miners.	
27.2.15	2 parties, each consisting of 1 officer and 40 men, arrived. All the men are miners, and belong respectively to the 1st and 3rd Mon. North Regiment (T.F.) They were attached to 1st Northumbrian Field Coy. R.E. and placed under the O. Liaot Coy for orders.	
28.2.15 Ypres.		

H. Jerome
Colonel.
C.R.E. 28th Division.

7.3.15

12/4865

HdQrs R.E. 28th Division

Vol II 1-31.3.15

Army Form C. 2118.

Headquarters.
78th Territorial Engineers.

WAR DIARY
INTELLIGENCE SUMMARY
(Erase heading not required)

Instructions regarding War Diaries and Intelligence Summaries are contained in F.S. Regs., Part II. and the Staff Manual respectively. Title pages will be prepared in manuscript.

Hour, Date, Place	Summary of Events and Information	Remarks and references to Appendices
1-3-15 to 31-3-15. Ypres.	General work — Companies in trenches, employed on trench work & preparation for attack, in workshops at Ypres. First importance given to training operations, to which primary importance was given as regards provision of relief, etc. The Company employed in vicinity of Hauwerlinghe, were being relieved. This was the 1st North Midland Field Coy. R.E. until 13.3.15, & which day it came to Ypres, being relieved by the 4th (Siege) Coy. R. Lanark R.E.	
5.3.15	2 Lieut. R.E. Clark, 1st Northumbrian Field Cor. R.E. (wounded) 15.2.15, died of wounds.	
7.3.15	2 Lieut. F.L. Beck, R.L.R.E. killed.	
14.3.15	Captain A.J. Constantin, 1st North Midland Field Cor. placed temporarily in command of 2nd London Field Coy. on account of serious breakdown of Captain W.S. Kelly. (No. Sel- ..... went to hospital.	

Army Form C. 2118.

WAR DIARY
INTELLIGENCE SUMMARY.
(Erase heading not required.)

Instructions regarding War Diaries and Intelligence Summaries are contained in F. S. Regs., Part II. and the Staff Manual respectively. Title pages will be prepared in manuscript.

Hour, Date, Place	Summary of Events and Information	Remarks and references to Appendices
19.3.15	Lieut: Bunyat, 1st Monmouth Regt (T.F.), attached to 1st Northumbrian Field Coy in charge of attachment of Miners. Wounded.	
26.3.15	2nd Lieuts (Portion) Coy. R.E. & Cornwall (Portion) Coy. R.E. placed under orders of O.C. 2nd F.Coy. 28th Division. Both Companies supplying to form subsidiary twin of Defence.	
29.3.15	2/Lieut: W.H. Hodges, 1st Northumbrian (and) Field Coy. R.E. wounded.	
31.3.15	1 section of 4th (Siege) Coy. R. Monmouth R.E. came from vicinity of Kemmel Single for attachment to 1st Northumbrian Field Coy. for trench work. (Officer - 2nd Lt. Hill)	

2.4.15

H. Jerome
Colonel.
C.R.E. 28th Division.

12/5320

H^d Qrs: R.E. 28th Division

Vol III 1 — 29.4.15

April 1915

● Bradgeworth
28th Divisional
Engineers

Army Form C. 2118.

WAR DIARY
OF
INTELLIGENCE SUMMARY.
(Erase heading not required.)

Instructions regarding War Diaries and Intelligence Summaries are contained in F. S. Regs., Part II. and the Staff Manual respectively. Title pages will be prepared in manuscript.

Hour, Date, Place	Summary of Events and Information	Remarks and references to Appendices
1-4-15 to 5-4-15 Ypres.	Companies employed on general trench work.	
5-4-15 to 9-4-15	Return retiring old & new divisional frontage. Old frontage handed over to 5th Division. New frontage (left half m.w.) on left of 27th Division. Taken over from Pandr 6-4-15.	×
8-4-15	1st North Midland Fd Coy left division to join its own terr— 2nd Division. — 8th N London Fd Coy.	
8-4-15	38th (Field) Coy (Major P.R. Roome, D.S.O. commanding) joined division.	
11-4-15	2nd (Sig) Coy Royal Engineers R.E. (S.R.) (Major Colson commanding) joined division.	
10-4-15 to 30-4-15 Ypres	Companies employed on general trench work.	
21-4-15	On account of heavy shelling moved H.Q. to house on N.W. edge of town.	
28-4-15	Heavy German attack on front on left of British	
23-4-15	H.Q. (moved) to Vlamertinghe (Château).	
15-4-15	2nd Lt. E.C. Osborn (38th Fd Coy) killed.	

Army Form C. 2118.

WAR DIARY
or
INTELLIGENCE SUMMARY.
(Erase heading not required.)

Instructions regarding War Diaries and Intelligence Summaries are contained in F.S. Regs., Part II. and the Staff Manual respectively. Title pages will be prepared in manuscript.

Hour, Date, Place	Summary of Events and Information	Remarks and references to Appendices
26-4-15	2/Lieut. F.S. Vavasour (2nd Coy. 7th P.F.E.) killed.	
27-4-15	Major D.E. Griffith. H.Q. 7th Engr. (wounded).	
29-4-15	Captain M.G. Dyer (38th Fd Coy) wounded	
11-5-15		J M Bristow Major R.E. A/C.R.E. 28th Division

121/5336

H.d Q.rs R.E. 28th Division.

Vol IV. 1 — 31.5.15.

Headquarters
28th Divisional Engineers

WAR DIARY

INTELLIGENCE SUMMARY.

Army Form C. 2118.

(Erase heading not required.)

Hour, Date, Place	Summary of Events and Information	Remarks and references to Appendices
1-5-15 to 30-5-15 Ypres.	Companies Employed on trench work	
2-5-15	54th & 155th Coys attached for work in connection with new line through Frizenberg (for 2 days)	
3-5-15 /4	Division moved back to Busseboom – presumably Cam's ork.	
5-5-15	H.Q. 28th Div'l Engrs moved from Chateau, Vlamertinghe to farm down H.Q.A.	
10-5-15	Colonel H. Jeudwine C.R.E. left Division on 3 weeks' leave/on sick certificate/ & replaced by Lt.Col. A.R. Winsloe R.E.[O] Major R.R. Brown D.S.O. acting CRE.	
12-5-15	1st Cav. Bwi took over command of front 28th Div'l Engrs placed under command (for work) of [illeg] 14 Cav. Bwi.	
15-5-15	Coys placed under orders of C.E. E. Corps for work.	
16-5-15	456 Coys & 4th Durhams with [Engr] Coy, working on Canal Line. with Belgian working parties.	
21-5-15	28th Div. Assumed Command of Front – Was taken over by 85th Inf. Brigade which 2nd Lowthrian Field Coy was attached for work.	

Army Form C. 2118.

WAR DIARY
— of —
INTELLIGENCE SUMMARY.
(Erase heading not required.)

Instructions regarding War Diaries and Intelligence Summaries are contained in F.S. Regs., Part II. and the Staff Manual respectively. Title pages will be prepared in manuscript.

Hour, Date, Place	Summary of Events and Information	Remarks and references to Appendices
22-5-15	25th Inf. Brigade (with 1st Northumbrian RE Coy) in to trenches (under Cavalry Corps)	
24-5-15	Gas attack by enemy in early morning. 2 W. Lcrk's RE Coy.	
25-5-15	A Lectr. attached to remains Div. Lieut. Col. A.R. Winsloe joined as CRE. 28th Division.	
30-5-15	35th (RWF) Coy. returned to Bertaine, was Hazgrela.	
31-5-15	1 W. Northumbrian RE Coy joined 6th Division.	
3-6-15		

Brigadier for C.R.E.
C.R.E. 28th Division.

28th Division

Hd Qrs RE 28th Division

Vol I 1 - 30.6.15

10/5993

as7
DFW

10.

Army Form C. 2118.

WAR DIARY
or
INTELLIGENCE SUMMARY.
(Erase heading not required.)

Radgeon Ris.
28th Div Engrs.

Instructions regarding War Diaries and Intelligence Summaries are contained in F.S. Regs., Part II and the Staff Manual respectively. Title pages will be prepared in manuscript.

Hour, Date, Place	Summary of Events and Information	Remarks and references to Appendices
1-6-15	H.Q. R.E. moved to rest area at Watou Reking.	
1-6-15 to 14-6-15. Watou 14-6-15.	H.Q. R.E. moved to Boeschepe. 51st (Fed) Coy came under orders of 28th Div.	
15-6-15	1/2 38th (Fed) Coy moved from rest area to Canada huts, sticking huts and the other half Coy to vicinity of Ballerul for work under C.E. II Corps.	
19-6-15	1/2 38th (Fed) Coy rejoined Coy H.Q. at Canada huts from work under C.E. II Corps.	
19-6-15	61.2nd (Fed) Coy left 28th Division and rejoined 14th Div.	
19-6-15	2/1st South Midland Field Coy R.E. (T) joined 28th Division 3 sections at R.E. Farm, Kanned and 1 section at Loes (with Transport).	
15-6-15 to 30-6-15	H.Q. at Boeschepe. Companies employed in general R.E. work in trenches. 2/1st South Midland 3rd Coy with 83rd Inf. Brigade on right of frontage; 38th (Fed) Coy with 84th & 85th Inf. Brigades on left of frontage. Digging and running mining of natures (carried on) to prevent Enemy running mines & to under our own trenches;	

(73989) W4141—463. 400,000. 9/14. H.&J.Ltd. Forms/C. 2118/10.

Army Form C. 2118.

WAR DIARY
OF
INTELLIGENCE SUMMARY.
(Erase heading not required.)

Headquarters
28th Divl. Engrs.

Instructions regarding War Diaries and Intelligence Summaries are contained in F.S. Regs., Part II. and the Staff Manual respectively. Title pages will be prepared in manuscript.

Hour, Date, Place	Summary of Events and Information	Remarks and references to Appendices
20-6-15.	Infantry mining section, consisting of 50 men with 2 Officers from each infantry brigade organized and employed. Lieut. Taylor from 177 (Mining Coy. Employed). Quarry consisting 2L. Lyle or 29-6-15. 2/Lt. J. R. Troop, 38th (Field) Coy. R.E. wounded.	
4-7-15	Isogelwarth Captain for CRE 28th Division.	

28th Division

12/6461

HdQrs RE. 28th Division

Vol VI

Army Form C. 2118.

Headquarters,
28th Field Coy.

WAR DIARY
INTELLIGENCE SUMMARY.
(Erase heading not required.)

Instructions regarding War Diaries and Intelligence Summaries are contained in F.S. Regs., Part II. and the Staff Manual respectively. Title pages will be prepared in manuscript.

Hour, Date, Place	Summary of Events and Information	Remarks and references to Appendices
1-7-15 to 31-7-15.	Companies employed in general R.E. work in trenches 38th (up) Company working with 84th & 85th Infantry Brigades and 21st North Midland – and subsequent 21st Northumbrian Field Coy – working with 83rd Infantry Brigade. Separate coming of work carried out by Infantry Brigade Mining Sections, without exception at first under Officers commanding Field Coys concerned, and from the middle of the month all under O.C. 2/1st Northumbrian Field Coy. R.E.	
10-7-15	21st North Midland Field Coy R.E. left to join the 5th Division.	
10-7-15	21st Northumbrian Field Coy. R.E. joined for duty from 50th Division.	
29-7-15	Lieut. R.B. Murray 171st (Tunnelling) Coy. R.E. (and) division to report in mining work here	

12.

Army Form C. 2118.

WAR DIARY
or
INTELLIGENCE SUMMARY.
(Erase heading not required.)

Headquarters,
28th Divl Engrs.

Instructions regarding War Diaries and Intelligence Summaries are contained in F. S. Regs., Part II. and the Staff Manual respectively. Title pages will be prepared in manuscript.

Hour, Date, Place	Summary of Events and Information	Remarks and references to Appendices
23-7-15	War attached to 2/1st Northumbrian Fd Con. R.E.	
	Lieut. E.F.Tickell joined 38th (Fds) Coy. R.E. for duty.	
15-7-15	38th (Fds) Coy moved from Canada Huts, Dickebusch, and ultimately were billetted at Drouvin, spending one day in vicinity of Krumel and one day at Lees en route.	

W. Cruickshank. Col.

George Walker Capt.
for
C.R.E. 28th Division.

10-8-15

28th Division

B/
6787.

HdQrs R.E. 28th Division

for VII

August. 15

Original.

Army Form C. 2118.

Headquarters
28th Div'l Engrs.

WAR DIARY
or
INTELLIGENCE SUMMARY.
(Erase heading not required.)

Instructions regarding War Diaries and Intelligence Summaries are contained in F.S. Regs., Part II. and the Staff Manual respectively. Title pages will be prepared in manuscript.

Hour, Date, Place	Summary of Events and Information	Remarks and references to Appendices
1-8-15 to 31-8-15	Companies employed on General R.E. work in trenches. 38 (F'd.R'y.Co) Coy working with 84th & 85th Infantry Brigades and 2/1st Northumbrian Field Coy working with 83rd Infantry Brigade. Defensive wiring & draining carried on by Infantry Brigades. Mining Sectors under O.C. 2/1st Northumbrian Field Coy. R.E.	
27-8-15	Lieut. G.K. Walker, 2/1st Northumbrian Field Coy. R.E. wounded.	
28-8-15	Lieut. G.K. Walker, 2/1st Northumbrian Field Coy. R.E. returned to duty.	

George Walker
for Captain,
C.R.E. 28th Division.

3.9
10-9-15

Army Form C. 2118.

15.

WAR DIARY
INTELLIGENCE SUMMARY.

Headquarters. 105th Batt Engrs.

(Erase heading not required.)

Instructions regarding War Diaries and Intelligence Summaries are contained in F.S. Regs., Part II. and the Staff Manual respectively. Title pages will be prepared in manuscript.

Hour, Date, Place	Summary of Events and Information	Remarks and references to Appendices
30-9-15	Rolunzollern Redoubt & Big Willie, captured from enemy.	
30-9-15.	Major P. H. Brown. D.S.O. (O.C. 38th Coy.) mortally wounded. Lieut J. H. Forster 2/Lt Northumbrian Field Coy. killed.	
5-10-15		Fitzgerald Captain for O.C. 28th Division.

121/7466

Cal.E. 28th June

Doc 15

Vol IX

WAR DIARY
or
INTELLIGENCE SUMMARY.

(Erase heading not required.)

Army Form C. 2118.

9 ? C.R.E. 2Fr Divn
Major Sundys

Instructions regarding War Diaries and Intelligence Summaries are contained in F.S. Regs., Part II and the Staff Manual respectively. Title pages will be prepared in manuscript.

Hour, Date, Place	Summary of Events and Information	Remarks and references to Appendices
1-10-15. Sailly-Labourse	101st Fd Coy R.E. joined division for work.	
1-10-15 — 5-10-15	All 3 Coys employed consolidating WEST FACE until its reception by enemy, also BIG WILLIE, QUARRY TRENCH and communications to same. A.S.O. appointed C.R.E. vice Lt-Col. Lt-Col. Sandys appointed C.R.E. vice Lt-Col.	
4-10-15	Winter A.S.O. to G.H.Q. M. Ranziers, Belgium Interprete aft H.Q. Liek R.E. & M. Roolenbruck, French Interprete, joined.	
4-10-15 — 6-10-15	Coys employed on consolidating ground in rear near BIG WILLIE. 4th R. Welsh Fusiliers (Reserve) joined Division for work under C.R.E. Handed over R.E. work to C.R.E. Guards Division and left BUSNES.	
6-10-15. BUSNES		
7-10-15 — 8-10-15.	at BUSNES. Companies employed on Drill, Route marching and R.E. training. Lt-Col. D. Tate appointed adjutant 2nd Divl. Engineers vice Capt. J. Martin to command 38th Fd. Coy.	
9-10-15.		

Army Form C. 2118.

WAR DIARY
or
INTELLIGENCE SUMMARY.
(Erase heading not required.)

Instructions regarding War Diaries and Intelligence Summaries are contained in F.S. Regs., Part II. and the Staff Manual respectively. Title pages will be prepared in manuscript.

Hour, Date, Place	Summary of Events and Information	Remarks and references to Appendices
8-10-15 BUSNES	38th Fd Co. inspected by G.O.C. 28th Divn & by G.O.C. 1st Corps & marched past.	
10-10-15.	Conference held by G.O.C. 28th Divn to work out orders by 1st Corps for attack on FONE No 8 contemplated for 5/10/15. C.R.E. & Staff attended.	
11-10-15	101st Fd Coy & 2/1st Northumbrian Fd Coy left for BETHUNE to work under C.E. 1st Corps.	
12-10-15 to 16-10-13 16-10-15	Resting at BUSNES. C.R.E. visited front line trenches between BETHUNE - LA BASSÉE road and CANAL, which was taken over by 83rd Bde from the 2nd Division the following day.	
17-10-15 LEGUESNOY 18-10-15 BETHUNE	Hd. Qrs. R.E. moved into billets at QUESNOY. C.R.E. visited second and third line trenches behind 83rd Bde front. Plans and returns of work along front CANAL to THE LOOP taken over from C.R.E. 2nd Division 2/1st Northumbrian Co attached to 83rd Bde to work from BETHUNE. 38th Field Co took over work of Northumbrian Co under O.C 1st Corps Commander inspected 2nd line defences and w[orks?]	
19-10-15	[ ] on 83rd Bde front.	
20-10-15	101st Field Co left to rejoin 3rd Corps.	

Army Form C. 2118.

WAR DIARY
or
INTELLIGENCE SUMMARY.
(Erase heading not required.)

Instructions regarding War Diaries and Intelligence Summaries are contained in F.S. Regs., Part II. and the Staff Manual respectively. Title pages will be prepared in manuscript.

Hour, Date, Place	Summary of Events and Information	Remarks and references to Appendices
21-10-15 to 22-10-15 BETHUNE.	At BETHUNE. Handed over plans etc. of portion of front between CANAL and BETHUNE-LA BASSÉE road to C.R.E. 2nd Division. Handed over plans etc. of portion of front between CANAL and THE LOOP to C.R.E. 7th Div.	
23-10-15 to 25-10-15 In the Train.	Entrained at LILLERS at 10 a.m. Travelled via DOULLENS — AMIENS — CHANTILLY — VILLENEUVE ST GEORGES — MONTARGIS — MOULINS — LYONS — LE TEIL. Here owing to line having been flooded, train reversed evening of 24th at LA VOULTE-SUR-RHONE & proceeded via PIERRELATTE — AVIGNON arriving MARSEILLES (PRADO Station) at 10 p.m.	
26-10-15 to 31-10-15 MARSEILLES	Arrived at camp en racecourse at PARC BORÉLY where remained.	

6095/22703

6095/22703

28TH DIVISION
DIVL TROOPS

D. A. D. O. S.
DEC 1914 — SEP NOV 1915

121/6754

28th Division

DADOS. 28th Division

Vol V

14th DEC TO 1915 August 15

121/6033

28th Division

DADOS. 28th Division

Vol I.

Army Form C. 2118.

WAR DIARY
INTELLIGENCE SUMMARY
(Erase heading not required.)

Instructions regarding War Diaries and Intelligence Summaries are contained in F.S. Regs., Part II. and the Staff Manual respectively. Title pages will be prepared in manuscript.

Hour, Date, Place	Summary of Events and Information	Remarks and references to Appendices
	Confidential War Diary of D.A.D.O.S. 27 Division. From 15-10-14 to 30-4-15. " 1-6-15 to 30-6-15.	

WAR DIARY
or
INTELLIGENCE SUMMARY.
(Erase heading not required.)

Army Form C. 2118.

Instructions regarding War Diaries and Intelligence Summaries are contained in F.S. Regs., Part II. and the Staff Manual respectively. Title pages will be prepared in manuscript.

Hour, Date, Place	Summary of Events and Information	Remarks and references to Appendices
1914. December 15	Reported to Brigade at WINCHESTER - none of the Staff of 2nd Division have yet arrived - having to manage till — 2 Regiment K.O.Y.L.I.s — Suffolks are encamped at HURDLEY PARK and a certain amount of work near WINCHESTER — the remain of the Artillery of the 27th Division. The 27 Division have not yet finished their mobilization	
December 16	Staff an office in the CORN EXCHANGE - my Staff began issuing tents which I saw in Manchester a few G.1098's	

Army Form C. 2118.

WAR DIARY
or
INTELLIGENCE SUMMARY.
(Erase heading not required.)

Instructions regarding War Diaries and Intelligence Summaries are contained in F. S. Regs., Part II. and the Staff Manual respectively. Title pages will be prepared in manuscript.

Hour, Date, Place	Summary of Events and Information	Remarks and references to Appendices
December 18"	Arrange skate over the CORNEXCHANGE Wher the 27 Division move into —	
December 24"	Difficulties in Transport arrangements	
	driver urgent work.	
December 28"	Civilian Transport stuck work again.	

Army Form C. 2118.

WAR DIARY
or
INTELLIGENCE SUMMARY.
(Erase heading not required.)

Instructions regarding War Diaries and Intelligence Summaries are contained in F. S. Regs., Part II. and the Staff Manual respectively. Title pages will be prepared in manuscript.

Hour, Date, Place	Summary of Events and Information	Remarks and references to Appendices
Jan 5 1915	About the enhance of mobilization Intents or interior in general — checks begin a month taken & then proceeded to Portsmouth — Portsmouth devoid on trek from Wolverine — opposition the required details for the detachment told the Gloria and defender Dagmeister Corie a Engrais Winchester. Stone are offloaded into the CORNFLOWER either moved from the lorries or by motor lorries from the station — mules attend at the station — daily trains what arrive for them —	

Army Form C. 2118.

WAR DIARY
or
INTELLIGENCE SUMMARY.
(Erase heading not required.)

Instructions regarding War Diaries and Intelligence Summaries are contained in F.S. Regs., Part II. and the Staff Manual respectively. Title pages will be prepared in manuscript.

Hour, Date, Place	Summary of Events and Information	Remarks and references to Appendices
3 Jan 1915 Mintzaben (India)	Army Form C.2098 anxiously awaited news from the War Office. The two horses tent equipment & other arms to this unit — Considerable assistance in mobilization given by the following Supplementary Staff — 1 Commissioner } These have been 1 Corporal } employed the 1 Private } mobilization of the 8th & 27th Divisions and I am thus able to profit immensely by their experience. A clothing store to also run by O.O. Wonderful with the assistance of a temporary Assistant	

WAR DIARY
or
INTELLIGENCE SUMMARY.
(Erase heading not required.)

Army Form C. 2118.

Instructions regarding War Diaries and Intelligence Summaries are contained in F.S. Regs., Part II. and the Staff Manual respectively. Title pages will be prepared in manuscript.

Hour, Date, Place	Summary of Events and Information	Remarks and references to Appendices
5 Jan 1915 mobilization (Continued)	and trousers are blankets, the above we of all the men of clothing which by any chance in the hands of the division have just come home from India. The Ordnance Officers at WINCHESTER and HURSLEY Park clearfors also deal with the want of rifle (the Division has late Enfields haired with Mark VII rifle) and also all details of ambs equipment also of from multigation equipment. There also of field ambulance tops in the want of Ammunition qui many other wats. I am also arrives by a staff-sergeant at the various stations	

Army Form C. 2118.

WAR DIARY
or
INTELLIGENCE SUMMARY.
(Erase heading not required.)

Instructions regarding War Diaries and Intelligence Summaries are contained in F.S. Regs., Part II. and the Staff Manual respectively. Title pages will be prepared in manuscript.

Hour, Date, Place	Summary of Events and Information	Remarks and references to Appendices
7 Jan. 6pm (Wednesday) (continued)	My experience at PORTSMOUTH when I was Ordnance Officer for the preceding two months in motor cycles home – I knew the officers whom I am working with – their methods their capabilities	
8 Jan.	The tour exchange has been hired as an office accommodation in which worked auxiliaries store Some Bogart Square where it had been a store room and attached both is one office. The whole 6.10" which is used as an office. The whole is warmed by the workshops and lit by electricity. A telephone is fitted up. The station is about ½ mile distant.	

Army Form C. 2118.

WAR DIARY
or
INTELLIGENCE SUMMARY.
(Erase heading not required.)

Instructions regarding War Diaries and Intelligence Summaries are contained in F.S. Regs., Part II. and the Staff Manual respectively. Title pages will be prepared in manuscript.

Hour, Date, Place	Summary of Events and Information	Remarks and references to Appendices

Jan 1st onwards (Malagasha).

The troops are about 3 to 5 mile distance. The 83ord Brigade as at HURSLEY PARK Camp which is 5 miles away to the East of MORNE HILL CAMP where is 3 miles away.

Jan 9th

Friends — A report of intend to keep in touch — A record showing the date the G6098s were [issued] to the units, when returned, when [completed] & when all pridence [forwarded] to PORTSMOUTH. Before being sent out to march the G6098s was [divided] in 2 columns (1) [numbers] [reasons] [wrongful] (2) [mistake] [wrongwise] Men returning complete forwards — they accepted the [investigated] COs kept to [reserve]

Forms/C. 2118/10.

Army Form C. 2118.

WAR DIARY
or
INTELLIGENCE SUMMARY.
(Erase heading not required.)

Instructions regarding War Diaries and Intelligence Summaries are contained in F.S. Regs., Part II. and the Staff Manual respectively. Title pages will be prepared in manuscript.

Hour, Date, Place	Summary of Events and Information	Remarks and references to Appendices
Jan 10th 1915 Jan 15th Mi Winjalin (continued)	This found impossible to keep a record of observations in the wire in the trench — the packages came without packing rolls and without wrapping every case of fuse — an impossibility from an accurate [time] and at a glance of [unreadable] labour, it is impossible to say what the actual air — it has been brought to notice that the storm do not [unreadable] with the webs on the inside & have have been many cases of [unreadable] mines.	

Army Form C. 2118

WAR DIARY
or
INTELLIGENCE SUMMARY
(Erase heading not required.)

Instructions regarding War Diaries and Intelligence Summaries are contained in F. S. Regs., Part II. and the Staff Manual respectively. Title Pages will be prepared in manuscript.

Place	Date	Hour	Summary of Events and Information	Remarks and references to Appendices
WINCHESTER	Jan 15th		Mobilisation (continued). Owing to rainstorms and continued bad weather it is found impossible to keep the troops under canvas — the whole division with the exception of the Yeomanry RE & field ambulances have been moved into billets in WINCHESTER. This has caused great inconvenience as regards Mobilisation. Entrainment must be postponed a week or some such taking as return — they are wheeling on their mobilisation equipment in their lorries which are not to be interchanged. They have no idea what they have got rolled they have collected. The remnants in a muddle —	

1875 Wt. W593/826 1,000,000 4/15 J.B.C. & A. A.D.S.S./Forms/C. 2118.

WAR DIARY
or
INTELLIGENCE SUMMARY

(Erase heading not required.)

Army Form C. 2118

Place	Date	Hour	Summary of Events and Information	Remarks and references to Appendices
WINCHESTER	Jan. 15		The division is now supposed to have drawn all its mob-equipment — all indent-paperwork has been stopped. There is a conference of quartermasters every evening at which the Asst Qmt presides. Every unit brings a list of the articles which are deficient. Their list are passed to Portsmouth & the article are sent by motor lorry. There is indeed that a lot of confusion is caused by the ignorance of the quartermasters (who have had no time to get and have been reported) A unit has demanded 1000 packs, their pouch have been supplied from Portsmouth & a fortnight later the unit has returned them as not required!	

WAR DIARY
or
INTELLIGENCE SUMMARY
(Erase heading not required.)

Army Form C. 2118

Place	Date	Hour	Summary of Events and Information	Remarks and references to Appendices
WINCHESTER	Jan 16		The division marches down to SOUTHAMPTON and embark for LE HAVRE	
	Jan 18		The division is in billets in the HAZEBROUCK area	
	Jan 19		The railhead is at EBBLINGHEM.	
	Jan 30		Blankets, braziers & gumboots are sent up and issued to the division - review this item in months of stores - The host moves to the division at WINCHESTER have turned out very badly - Many of them gave out during the march to SOUTHAMPTON. This is no doubt the South African boots is poor, but the conditions leave	

Army Form C. 2118

WAR DIARY
or
INTELLIGENCE SUMMARY
(Erase heading not required.)

Instructions regarding War Diaries and Intelligence Summaries are contained in F. S. Regs., Part II. and the Staff Manual respectively. Title Pages will be prepared in manuscript.

Place	Date	Hour	Summary of Events and Information	Remarks and references to Appendices
FEB 15 BOMETHEK.			The division moves up into the fighting area. During the Greater Lie in at the place named in the margin. A dump has been formed at OUDERDOM to my office is also at OUDERDOM. I find it very difficult to keep our Office away from my staff — The Administration staff with this and so my Office is nominally here —	
POPERINGHE	Feb 6th		Headquarters moved to POPERINGHE. My Office has been moved up to this place and indeed an well a general correspondence is being done here. My chief clerk 4 assistants are with me — The three warrant officers with their assistants are at the "dump"	

WAR DIARY or INTELLIGENCE SUMMARY

Army Form C. 2118

Place	Date	Hour	Summary of Events and Information	Remarks and references to Appendices
POPERINGHE	Feb/15		Col Willans arrived as NCO in attached which is at BRODWATERSTEEN	
	16		A considerable amount of work overhead — The French are in an exposed position and great difficulty is experienced in getting rations up to the men. I have bought a lot of "Orilux" hand-lamps for them to enable them to use up tender fire — 83 rifle grenades in particular invaluable & I have been asked to buy them yellow balloons to blow up the Huns !! There is also a great request for lanterns — The rising line lamps provided are hopeless — They give a poor light in all weathers except one — becomes unbearable viz. quickly & do not burn well unless constantly attended to	

Place	Date	Hour	Summary of Events and Information	Remarks and references to Appendices
POPERINGHE	Feb 16		I find it absolute necessary to have a motorcar completely at my disposal — A visit bradhead is a necessity and there is so much bread nowhere else done that it is in a case of always having to ask for a car to work council help Power. Although I had great difficulty in getting a car to myself at this beginning in spite of the fact that it is definitely laid down in War Establishments that the D.A.D.S. is entitled to one — the first motorcar Bradage the recently and it is possibility allotted to me. I use it all day and every day —	

WAR DIARY
or
INTELLIGENCE SUMMARY

(Erase heading not required.)

Army Form C. 2118

Place	Date	Hour	Summary of Events and Information	Remarks and references to Appendices
POPERINGHE Resting			A large amount of equipment returned by units breakings 1st & 3rd Monmouths & 5th Scottish join the division - I notice them today & find that their muhlespolin has been partly completed. They have only come out with 2 machine guns a piece instead of 4. The rickshaw is here at APEELE. There is only 3½ miles from POPERINGHE. The roads are very bad. The divmtp is at DUNERDOM and that found the train revised to have the office separated from the Steen -	

WAR DIARY
or
INTELLIGENCE SUMMARY

(Erase heading not required.)

Army Form C. 2118

Place	Date	Hour	Summary of Events and Information	Remarks and references to Appendices
POPERINGHE	Mar 22		The motor car has broken down — it has broken a tail bearing in the back axle — wired for spare parts.	
	23		Visited dumps & railheads in S.S.O's car — it is quite hopeless hyperways my work using this means of getting about — but — it is very difficult knowing for M.L.S.O. While he referred his decipher — 9 involved — he has bruised which I do my work — this method would not work if there were [?] —	
	28		No 3 Motor machine gun battery join the division	

WAR DIARY
or
INTELLIGENCE SUMMARY

(Erase heading not required.)

Army Form C. 2118

Place	Date	Hour	Summary of Events and Information	Remarks and references to Appendices
POPERINGHE	March			
	2	—	Battn. has left OUVERDOM. Office will be at quarters —	
	3	6	Lieut. Holbrook above Liverpool Regt. join this Bn.	
	4		Remained in headquarters with local alerts —	
	5		Battalion busy standing orders.	
			Mosspark arrived from — it has been handed — bought for the bath service — it is likely there might be to shower onto the area, an offensive is being tried but have been made to obtain.	
			A car it uses will have been made to obtain.	
	7		A certain amount of the push is less possible	
			to YPRES — the trenches as shown as possible by degree	

Army Form C. 2118

WAR DIARY
or
INTELLIGENCE SUMMARY
(Erase heading not required.)

Place	Date	Hour	Summary of Events and Information	Remarks and references to Appendices
POPERINGHE	March 8"		Am informed that I have to move my unit from OUDERDOM - look tomorrow - locations intermediate. Huts have to be furnished - the motives emerged.	
	15.		Isaacpuchaer of booms, tackles, hairs, etc -	
	24.		Brudpuchaer in Dunkirk - represent trader as airships come from PARIS.	
	29.		The Question of taking in warm underclothing is conjured up - it is decided not taken in any hut	
	20"April			

Army Form C. 2118

WAR DIARY
or
INTELLIGENCE SUMMARY
(Erase heading not required.)

Place	Date	Hour	Summary of Events and Information	Remarks and references to Appendices
POPERINGHE	Mar 29		DUNKERQUE - Local purchase franc togs - The A.D. dev to R.E. Lut run wireless instruments can - Fixed up for 2 longshots with Saint Omer. The question arises as to whether whonies do the office work in which case such as an application for renewal approval be taken - whether the letter shd be made by the headquarter office or by any office. Seem Isle considerate friction between the two offices.	

WAR DIARY
or
INTELLIGENCE SUMMARY
(Erase heading not required.)

Army Form C. 2118

Place	Date	Hour	Summary of Events and Information	Remarks and references to Appendices
POPERINGHE	April 1st		Three with each guide — dumps & the ABRIS-DROOM railhead - me at ABEELE - looked afrin for ammo dump —	
	2d		Our original brigade come back to-in.	
	3d		looked for new dump in YPRES, with O.C. train as am not on similar lines & the place of any dump depends to a great extent on where the supply dumps are going to be - It is an excellent plan that D.A.D.O.S. & O.C. train should both for new dumps together —	

Army Form C. 2118

WAR DIARY
or
INTELLIGENCE SUMMARY
(Erase heading not required.)

Instructions regarding War Diaries and Intelligence Summaries are contained in F. S. Regs., Part II. and the Staff Manual respectively. Title Pages will be prepared in manuscript.

Place	Date	Hour	Summary of Events and Information	Remarks and references to Appendices
POPERINGHE	April 6th		Moved HQrs. from OUDERDOM to YPRES — Hire 3rd MO 27 Div is in Lovenworth — Chose a hop factory near the station. He brought exchange with 27 Div as he is my senior & saw in him. Senior in the meanwhile are waiting loaded up outside the Hop factory.	
	April 7th		Moved into Lovenworth - YPRES	
	8th		Advance Moved from ABEELE to VLAMERTINGHE Rail Head. The 3rd ship truck unloaded — no train today.	

1875 Wt. W593/826 1,000,000 4/15 J.B.C. & A. A.D.S.S./Forms/C. 2118.

Army Form C. 2118

WAR DIARY
or
INTELLIGENCE SUMMARY
(Erase heading not required.)

Instructions regarding War Diaries and Intelligence Summaries are contained in F. S. Regs., Part II. and the Staff Manual respectively. Title Pages will be prepared in manuscript.

Place	Date	Hour	Summary of Events and Information	Remarks and references to Appendices
POPERINGHE				
	Friday 9th April		Saturday's mail came in answer unknown "By R.T.O. in top bottom - not a photo thing into but no doubt the R.T.O. had no alternative.	
	April 10th		Stephen drove officer to YPRES. Man returned	
	April 13th		Put in telephone into dump at YPRES	
	April 14th		Leave given to move office up to YPRES.	
	— 19.		YPRES is being shelled continuously by his guns, have great difficulty in arranging move of HdQrs. for Brigade. This I mentioned before that it is my duty to move forward from ang. — Notwithstanding shells come and drop from me 8 that area the slow have been	

1875 Wt. W593/826 1,000,000 4/15 J.B.C. & A. A.D.S.S./Forms/C. 2118.

WAR DIARY
or
INTELLIGENCE SUMMARY
(Erase heading not required.)

Army Form C. 2118

Place	Date	Hour	Summary of Events and Information	Remarks and references to Appendices
YPRES.	April 19		Invited my superiors with their end — The Staff seem to think otherwise and am anxious to see later what they are wanted — to myself know them from one place to another — When are many persons coming up then to show very difficult full improvised beds.	
	April 23rd		YPRES shelling [illegible]	
	April 24th		Office and Sheri at YPRES with Mrs L her aunt had both gone — The Staff were withdrawn in breathing afternoon so lucky there were no casualties —	

Army Form C. 2118

WAR DIARY
or
INTELLIGENCE SUMMARY

(Erase heading not required.)

Place	Date	Hour	Summary of Events and Information	Remarks and references to Appendices
CMESTRE	April 98		Moved down from office to CMESTRE which is mr morai head — The 9lon are hurriedpt a week + I have no shin — The lorries go out to the Supply dumps and deliver short to the brothe with the ration — This method seems stronge to us but — the Supervision of rations is difficult but there is no longer floor of wh — Headquarters and PROVEN which is to hours ride in another — I go up to 10/11/5pm once a day — Generally after tea — C H Saunder Maj	

DADOS. 28th Division

Vol I. 1 — 31.5.15.

Army Form C. 2118.

WAR DIARY
or
INTELLIGENCE SUMMARY.
(Erase heading not required.)

Instructions regarding War Diaries and Intelligence Summaries are contained in F.S. Regs., Part II. and the Staff Manual respectively. Title pages will be prepared in manuscript.

Hour, Date, Place	Summary of Events and Information	Remarks and references to Appendices
May 1st 1915	Office at Caestre. No storm – a few items kept in a barn at CAESTRE. mostly stores returned from dumps not wanted brands because they have not called for them – there are not sent down to the base because it is known that they are required by units – Headquarters at PROVEN – Chateau COUTTOUD.	
May 3rd	2 dumps near POPERINGHE which is being shelled. Car broke its spring	
May 4th	Visited advanced headquarters went from DIKEBUSH to new shelter huts for wood men – now available	

WAR DIARY
or
INTELLIGENCE SUMMARY.
(Erase heading not required.)

Army Form C. 2118.

Hour, Date, Place	Summary of Events and Information	Remarks and references to Appendices
May 30th	Further complaints of long time in obtaining flags owned — These flags were ordered in POPERINGHE just before it was bombarded — the inhabitants paid a hurried exit — before the flags were ready hence the delay — Red and yellow flags too — to be used in the case of an advance if our own Artillery shelled trenches occupied by our own men — There does not seem to be a good one for his man — (1) It is unlikely that this would be seen by our artillery (2) The Germans would probably take them and use them however disadvantage.	

WAR DIARY
or
INTELLIGENCE SUMMARY.

(Erase heading not required.)

Army Form C. 2118.

Instructions regarding War Diaries and Intelligence
Summaries are contained in F. S. Regs., Part II.
and the Staff Manual respectively. Title pages
will be prepared in manuscript.

Hour, Date, Place	Summary of Events and Information	Remarks and references to Appendices
May 9th	Marching with breal ourstrie - Bailleul, WESTOUTRE, OUDERDOM, HAZEBROOK. 24th Brigade hastily cut up in attacking.	
May 11th	Another received from Headquarters to move 750 sets of rifles and equipment - sent some to BAILLEUL and HAZEBROOK to clearing hospital and railhead. Capt Frazr went to HAZEBROOK permanent. I went to BAILLEUL. Collected some 500 sets and took them to points along YPRES-POPERINGHE road also to railway points. Master this transport - More men found had struck 50 only were the average strength to work with - A day worked.	

Army Form C. 2118.

WAR DIARY
or
INTELLIGENCE SUMMARY.
(Erase heading not required.)

Instructions regarding War Diaries and Intelligence Summaries are contained in F. S. Regs., Part II. and the Staff Manual respectively. Title pages will be prepared in manuscript.

Hour, Date, Place	Summary of Events and Information	Remarks and references to Appendices
May 12th	Byrone & others — one Sergeant to ST OMER to fetch reparation, one to Evacua: ang: from YPRES. Interpretation — one to dump with increase. Shells — Then continue un if time for Thursday. Fair Bushel pumper (ie conveying Ordnance Stores from lighters to the dump) is very exacting — the first the men a lot of extra work and interferes with the routine of Ordnance Battalion.	
May 14th	Two motor lorries arranged — troops on the mine field rat course — transportation issued.	
May 15th	Two Field motor lorries — Divisional & Provisional Brigade. S.F. POPERINGHE 3 Brigade's dumps at WINNEZEELE	

WAR DIARY
or
INTELLIGENCE SUMMARY.

(Erase heading not required.)

Army Form C. 2118.

Hour, Date, Place	Summary of Events and Information	Remarks and references to Appendices
May 17th	8th/10th 2 Army Corps brigade informed in despatch immediate order for — unnecessary interference. Large quantities stores expected up — 2 additional lorries asked for from 5th Corps — these were eventually procured from Ord. Park — 8 proved unnecessary and worthy. The division particularly required nothing in the way of unusual thing else — During the recent heavy fighting much teamstore lost. Two Spare Shirts 2pr's trucks issued on the person. Postings have been taken into wear and the other known army. All men as steps taken to avoid waste —	

Army Form C. 2118.

WAR DIARY
or
INTELLIGENCE SUMMARY.
(*Erase heading not required.*)

Instructions regarding War Diaries and Intelligence Summaries are contained in F.S. Regs., Part II. and the Staff Manual respectively. Title pages will be prepared in manuscript.

Hour, Date, Place	Summary of Events and Information	Remarks and references to Appendices
May 19th	In addition to the baths at POPERINGHE there are baths at the station – at WINNEZEELE, WINZEELE and HOUTKERQUE where the Brigades are resting – the figures are enormous generally – under clothing to last them & as the brigades have been complete up with underclothing will complicate matters. Understanding was moved to the south on the orders for headquarters & then it was decided to start the baths.

12th London is hard on another train and move to Sevenchre near ST OMER as it is intended to bring them up to strength again | |

Army Form C. 2118.

WAR DIARY
or
INTELLIGENCE SUMMARY.
(Erase heading not required.)

Instructions regarding War Diaries and Intelligence Summaries are contained in F. S. Regs., Part II. and the Staff Manual respectively. Title pages will be prepared in manuscript.

Hour, Date, Place	Summary of Events and Information	Remarks and references to Appendices
May 21st	Summary lecture — in order that the travelling efficiency of three cookers those pairs of horses were sent down to the station than permeable cookers selected — These moved off on a 8 mile trek over bad roads & then fed 15 men 5 carts for inspection. I propose to examine their harness & report on their condition. Considerable demands for new clothing and greatcoats & others which all address tents soon to hand — Orders issued to concentrate Monmouth Regiment. Permission notes to apply to Lord Roberts fund for transculars — available in London Depot — There was refused. A large quantity of red sealed wax handed in R.F.A. ordered to retain their branch forth forward.	

WAR DIARY
or
INTELLIGENCE SUMMARY.
(Erase heading not required.)

Army Form C. 2118.

Hour, Date, Place	Summary of Events and Information	Remarks and references to Appendices
May 22nd	Practically a fine day & blankets were dried in the sun before being despatched to PARIS. 85 Brigade move into trenches 83rd to BRANDHOEK. Reverend lift of workers LONE VALLEY — 5 Offrs & 76 O.R. being war found to the leaks after the lift — the 10m 5ft 0% Sent in a report on these generally undermining them — It been an accident would probably be indicated by being pierced and the nature is too thin — Burden the view the general thread of the cotton is invariably and flimsy. Mr G. Gardener reports that they are hilft for travelling an overland road not here — The bales of all the cotton of the station are held & only 10% war found to be sound. NCO and 2 men Sent up as additional help	

Army Form C. 2118.

WAR DIARY
or
INTELLIGENCE SUMMARY.
(Erase heading not required.)

Instructions regarding War Diaries and Intelligence Summaries are contained in F. S. Regs., Part II. and the Staff Manual respectively. Title pages will be prepared in manuscript.

Hour, Date, Place	Summary of Events and Information	Remarks and references to Appendices
May 23rd	Inspection by Col. Parsons DOS. Southern views — addresses transport to be given to — wait for ordnance stores — Percentage WO's & drivers to be authorized. Subalterns lecture — Stoked down 15 case.	
May 26th	Am to send to STOMETR & Felix Inspection — these were regards required that evening by works in lorry lines — I arranged to send him up to the Lunatic Asylum, but they arrived too late — to call 115 Indian Transport — Visited Lunatic Asylum. 110/5c 8 Inf. Brigade. 130 Tsau RFA	

(73989) W4141—463. 400,000. 9/14. H.&J.,Ltd. Forms/C. 2118/10.

WAR DIARY
or
INTELLIGENCE SUMMARY.
(Erase heading not required.)

Army Form C. 2118.

Hour, Date, Place	Summary of Events and Information	Remarks and references to Appendices
May 27=	Took Army both on car — Lord purchase at HAZEBROUK	
May 31=	Railhead moved to ARNEKE — Office moved Men and aeroplane store. Cut down to base holding 50 Lewis buckets — 2 extra lorries shed in position from Ronin=Park boxing Motorbike.	

A Saunders
May DADS 2nd Div

28th Division

DADOS. 28th Division.

Vol III

WAR DIARY
or
INTELLIGENCE SUMMARY.
(Erase heading not required.)

Army Form C. 2118.

Instructions regarding War Diaries and Intelligence Summaries are contained in F.S. Regs., Part II. and the Staff Manual respectively. Title pages will be prepared in manuscript.

Hour, Date, Place	Summary of Events and Information	Remarks and references to Appendices
June 2nd 1915	Moved down to ARNEIKA during February break head from this place — Headquarters about 3/4 went by motor over good road — round the way — thence at IMREELE. Troops running at IMREELE, NUMMEREFLE and HOUTIQ RQUE — Too far from headquarters to be pleasant — but there are being relieved without difficulty — Practically nothing in rest at ARNEIKA and the stores are kept in sheds. The chief objection to this station is the difficulty of good supervision over the horses — wet weather is a serious disadvantage.	

WAR DIARY
or
INTELLIGENCE SUMMARY.
(Erase heading not required.)

Army Form C. 2118.

Instructions regarding War Diaries and Intelligence Summaries are contained in F.S. Regs., Part II. and the Staff Manual respectively. Title pages will be prepared in manuscript.

Hour, Date, Place	Summary of Events and Information	Remarks and references to Appendices
June 2nd	G.O.C. visits a station of Sprayer kept up (50 atleast) in which Calcium Bisulphide KNO₃ and purchase locally whilst various arrangement can be made to procure from Paris.	
June 3rd	Two reduction at horses borrowed from the "Anna" Park returned – these horses have proved most unfit – 4 horses are not enough when the division is refitting. Difficulty experienced in obtaining rifles and equipment for completing up the Cheshire regiment. There are however to 40 rifles and equipment are issued in both machines.	

Army Form C. 2118.

WAR DIARY
or
INTELLIGENCE SUMMARY.
(Erase heading not required.)

Instructions regarding War Diaries and Intelligence Summaries are contained in F.S. Regs., Part II. and the Staff Manual respectively. Title pages will be prepared in manuscript.

Hour, Date, Place	Summary of Events and Information	Remarks and references to Appendices
June 1st	A certain number of sprayers are available at dumps at BAILLEUL and HAZEBROUCK. 85" hose have become a separate dump near DICKEBUSCH — they have moved into the French	
June 7th	25 rifles sent to Armourers workshops for overhaul of O.P. carbines	
June 12th	2 Army workshops Armourers — new RE for local manufacture of Sniper's open bomber do's attendant stones to be taken over by RE on the 25th for working both with Ordnance	

WAR DIARY
or
INTELLIGENCE SUMMARY.
(Erase heading not required.)

Army Form C. 2118.

Instructions regarding War Diaries and Intelligence Summaries are contained in F. S. Regs., Part II. and the Staff Manual respectively. Title pages will be prepared in manuscript.

Hour, Date, Place	Summary of Events and Information	Remarks and references to Appendices
June 14th	Office & dumps moved to WESTOUTRE. Headquarters are disarmed police & the method is now the same as that worked during the winter — the gun is an enemy one — two have arrived & so long as the Brutin remain stationary it is to be preferred. WESTOUTRE attacks. We protected by well in Rifle Brigade dumping ground & it is intended to form a large collection of dosé here.	
June 15th	2nd Army Workshop dismantles parts unsers. factors are continually being issued by G.S.I. 15th Divn travellers.	

WAR DIARY
or
INTELLIGENCE SUMMARY.
(Erase heading not required.)

Army Form C. 2118.

Instructions regarding War Diaries and Intelligence Summaries are contained in F.S. Regs., Part II. and the Staff Manual respectively. Title pages will be prepared in manuscript.

Hour, Date, Place	Summary of Events and Information	Remarks and references to Appendices
June 8th	Road purchase work in anyhears — huts being got be made comfortable — Camps Latrines Cookries etc prepared.	
June 16th	The Squadron straying with horses outlined — No sign in Channels lovely — a number of ricker and copper sulphate to horses satisfactory to been up from the base late on. Officers & individual horseplace concealed tomasophila with the 8th army	
June 24th	Flies are getting troublesome — the horses in long jumbin conditions take breezy.	

WAR DIARY
or
INTELLIGENCE SUMMARY.

(Erase heading not required.)

Army Form C. 2118.

Hour, Date, Place	Summary of Events and Information	Remarks and references to Appendices
June 26th	Leave parties still heavy. Application for men cleared half - my total at 165 have consists of — 1 Tocamill, 1 Blomin, 1 Kichener's own men } 3 N.C.O.'s All to indent work in the thrown on injured clerk and S/ Renie.	
June 30	Dunkirk 1st In Jas being shelled late— Offeuneur	May DHS 28 Jun.

12/6272

28th Division

D.A.D.O.S. 28th Division
Vol IV

Army Form C. 2118.

WAR DIARY
~~INTELLIGENCE~~ SUMMARY.

(Erase heading not required.)

Instructions regarding War Diaries and Intelligence Summaries are contained in F.S. Regs., Part II and the Staff Manual respectively. Title pages will be prepared in manuscript.

Hour, Date, Place	Summary of Events and Information	Remarks and references to Appendices
	Confidential War Diary of:- D.A.D.S. 28th Division. (Major Saunders a.v.s.) From: 1: 7: 15. To 31: 7: 15.	

Army Form C. 2118

WAR DIARY
or
INTELLIGENCE SUMMARY
(Erase heading not required.)

Instructions regarding War Diaries and Intelligence Summaries are contained in F.S. Regs., Part II. and the Staff Manual respectively. Title Pages will be prepared in manuscript.

Place	Date	Hour	Summary of Events and Information	Remarks and references to Appendices
WESTOUTRE	July 2nd	10.15	Store at headquarters. Office also - which cases WESTOUTRE here - only 3 lorries at present but under the circumstances 3 are enough - One Supply column is astride of two lorries. A certain amount of difficulty as regards billeting the men, but this has been solved by erecting 2 tents between them - Am in possession of that hextomy and 1 staff tent. Received at WESTOUTRE.	
	July 3rd		A considerable amount of local purchase - toys or and and the branches are being sprayed with turpentine - Our supplying Supplies for their purpose but they are difficult to get. The question as to who is in need or payment from Store requires close supervision. There is nothing laid down which subject as regards issues to anybody other than officers - Belgium & French outfits for store. It is not clear whether French, Belgian, India, etc should have free issue in the case of Officers. Issues on payment are being made.	

1875 Wt. W503/826 1,000,000 4/15 J.B.C. & A. A.D.S.S./Forms/C. 2118.

Army Form C. 2118

WAR DIARY
or
INTELLIGENCE SUMMARY
(Erase heading not required.)

Instructions regarding War Diaries and Intelligence Summaries are contained in F. S. Regs., Part II. and the Staff Manual respectively. Title Pages will be prepared in manuscript.

Place	Date	Hour	Summary of Events and Information	Remarks and references to Appendices
WESTOUTRE	July 3. July 4th		Occupation of Scyngo – Remain now in Cave. Visit of D.O.S, Railhead – found rations (1) a certain amount of rations in case draw to-day, there is one at Railhead to take this in hand, O.O.S. decides to approach Reinforcing Battalions at Railhead. (2) Issue of Rum to trenches" Still 1 per man & 1 pr man in reserve. A certain amount of the reserve is in the hands of the battalions in the division – draw whereas the quota in accordance with noted W.D.S. Truck Shelters made to Welsh Regiment – the Lorries are being used for this purpose – appeals regimental transport is out of the question. The use of Lorries upsets" the present method of watering as it means that the Blois lorries on leaving the mooring have to be watered into the Blois before yesterday Blois can be cleaned – This increase arrangements at the moor in Boileau.	

Army Form C. 2118

WAR DIARY
or
INTELLIGENCE SUMMARY
(Erase heading not required.)

Instructions regarding War Diaries and Intelligence Summaries are contained in F. S. Regs., Part II. and the Staff Manual respectively. Title Pages will be prepared in manuscript.

Place	Date	Hour	Summary of Events and Information	Remarks and references to Appendices
WESTOUTRE	July 6		Prophylactic billets in POPERINGHE to put the 3rd Div. near railhead so as the men in case of a move — The we considered advisable to keep the men in BAILS WESTOUTRE — paths become stony in wet weather and also because the mean an accumulation of traffic which is inconvenient both from a sanitary point of view and also because it is liable to draw shellfire onto Divisional Headquarters.	
	July 7th		The record of movement of helicopter Squads has not been worked up to & it is difficult to know which Brigades have which Squads.	
	July 8th		Lorries are taken for transporting a hut by Brigades, running from 3 to 8 p.m.	
	July 10.		Divisions gone on leave — Park of transport have a long time to come up from the base, a certain number are available or railheads by local purchase.	

Army Form C. 2118

WAR DIARY
or
INTELLIGENCE SUMMARY
(Erase heading not required.)

Instructions regarding War Diaries and Intelligence Summaries are contained in F. S. Regs., Part II. and the Staff Manual respectively. Title Pages will be prepared in manuscript.

Place	Date	Hour	Summary of Events and Information	Remarks and references to Appendices
NEFOUTRE	July 11th		Have made arrangements to repair experience of Smoke helmet at a Stay factory in BAILLEUL at a cost of 11 am par helmet. These is obtained from 2nd Army. G.O.	
	July 15th		Visits 2nd Corps & BEF rifles — now were issued by them. Arrangements in weeks return of pace experiences, also diary up to 30th June. Gasmask comp lot in line at YPRES — this means shoving it from the beginning. — The moment is where we is the depressed on active service.	
	July 16		Visited BOULOGNE — had both bombardiers made strained — it was not possible to get anyone to wrestle like this work — Valerie about a great difficulty — Gave it up as a bad job here.	
	July 17		McParrish's sure on leave.	
	July 19th		Railhead moved to STEENWERKE. Saw 50 refills water carts — the dew war is to be our hearing cylinder on each cart and a pump to the people — this is found to be the best arrangement at present.	

1875 Wt. W 593/826 1,000,000 4/15 J.B.C. & A. A.D.S.S./Forms/C. 2118.

WAR DIARY
or
INTELLIGENCE SUMMARY

(Erase heading not required.)

Army Form C. 2118

Instructions regarding War Diaries and Intelligence Summaries are contained in F.S. Regs., Part II. and the Staff Manual respectively. Title Pages will be prepared in manuscript.

Place	Date	Hour	Summary of Events and Information	Remarks and references to Appendices
MESTOUTRE	July 21st		SBO Snelden arrived from base - there were orders for some time ago with no authority, but demands were received so the matter was cancelled - they were sent up. The lorry arrived & stopped train to bring stragglers - it did not come up till 12 pm lorry - stragglers came in at 9 to 9.30 am.	
	July 22		A drunk mechanic found in BAILLEUL who is able to make reconnaissance part of sight by BSA sights - reconnoitered LOCRE with a view of improving the store there. There is an excellent house at the cross roads but which would do as an office and store. The houses in a bad place as regards proofs and in my opinion too near the firewalks.	
	July 23rd		Reconnoitered railhead possibilities of finding a store here - Can i- celled thus and others put me via Lys & Bois. but this too far from the railway station to be worth pursued when we've the orderly system.	

Army Form C. 2118

WAR DIARY
or
INTELLIGENCE SUMMARY
(Erase heading not required.)

Instructions regarding War Diaries and Intelligence Summaries are contained in F. S. Regs., Part II. and the Staff Manual respectively. Title Pages will be prepared in manuscript.

Place	Date	Hour	Summary of Events and Information	Remarks and references to Appendices
WESTOUTRE	July 26		Visited GRAVELINES with a view to practice of local procedure — not good. Re Spring Waterproof or Fly proper armature	
	July 28		Stokes petrol carrier — the manufacture of an article like a Brushthrower is very difficult to select — either the material is insufficiently following or else no workmen are available. The greatest difficulty was experienced at BOULOGNE obtained place I was unable to obtain brushes like the work.	
	July 29		Local purchase in the Flanders — chiefly for article recommended by the AD.M.S. for the health of his troops such as Fly papers muslin etc. Question of issue of straw hats worthwhile	

O.N Launder
Major DADOS
29/7/17

1875 Wt. W593/826 1,000,000 4/15 J.B.C. & A. A.D.S.S./Forms/C. 2118.

CONFIDENTIAL

War Diary
of
D.A.D.O.S. 28th Division
from August 1st to August 31st
1915.
(Volume 1)

Army Form C. 2118

WAR DIARY
or
INTELLIGENCE SUMMARY
(Erase heading not required.)

Instructions regarding War Diaries and Intelligence Summaries are contained in F. S. Regs., Part II. and the Staff Manual respectively. Title Pages will be prepared in manuscript.

Place	Date	Hour	Summary of Events and Information	Remarks and references to Appendices
WESTOUTRE	August 1st		Headquarters, Office and store in the same place - see. Only 3 lorries, but no difficulty in towards at present in arranging stores from lt. reached STEENWERKE here — However it is most important to have details up in case of a sudden move — 3 lorries would not be sufficient to move the store here. O/S	
	August 2nd		Motor car under repair — answer in BAILLEUL. O/S	
	4th		Store was dumped on the platform at 9am by R.T.O. — This arrangement division until STEENWERKE as a railhead and lorries carried be Shunted or Entraining to be undecided — This would prove awkward at the Division was on the move as the lorries would not be available at any moment blend up from the Railway tracks. In this event in bad weather the store would suffer from being dumped on the railway platform. Best precedence at 9/Oman — O/S	

Army Form C. 2118

WAR DIARY
or
INTELLIGENCE SUMMARY
(Erase heading not required.)

Instructions regarding War Diaries and Intelligence Summaries are contained in F. S. Regs., Part II. and the Staff Manual respectively. Title Pages will be prepared in manuscript.

Place	Date	Hour	Summary of Events and Information	Remarks and references to Appendices
MESTOCKRE.	August 5th		A complaint received from Bing gen conby 83rd Brigade that I was making insinuations. The ROHLI have withstanding demands for over 300 litres. Was put in a further demand for 200 — I wrote them a memo stating that there was some confusion in the preparation of demands — (it appears puller in fact that demands have been duplicated.) The matter has been taken up by MA RGNG + have head no movement it. It is my duty to check waste and the case allowed to attempt demands — it is impossible into the without insinuating that the units do not do this work correctly. In the case there was no insinuation — I stated the fact. OAS	
	August 6th		STOMER. breakfasted if 100 bomb carriers — Now been promised for to-day but only 30 br available — the un-van Rep told with be finished before Tuesday next — QOTS.	

WAR DIARY
or
INTELLIGENCE SUMMARY

(Erase heading not required.)

Army Form C. 2118

Instructions regarding War Diaries and Intelligence Summaries are contained in F. S. Regs., Part II. and the Staff Manual respectively. Title Pages will be prepared in manuscript.

Place	Date	Hour	Summary of Events and Information	Remarks and references to Appendices
MESTOUTRE	August 7th		Asked for another lorry transport. Column – 4 lorries should now be kept here in case of emergencies – there with 158 with= from O.O. 2nd lorry to deliver their biscuits. 1st/3rd Mourmelle an late split up again – 1st line transport has to be supplied – the will to available in the lots each come up 21 are due & it is reported that these are on their way. O.A.S.	
	August 8th		2nd Corps head over a lot of tech– C&L Clin with transpires at railhead – extra transport supplied by Div Sup Col. – I have 4 lorries – B.M.S.Vehicle are used for bringing up the rest and distributing them. 158 with C&L are distributed in return place under orders from D.Sup.oth. The remainder are handed over to the brigades for distribution later.	

1875 Wt. W593/826 1,000,000 4/15 J.B.C. & A. A.D.S.S./Forms/C. 2118.

WAR DIARY
or
INTELLIGENCE SUMMARY

Army Form C. 2118

Place	Date	Hour	Summary of Events and Information	Remarks and references to Appendices
WESTOUTRE	Aug 29		Great forwardness of hurricane lamps & two hand bombs for holding what in the trenches for B's Bath. — I asked Hogan if I should try these clubs — it seems that an enormous amount of money is being spent on trench horsism that it will be useful to know if we leave the trenches. OHS	
	Aug 30		No truck from CALAIS 15 day — About moved by motor — Showed the extra stuff to cement the men — it is found that in trenches whatever stuff the extra stuff is carried the numbers known by them is very much greater than in battalions where nothing is carried. The numbers varying from 700 in 3 weeks to nil! The matter has been referred to Sir Hogan. OHS	

Army Form C. 2118

WAR DIARY
or
INTELLIGENCE SUMMARY
(Erase heading not required.)

Instructions regarding War Diaries and Intelligence
Summaries are contained in F.S. Regs., Part II.
and the Staff Manual respectively. Title Pages
will be prepared in manuscript.

Place	Date	Hour	Summary of Events and Information	Remarks and references to Appendices
WESTOUTRE.				
	August 11th		Rifle fired with telescope drawn from 2nd Corps. Locusphones – Shelter huts withdrawn from some units & handed to others. O.K.	
	August 12th		8th Divn. Breast pushers – Measurement of head covers. O.K.	
	August 19th		Things very quiet – all units as being carefully checked to search back records for explanations why men in any character this is difficult too much of the attitude causing ill-feeling amongst the quarter masters and foreman has to be taken not to hurt their feelings or interfere. Have their men carefully opening away their cap badges. C.M.S.	
	August 22nd		2 lorries has to be sent dir to DRANOUTRE at 7.30 pm at the request of the D.A.Q.M.G. to assist in moving a camp –	

WAR DIARY
or
INTELLIGENCE SUMMARY

Army Form C. 2118

Place	Date	Hour	Summary of Events and Information	Remarks and references to Appendices
NESTOUTRE	22 (continued)		Happens that one of the sleeping partners or amateur month kite balloon was ready his by asking brother move their camp into an adjacent field — lorries were provided for the purpose by the Corps but the lorries were allowed to go home having dumped the tents in the field (sic) of the field — The OxBaen lorries had then to be turned out to move the tents from one bed of the field to the other! AHS	
	23rd		Orders to provide chain for nos: 6,8 offices — there is no authority for this but as the chains cannot be obtained in any other way, their terms to be established. CRS.	
	24th		Purchased chain at MAESTRE. 8f some 5wire cheap, made by French Breon a little before the war. CRS	

Army Form C. 2118

WAR DIARY
or
INTELLIGENCE SUMMARY

(Erase heading not required.)

Instructions regarding War Diaries and Intelligence Summaries are contained in F.S. Regs., Part II. and the Staff Manual respectively. Title Pages will be prepared in manuscript.

Place	Date	Hour	Summary of Events and Information	Remarks and references to Appendices
WESTOUTRE	Aug 26th		Heard a Zeppelin in the evening but came in for its AA.	
	Aug 27th		Was getting my photo taken - Bear chief clerk in motor down to town. Saw about fitting for stores essentials etc. OAR.	
	29th		Ordered to arrange Brens ambulance W.O. 15th Division. Arrange Brens Divan. 2 rifle with telescope sight - came at via the A.M.F.O. from the town - it is not understood why this method of armour is adopted - it only leads to confusion - the rifle were eventually handed over to the Supply Column and arrived here two days later OAR.	

Army Form C. 2118

WAR DIARY
or
INTELLIGENCE SUMMARY
(Erase heading not required.)

Instructions regarding War Diaries and Intelligence Summaries are contained in F. S. Regs., Part II. and the Staff Manual respectively. Title Pages will be prepared in manuscript.

Place	Date	Hour	Summary of Events and Information	Remarks and references to Appendices
MESDURE	August 31st		Some trouble with Cond. Brassler — does not appear quite happy. Ausask to be sent to 6 Div. This cannot be done, but am arranging Brensly mallets as far as possible. Sent Brassler down to Cashier 9.15 pm. Return of telephones done — NIL. This is the first time a return has been Known. We have always been a bit different before — Anxiety enquiries it is found out that signals have recused a lot direct from the Corps. CH Lawrence Lieut Amer 2nd Div.	

1875 Wt. W593/826 1,000,000 4/15 J.B.C. & A. A.D.S.S./Forms/C. 2118.

121/7100

28th Division

D A D O S. 28th Division
Vol VI
Sept. 15

Army Form C. 2118

WAR DIARY
or
INTELLIGENCE SUMMARY

(Erase heading not required.)

WAR DIARY
of
D.A.D.D.S. 28th Division

from Sept 1st to Sept 30th

Volume 1.

1915

WAR DIARY or INTELLIGENCE SUMMARY

Army Form C. 2118

Place	Date	Hour	Summary of Events and Information	Remarks and references to Appendices
WESTOUTRE.	Sep. 1st		All units drawing from Store in WESTOUTRE. Office and Divisional Headqrs in Same place. Received at Kemmerch - CAP. Am carrying on taking all wounds and trying to teach the two new officers Stongues in the hope that eventually they may be shown use in their respect - Apparently it takes quite no long before their work is so to do it ourself.	
	2nd		The day is moderate from the fact that the division is reported complete in telephones both from time in its container! CAP. Office accommodation in bed — is word free invite hand for myself a chief clerk. Unit according for Hrs of occupation — Am enjoying the papers which arrive are not empty. This though that the running of this recent have been for now and results of Kitchener promise from England. CAP.	
	3rd		Mind local practice. CAP.	

WAR DIARY or INTELLIGENCE SUMMARY

Place	Date	Hour	Summary of Events and Information	Remarks and references to Appendices
WESTOUTRE	Sept 4th		I have been directed to remain [Kestral?] but to proceed to Poperinghe in the absence of Lieutenant Colonel ... This is exceptionally serious affliction. 5th Home Battalion has joined the regiment and we being transferred in turn - All the honors of promotion on my 4 [tomes?] when we any an unknown amount of goodwork. I have also managed to manage 3 bomo-trou to Sergt. - Major Coleman. (A)	
	5th		A day marked of [links?] and business to notify Hats [hanging?] up by Coventry's Division. 65th Battalion received from the base - again [minstrel?] in Buxton - Handfast. (A)	
	7th		Went to DUNKERQUE to try and get some more boots - cannot receive authority to pay up to £100 per coverage together made by Mr Dixon SRS.	
	8th		Spoke on telephone to Mr Dixon + [find?] he is unable to supply the kind wanted. He has intention to attend interview who knows with a responsible [officer?]. (A.F.)	

Army Form C. 2118

WAR DIARY
or
INTELLIGENCE SUMMARY
(Erase heading not required.)

Instructions regarding War Diaries and Intelligence Summaries are contained in F. S. Regs., Part II. and the Staff Manual respectively. Title Pages will be prepared in manuscript.

Place	Date	Hour	Summary of Events and Information	Remarks and references to Appendices
VISTO TRE	Sept. 8th		Visited Major Prior and arranged with him to buy him boots, camisoles etc. HARDINGUE at BÉTHUNE as it is easier as needs to BOULOGNE. There is constantly little than I can do anywhere else – OHS	
	11th		Lieut Jackson of Indian Cavalry (Veterinary Officer) at ARMENTIERES. Very difficult kept. Also bought shoes for 3rd S. Africa. Strongly pulling down for the Sea – But not been likely that an attempt was to made by us after 15	
			Germans failed to make change in April with everything in their favour. OHS	
	13th		Bombardment reaches from BETHUNE. OHS	
	14th		Railways office. The spare at Ordnance workshops has been increased –	
	15th		Heavy artillery workshops under the Army have been established at HAZEBROUCK – and Northern Park are now kept in instead of at the front with the travelling workshops. OHS	

Army Form C. 2118

WAR DIARY or INTELLIGENCE SUMMARY
(Erase heading not required.)

Instructions regarding War Diaries and Intelligence Summaries are contained in F. S. Regs., Part II. and the Staff Manual respectively. Title Pages will be prepared in manuscript.

Place	Date	Hour	Summary of Events and Information	Remarks and references to Appendices
VIEUX BERQUIN	Sept 17		Local pastoral dispersed but McNamara sprayers — to be improved together from the base today on the QM lorry — a large quantity of abnormal sprayers are unserviced found at front. OM	
	18th		Understand that 2 Canadian Division will forward with their air-Pan — visited DADVS 2 Canadian Div at HAZEBROUCK. Forward market. OM	
	19		2 pm came up to KRUYSTRAETE to get mud arrangement for hauling over. OM	
	20		Raillcars? Mule at STEENWERKE have had trains out for not having head lids on & the men have now no spare horses needed when a mare is to bring machine. OM	
	21		Visited horse dump in connection of STRAZEELE. OM	
	22		horse dump at STRAZEELE. Our requisite broken down. Let's have loads of remits from LOERE & BAILEUL at PRADELLES & 2 lorry loads from PRADELLES. Last B.G. at STRAZEELE — Received 2 horses from Canadian Division. OM	

WAR DIARY
or
INTELLIGENCE SUMMARY

(Erase heading not required.)

Army Form C. 2118

Instructions regarding War Diaries and Intelligence Summaries are contained in F.S. Regs., Part II. and the Staff Manual respectively. Title Pages will be prepared in manuscript.

Place	Date	Hour	Summary of Events and Information	Remarks and references to Appendices
WESTOUTRE	Sept. 23rd		Marconigrams broken down – moved all blankets from LOCRE to WESTOUTRE. Khaki trousers – Some applied under corps arrangement. Have formed a advance dump at STRAZEELE which is under control. Our Bgge [baggage] are at HOUTKERQUE – NIEPPE [?] where is a list about 2½ miles. Have managed to borrow one Leyland lorry for a spare there which is parked in 24 hr cars.	
	24th		All units drawing stores from Dump. Have petrol actual tabs lorries and stores – Burious reserve Dickebusch road Shire – Men sleeping in shelters – OCS from WESTOUTRE and Stores inside Stores tent – OCS	
	25th		Cars received truck from Loupe where at 1st Storm – Repairs temporarily. Caterpillar urgently repaired – returns up to Canadian Division to draw from Kew St lorries – My Maingun – OC Eaton – Evans – OCS	
	26th		Reached here at STEENVOORDE – Have done now interior for lorries respired by 12 Bn. Fire at Mine Hoa – Reconstruction Hut reached is being moved here by – WATERBROEK GARAGE – OCS	

WAR DIARY or INTELLIGENCE SUMMARY

Army Form C. 2118

Instructions regarding War Diaries and Intelligence Summaries are contained in F. S. Regs., Part II. and the Staff Manual respectively. Title Pages will be prepared in manuscript.

(Erase heading not required.)

Place	Date	Hour	Summary of Events and Information	Remarks and references to Appendices
STEENWERCK	26th	—	A great scarcity in hires and transport would have been effected if I had been allowed to move KYRKES ROTR instead of ESTEMINSTERCK to wander. Karmier remain for this CP.	
HAZEBROUCK	27th		Billets situated in a field near a village above certain farmer — another up slam to Supply dump near BETHUNE. Sickness seems of such behind. Lent news from STRAZEELE English to BETHUNE. Headquarters to be driven in at SAILLY la BOURSE CAI.	
do	28th		S Allies in Bethune observations again before (B1)	
FOUQUEREUIL	29th		Reached moved here — packed up and looked here short. Very anxious to know but managed somehow told when from all in but transport just in this village — The dinner are lent and 5 Supps refilling punts must be hard of finding 3 horses for infantry brigades to take their Ambulance places.	

WAR DIARY
or
INTELLIGENCE SUMMARY

(Erase heading not required.)

Army Form C. 2118

Place	Date	Hour	Summary of Events and Information	Remarks and references to Appendices
FOUQUEREUIL	Sept 29		Orders to take over LEWIS machine guns from Gordons in Sect. held by 2nd D. — to make arrangements — O.C. Officer arrangements to before — C.O.T.	
	30		Took over LEWIS machine guns and a certain amount of ammunition — Sergeant Dunn began — informants began — ammunition was short — as wasn't enough — so had to get it — Headquarters was running absolutely — on the report I sent kept from 10 pm to 12 am — I have the teams here and having my Mess cooks and the are supposed to make all my war and provisions & make which can be done early so everyone like a reasonable amount of time	
	30th Sept 1918			C.H. Alexander Maj D.A.D.O.S Div.

wo 05/02/2022 (木)
15am

wo 05/02/2022 (水)
130 am

28TH DIVISION
DIVL TROOPS

A. D. VETY SERVICES

~~JAN - NOV 1915~~

1915 JAN - 1915 OCT

ADMS 28th Division.
Vol I

121/4330

Jan 1915

Army Form C. 2118.

WAR DIARY
or
INTELLIGENCE SUMMARY.
(Erase heading not required.)

Instructions regarding War Diaries and Intelligence Summaries are contained in F.S. Regs., Part II. and the Staff Manual respectively. Title pages will be prepared in manuscript.

Hour, Date, Place			Summary of Events and Information	Remarks and references to Appendices
19.1.15.	Borre.	9. P.M.	Arrived at concentration area of 28th Division at midnight last night with Transport and horses of H.Q. of Division, and went into billets at BORRE.	Snow, sleet, hail, frost.
20.1.15.	Borre.	9. P.M.	Units still arriving.	Dull and cold. frost.
21.1.15.	Borre.	9. P.M.	Units still arriving.	Wet and cold.
22.1.15.	Borre.	9. P.M.	6th Field Amb from ENGLAND for the Division have now arrived, including the 14 M.V.S. which is billeted here.	Dull and cold. frost.
23.1.15.	Borre.	9. P.M.	Nothing to record. More than 75 per cent of horses in the Division are standing in the open.	Dull and cold. frost.
24.1.15.	Borre.	9. P.M.	D.D.V.S. arrived and gave general directions; also received copy of his general instructions. Obtained M.O.S. for sick cases. LIEUT. FORREST. A.V.C. 4/84 Inf. Bde. sick in quarters. Bronchitis; arranged for his duties to be carried out.	Dull and cold. frost.
25.1.15.	Borre.	9. P.M.	Nothing to record.	Very cold. frost.
26.1.15.	Borre.	9. P.M.	Received one Official Sheet Veterinary for use with Div:H.Q.	Very cold. frost.

Army Form C. 2118.

WAR DIARY
or
INTELLIGENCE SUMMARY.
(Erase heading not required.)

Instructions regarding War Diaries and Intelligence Summaries are contained in F.S. Regs., Part II. and the Staff Manual respectively. Title pages will be prepared in manuscript.

Hour, Date, Place		Summary of Events and Information	Remarks and references to Appendices
27.1.15. Boule.	9. P.M.	Arranged with D.A.D.O.S. for supply of Horse Blankets for sick horses in M.V.S. Recommended issue of one extra bag of Forage both to each Infantry Battalion, as they had each been allotted two Cooking Crucibles from the A.S.C. Wired continued rush of men of M.V.S. recommended for promotion to D.V.S.	Fine & cold frost.
28.1.15. Boule.	9. P.M.	Nothing to record.	Hard frost.
29.1.15. Boule.	9. P.M.	Inspected Ambulance in Horse of Surg. Kennedy which had died suddenly in the early morning. Sulphur & section of Spleen for examination etc., & gave necessary instructions re disposal of carcase etc. Reported case to Dir. M.R. and D.D.V.S.! Met all V.O.s of Division & gave directions on reorganisation.	Hard frost. V.G. Slight thaw. Fine frost.
30.1.15. Boule.	10. P.M.	Nothing to record.	

(73989) W4141—463. 400,000. 9/14. H.&J.Ltd. Forms/C. 2118/10.

Army Form C. 2118.

WAR DIARY
or
INTELLIGENCE SUMMARY.
(Erase heading not required.)

Instructions regarding War Diaries and Intelligence Summaries are contained in F.S. Regs., Part II. and the Staff Manual respectively. Title pages will be prepared in manuscript.

Hour, Date, Place	Summary of Events and Information	Remarks and references to Appendices
31.1.15. Bose. 12 P.M.	D.D.V.S. G.H.Q. visited and inspected M.V.S. 12th Bty of London Rangers joined the Division. A.Q. & O Battery R.H.A. sent their Ammunition to Army Reserve about 1000 rounds joined the Division. 1.9.2 Remounts arrived for the Division. During the present the influenza has been in this area. Horses have been admitted sick in their H over - 90 p.c. of these cases being so many hours after hours occurred from Pneumonia. With this exception the health of the horses has been good.	Total Horse Sick 757.

J B Tapley La/Col A.V.C.
D.D.V.S. 28th Div.

ADVS 28th Division.

121/4612

Vol II

Feb 1915

WAR DIARY.

FOR FEBRUARY 1915.

Army Form C. 2118.

WAR DIARY
or
INTELLIGENCE SUMMARY.

(Erase heading not required.)

Instructions regarding War Diaries and Intelligence Summaries are contained in F.S. Regs., Part II. and the Staff Manual respectively. Title pages will be prepared in manuscript.

Hour, Date, Place	Summary of Events and Information	Remarks and references to Appendices
Beauchop 1/2/15 10 P.M.	Division moved to YPRES-VLAMERTINGHE area, distance of march varying from 13 to 16 miles. M.V.S. remained at Borre.	Fine and cold. JST.
do 2/2/15 9 P.M.	Nothing to record.	Wet and cold. JST.
do 3/2/15 9 P.M.	Nothing to record.	Fine JST.
do 4/2/15 10 P.M.	D.D.V.S. Irenes 2nd Army H.Q. at HAZEBROUK. Was with D.D.V.S. to V.O. 2/3. R.H.A. Brits. 86th Howitzer Bde. joined the Division.	Fine JST.
POPERINGHE 5/2/15 10 P.M.	Went to HAZEBROUK and saw D.D.V.S. 2nd Army. Arranged for the M.V.S. from BORRE to move to near VLAMERTINGHE.	Fine. Bright. JST.
do 6/2/15 9 P.M.	M.V.S. arrived and went into Farms 1/2 mile S.W. of VLAMERTINGHE.	Dull. Raining at night. JST.
do 7/2/15 10 P.M.	Notified V.O's to Units that M.V.S. would take in cases. Received instructions from D.V.S. 2nd Army, re M.V.B. of the return.	Dull and rain ... JST.
do 8/2/15 10 P.M.	D.D.V.S. visited area. 22nd and 118th Batterys with 474 horses joined the Division.	Dull ... JST.

Army Form C. 2118.

WAR DIARY
or
INTELLIGENCE SUMMARY.
(Erase heading not required.)

Instructions regarding War Diaries and Intelligence Summaries are contained in F. S. Regs., Part II. and the Staff Manual respectively. Title pages will be prepared in manuscript.

Hour, Date, Place	Summary of Events and Information	Remarks and references to Appendices
POPERINGHE. 9/2/15 10 P.M.	Lieut T.L. SHEA A.V.C. joined for duty with R.H.A. 2 units.	Wet. yet.
do 10/2/15 9. P.M.	Nothing to record.	Bright. yet.
do 11/2/15 9. P.M.	Nothing to record.	Bright and warm. yet.
do 12/2/15 9. P.M.	11.3 a.m. Heavy Battery with 145 horses joined the Division. 37th Howitzer Battery with horses joined the Division. A.Q. and C. Batteries R.H.A. with their Ammunition Column left the Division. Lieut T.L. SHEA A.V.C. accompanied them.	Strong Snow & Sleet. yet.
do 13/2/15 9 P.M.	Nothing to record.	Wet. yet.
do 14/2/15 9. P.M.	Nothing to record.	Wet. yet.
do 15/2/15 9. P.M.	Visited 37th Howitzer Battery & its Ammunition Column & supplied them with Veterinary Wallets. Visited 86th Howitzer Battery.	Wet. yet.

(73989) W4141—463. 400,000. 9/14. H.&J.Ltd. Forms/C. 2118/10.

Army Form C. 2118.

WAR DIARY
or
INTELLIGENCE SUMMARY.

(Erase heading not required.)

Instructions regarding War Diaries and Intelligence Summaries are contained in F.S. Regs., Part II. and the Staff Manual respectively. Title pages will be prepared in manuscript.

Hour, Date, Place	Summary of Events and Information	Remarks and references to Appendices
POPERINGHE. 16.2.15 9 P.M.	Nothing to record.	Frost. Fine.
do 17.2.15 9. P.M.	Nothing to record.	Showery. frost.
do 18.2.15 9.P.M.	D.D.V.S. 2nd Army inspected the Div: Amm: Col: & impressed upon the D.M. of S. Officer the necessity of moving on to fresh ground, many of the horses standing in deep mud. He also inspected Nos. 1 & 2 Co. Y.A.S.C. Train.	Fine. frost.
do 19.2.15 9 P.M.	14th Reinforcement arrived for the Division. Visited 1st & 3rd M⁰ Furmouth Territorial Battalions also 5th K.O.R. Lancs. Territorial Battalion which had just joined the Division. Inspected their Transport animals & charges. 2.5th Inf: B⁰de north. LIEUT. BAMBRIDGE. A.V.C. left the Division. 13th Inf: B⁰de with LIEUT. DOYLE. A.V.C. joined the Division. 9th Inf: B⁰de with LIEUT. ANDERSON. A.V.C. joined the Division.	Showery. frost.
do 20.2.15 9. P.M.	Visited 13th Inf: B⁰de also LIEUT. DOYLE. A.V.C.	Heavy rain. frost.
do 21.2.15 9.P.M.	Visited the C.R.A. & arranged with him as to Veterinary care of two Units. LIEUT. CHOWN. A.V.C. o/c N⁰ 83rd Inf: B⁰de reported sick.	Fine. frost.

Army Form C. 2118.

WAR DIARY
or
INTELLIGENCE SUMMARY.
(Erase heading not required.)

Instructions regarding War Diaries and Intelligence Summaries are contained in F.S. Regs., Part II. and the Staff Manual respectively. Title pages will be prepared in manuscript.

Hour, Date, Place	Summary of Events and Information	Remarks and references to Appendices
POPERINGHE. 22.2.15. 9.P.M.	8th Howitzer Bde. R.F.A. with Capt. Fyrth A.V.C. in Veterinary charge arrived.	Frost. yst.
do. 23.2.15 9.P.M.	Visited Capt. FYRTH. A.V.C. and arranged to supply him with Veterinary equipment. Visited 13th Inf. Bde and met LIEUT. ANDERSON. A.V.C. Inspected No: 2 & 4 Sections of the Divisional Ammunition Column. Fine.	Some snow. yst.
do. 24.2.15 9.P.M.	Met D.D.V.S. 2nd Army at ABEELE.	yst.
do. 25.2.15 9.P.M.	Inspected No: 1 & 3 Sections of the Divisional Ammunition Column. Wet.	yst.
do. 26.2.15 9.P.M.	Nothing to record.	Fine. yst.
do. 27.2.15 9.P.M.	Arranged to include horses of 5th Corps in POPERINGHE requiring Veterinary attendance, daily. Inspected all horses of 31st Bde R.F.A. General condition of horses good, but horse standing in deep mud & very little attempt being made to improve their standing. Made dyffat Recommendation re this.	Cold. Sleet. yst.
do. 28.2.15 9.P.M.	1st & 3rd Monmouth Territorial Battalions left to-day.	Fine. Cold wind. yst.

J.S. Talley. Lt. Col. A.V.C.
A.D.V.S. 28th Div.
11.3.15.

No. 17, Mobile Veterinary Section.

Sick State of horses for period from 30=1=15. to 5=2=15.

In last Return.	Admitted since	Transferred sick	Died	Cured	Remaining	Remarks.
9	64	50	11*	1	11ˣ	* 7 Pneumonia, 1 Purpura, 1 Colic, 2 Destroyed (Incurable) x 1 left at Boore 1 Transferred to Pridelle 9 with section at Farm

(Signed) J.H.T. HERRICK, Lieut., A.V.C.

O.C., 17 M.V.S.,

6=2=15.

No. 17, Mobile Veterinary Section.

SICK STATE of Horses, for period from 6=2=15 to 11=2=15

In last Return	Admitted since	Total	Cured	Died	Destroyed	Abandoned at farms or missing	Transferred sick.	Remaining.
9	23	32	-	-	-	2	-	32

(Signed) H.J.T. HERRICK, Lieut. A.V.C.

O.C., No. 17, M.V.S., 12=2=15.

No. 17, Mobile Veterinary Section.

SICK STATE of Horses for period from 12=2=15, to 18=2=15..

In last Return.	Admitted Since.	Total	Cured	Died	Destryd	Abanded @ farms or missing.	Trans-ferred sick.	Remain-ing.	Remarks.
32	17	49	-	1*	2	-	13	33	*Colic Admitted 18=2=15 with Fistulas and was suffering from Colic.

(Signed) H.J.T. HERRICK, Lieut. A.V.C.,

O.C., No. 17, M.V.S.,

19=2=15.

No. 17, Mobile Veterinary Section.

SICK STATE of Horses for period from 19=2=15 to 25=2=15.

In last Return.	Admitted Since.	Total	Cured	Died	Destryd	Abandnd @ Farms or missing.	Transferred sick	Remaining.	Remarks.
33	44	77	-	-	2	-	41*	36	*Includes two Mares in foal taken over at Abeele Station.

(Signed) H.J.T. HERRICK, Lieut., A.V.C.,

O.C., No. 17, M.V.S.,

26=2=15

A.D.V.S.
28th Division

War Diary
March 1915

1/31st

Army Form C. 2118.

WAR DIARY
or
INTELLIGENCE SUMMARY.
(Erase heading not required.)

Instructions regarding War Diaries and Intelligence Summaries are contained in F.S. Regs., Part I. and the Staff Manual respectively. Title pages will be prepared in manuscript.

Hour, Date, Place	Summary of Events and Information	Remarks and references to Appendices
POPERINGHE. 1.3.15. 9. P.M.	Inspected all horses 146th Bde R.F.A., general condition satisfactory except 361st Battery, in which a large number of horses were out of condition. Most of the horses in the Brigade are standing in deep mud. Made verbal recommendations.	Bright. 9/st.
do. 2.3.15 9.P.M.	Nothing to record.	Fine 9/st.
do. 3.3.15 9.P.M.	Inspected all horses 3rd Bde R.F.A., general condition delicate, except 22nd Battery, in which a number of horses were out of condition. Made verbal recommendations. 83rd Inf. Bde left the Division. 15th Inf. Bde with Capt. R.E. BAELBY A.V.C. arrived.	
do. 4.3.15. 9.P.M.	D.D.V.S. 2nd Army arrived and inspected 16th M.V.S. also the 28th Divisional Squadron Scurly Yeomanry. Afterwards accompanied him to ABEELE & inspected the horses of 149th Batty. R.F.A.	Wet. 9/st.
do. 5.3.15 9.P.M.	Inspected and saw 60 horses at Mobile Veterinary Section which were sit for issue, arranged with D.A.R.M.G. as to their distribution.	Dull. 9/st.
do. 6.3.15 9.P.M.	Visited 10th Liverpool English Regt. inspected their horses & provided them with a shift feed. Visited 15th Inf. Bde & inspected horses with him the 6th Liverpool Regt. and A.V.C. Also visited, with him the 6th Liverpool Regt. and arranged for shoeing of their mules.	Dull. 9/st. Wet and cold 9/st.

Army Form C. 2118.

WAR DIARY
or
INTELLIGENCE SUMMARY.

(Erase heading not required.)

Instructions regarding War Diaries and Intelligence Summaries are contained in F. S. Regs., Part II. and the Staff Manual respectively. Title pages will be prepared in manuscript.

Hour, Date, Place		Summary of Events and Information	Remarks and references to Appendices
POPERINGHE.	7. 3. 15. 9. P.M.	Visited Town Commandant YPRES & arranged with him the Veterinary supervision & shoeing of horses there.	Wet. yet.
do	8. 3. 15. 9. P.M.	Nothing to record.	Fine cold wind. yet.
do	9. 3. 15. 9. P.M.	Nothing to record.	Fine. yet.
do	10. 3. 15. 9. P.M.	Nothing to record.	Fine. yet.
do	11. 3. 15. 9. P.M.	Inspected all horses of the Field Ambulances.	Dull. yet.
do	12. 3. 15. 9. P.M.	Inspected horses of Divisional Ammunition Column.	Fine. yet.
do	13. 3. 15. 9. P.M.	Visited Mobile Veterinary Section & inspected & issued horses. Lift for reserve & arranged with D.A.Q.M.G. as to their disposal.	Fine. yet.
do	14. 3. 15. 9. P.M.	Rode round ground occupied by the Division, the fine weather has greatly improved thy conditions under which the horses are living, but there is no fresh air - trodden ground on which to move. Many horses are going sick from a combination of Mud, Fevers and grease. Reached Hdqrs.	Fine. yet.

Army Form C. 2118.

WAR DIARY
or
INTELLIGENCE SUMMARY.
(Erase heading not required.)

Instructions regarding War Diaries and Intelligence Summaries are contained in F.S. Regs., Part II. and the Staff Manual respectively. Title pages will be prepared in manuscript.

Hour, Date, Place		Summary of Events and Information	Remarks and references to Appendices
POPERINGHE.	15.3.15 9.P.M.	Nothing to record.	Fine. yst.
do	16.3.15 9.P.M.	Inspected horses of 31st and 148th Brigades R.F.A.	Fine. yst.
do	17.3.15 9.P.M.	Inspected horses of 3rd Bde R.F.A. and 8th Howitzer Bde R.F.A.	Fine. yst.
do	18.3.15 9.P.M.	D.V.S. and P.D.V.S. 2nd Army visited and inspected 17 M.V.S. & met all V.Os of the Division.	Rain at night. yst.
do	29.3.15 9.P.M.	P.D.V.S. 2nd Army visited the Division.	Fine. yst.
do	30.3.15 9.P.M.	Accompanied G.O.C. 28th Division to 3rd Bde R.F.A. horse lines.	Fine. yst.
do	31.3.15 9.P.M.	Attended G.O.C. 5th Corps at his inspection of 31st Bde R.F.A. horses.	Fine. yst.

J.F. Tapley. Capt. A.V.C.
A.D.V.S. 28th Divn.

12/5216

ADVS. 28th Division

Vols. III & IV 1. H — 22.4.15

A.D.V.S.
28th Division

Maj. Keary
1/30th April 1915.

Army Form C. 2118.

WAR DIARY
or
INTELLIGENCE SUMMARY.
(Erase heading not required.)

Instructions regarding War Diaries and Intelligence Summaries are contained in F. S. Regs., Part II and the Staff Manual respectively. Title pages will be prepared in manuscript.

Hour, Date, Place	Summary of Events and Information	Remarks and references to Appendices
POPERINGHE. 1.4.15. 9 P.M.	Attended G.O.C. 5th boys at his instruction of horses of 146th Bde R.F.A.	Fine. J.S.T.
do 2.4.15 9 P.M.	Recognized D.A.R.M.O. to ABEELE STATION to meet Recruits.	Rain all night. J.S.T.
do 7.4.15 9 P.M.	M.V.S. moved to perishing post East of POPERINGHE STATION.	
do 9.4.15 9 P.M.	28th Division came out of firing line. Lieut. F.R. ADAMS. A.V.C. D.V.O. 3rd Bde R.F.A. wounded. Took over his duties myself.	Showery. J.S.T.
do 10.4.15 9 P.M.	D.D.V.S. 2nd Army visited and inspected Surrey Yeomanry No. 4 Section Div. Ammn. Col; and 83rd Inf. Bgde. Line transport; also 1 Y.M.V.S.	Fine. J.S.T.
do 11.4.15 9 P.M.	28th Division went into firing line again. Visited C.R.A. & obtained details of positions of Wagon lines etc.	Fine. J.S.T.
do 13.4.15 9 P.M.	Inspected 83rd Inf. Bde horses & reported on same to G.O.C. the Brigade.	Fine. J.S.T.
do 14.4.15 9 P.M.	Sent report on Offd R.F.A. V.C. to D.D.V.S. 2nd Army.	Showery. J.S.T.

Army Form C. 2118.

WAR DIARY
or
INTELLIGENCE SUMMARY.

(Erase heading not required.)

Instructions regarding War Diaries and Intelligence Summaries are contained in F. S. Regs., Part II. and the Staff Manual respectively. Title pages will be prepared in manuscript.

Hour, Date, Place		Summary of Events and Information	Remarks and references to Appendices
VLAMERTINGHE.	21.4.15. 9 P.M.	Moved to Chateau at VLAMERTINGHE.	Fine, yet.
do	22.4.15. 9 P.M.	LIEUT. F.R.ADAMS.A.V.C. returned to duty with 3rd Bde. R.F.A.	Fine, yet.
POPERINGHE.	23.4.15. 9 P.M.	Moved back to POPERINGHE.	Fine, yet.
PROVEN.	24.4.15. 9 P.M.	Office moved to PROVEN. The D.D.V.S. 2nd Army arranged to move M.V.S.to POPERINGHE – BOESCHEPE ROAD, leaving a collecting station sufficient in advance.	Fine, yet.

J.S.Tapley. Eqpt.A.V.C.
A.D.V.S. 28th Divn.

No. 17, Mobile Veterinary Section.

Sick State of Horses for period from 9=4=15 to 15=4=15.

n last eturn	Admitted since	Total	Cured	Died	Destroyed	Trans Sick	Remaining	Remarks.
22	38	60	4		2	27	27	

10=4=15.

(Signed) H.J.T. HERRICK, Lieut.,
O.C., No. 17, M.V.S.,

No. 17, Mobile Veterinary Section.

Sick State of Horses for period from 16=4=15 to 22=4=15.

In last Return	Admitted since	Total	Cured	Died	Destroyed	Trans Sick	Remaining	Remarks.
27	30	57	1		1	29*	26	*Includes one Mare in foal.

23=4=15.

(Signed) H.J.T. HERRICK, Lieut., A.V.C
O.C., 17, M.V.S.,

No. 17, Mobile Veterinary Section.

Sick State of Horses for period from 23=4=15 to 29=4=15.

n last return.	Admitted Since.	Total	Cured	Died	Destroyed	Trans Sick	Remaining	Remarks
26	58	84	5	6	1	55*	17	* Includes One Mare in foal stray

30=4=15.

(Signed) H.J.T. HERRICK, Lieut., A.V.C.,
O.C., 17, M. V. S.

No. 17, Mobile Veterinary Section.

Sick State of Horses for period from 2=4=15 to 8=4=15.

In last Return	Admitted Since	Total	Cured	Died	Destroyed	Trans Sick.	Remaining	Remarks
51	41	92	5	1	8	56*	22	*Includes six Mares in foal.

(Signed) H.J.T. HERRICK, Lieut., A.V.C

O.C., 17, M.VMS.,

9=4=15.

121/5543

ADVS. 28th Division

Vol V 1. — 31. 5. 15

War Diary
March ending 31st March 1915

WAR DIARY
or
INTELLIGENCE SUMMARY.

(Erase heading not required.)

Army Form C. 2118.

Instructions regarding War Diaries and Intelligence Summaries are contained in F.S. Regs., Part II. and the Staff Manual respectively. Title pages will be prepared in manuscript.

Hour, Date, Place		Summary of Events and Information	Remarks and references to Appendices
Proven	4. 5. 15 9 P.M.	No: 11 M.V.S. moved to section on ABEELE – STEENVOORDE Road, it's advanced collecting station received as before.	Fine. Rain at night.
do	5. 5. 15 9 P.M.	Visited M.V.S. in new billet, & met D.D.V.S. 2nd Army there.	Fine. Rain at night. 7st.
do	10. 5. 15 9 P.M.	Lieut. F.R. ADAMS. A.V.C. V.O. Y.S. 3rd Bde R.F.A. int. Took over veterinary charge of this units.	Fine. 7st.
do	14. 5. 15 9 P.M.	The Infantry of the Division went into rest areas with exception of 15 Battalions which were formed into a composite Brigade at VLAMERTINGHE. Visited H.R. of this Brigade & made Veterinary arrangements	Misty rain. 7st.
do	16. 5. 15 9 P.M.	1st Lieut. FORREST. A.V.C. being sick charge. Finished with report to 2nd Division on the Veterinary work from 22nd April to 13th May.	App. I. A.V. 49 attd.
do	21. 5. 15	Gave LIEUTS. NICHOLSON and MITCHELL and CAPT. WILLIAMS. A.V.C. 5 days leave (16th to 20th) Gave LIEUT. HERRICK. A.V.C. 4 days leave (21st to 24th)	Fine. 7st. Fine. 7st.
do	23. 5. 15	D.D.V.S. 2nd Army inspected 8th How. Bde R.F.A.	Fine. 7st.

Army Form C. 2118.

WAR DIARY
or
INTELLIGENCE SUMMARY.
(Erase heading not required.)

Instructions regarding War Diaries and Intelligence Summaries are contained in F.S. Regs., Part II. and the Staff Manual respectively. Title pages will be prepared in manuscript.

Hour, Date, Place	Summary of Events and Information	Remarks and references to Appendices
Watou. 31/5/15 9. P.M.	28th Division moving into Rest area. Divisional Headquarters moved to WATOU. 11 M.V.S. moved to WINNIZEELE area. 4/6/15.	J. Stopley Capt. A.S.C. A.D.V.S. of 28th Divn.

(73989) W4141—463. 400,000. 9/14. H.&J.Ltd. Forms/C. 2118/10.

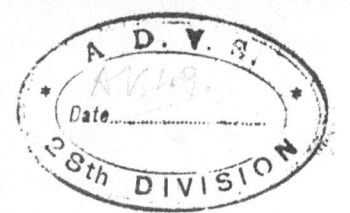

Work of Army Veterinary Services, 28th Division, from April 22nd, to May 13th 1915.

※-※

An Advanced Collecting Station for the Mobile Veterinary Section was established just East of POPERINGHE Station, and the Mobile Veterinary Section was situated just West of ABEELE.

425 Horses and Mules have been treated for injuries and sickness, of which 264 have been sent to Mobile Veterinary Section, and from there evacuated to the Base.

232 animals have been killed, and 120 have had to be destroyed, as the result of Shell and Bullet wounds.

During the period from 22nd April to 4th May, Lieuts. F.R. ADAMS and E.J. NICHOLSON, A.V.C., Veterinary Officers in charge respectively of the 3rd and 31st Brigades, R.F.A., did excellent work amongst their horses in the wagon lines in neighbourhood of FREZENBERG and VERLORENHOEK.

Sergeant D. SHADBOLT, A.V.C., efficiently carried out his duties as N.C.O. in charge of Advanced Mobile Veterinary Section, and

Lance Corporal J. LYALL, A.V.C., did very good work amongst the Transport Horses of the 83rd Infantry Brigade in the neighbourhood of YPRES.

Headquarters,   (Signed) J.J.B. TAPLEY, Capt., A.V.C.,
16=5=15.   A.D.V.S., 28th DIVISION.

No. 17. M.V.S. A.V.C

Sick State of Horses for period from 30.4.15 to 6.5.15

LAST RETURN	ADMITTED SINCE	TOTAL	CURED	DIED	DESTROYED	TRANS SICK	REMAINING	REMARKS
16	122*	138	—	—	7	113	18	*Includes 19 Horses other than 28th Division

7/6/15.

(Sgd) J.B Hapley Capt.
for Lieut A.V.C.
O.C. 17th M.V.S.

No. 17. M.V.S. A.V.C.

Sick State of Horses for period from 7-5-15 to 13-5-15

LAST RETURN	ADMITTED SINCE	TOTAL	CURED	DIED	DESTROYED	TRANS SICK	REMAINING	REMARKS
18	89	107	1	–	1	*96	11	*Includes 2 Section Horses.

No 14. M.V.S. A.V.C.

Sick State of Horses for period from 14-5-15 to 20-5-15.

LAST RETURN	ADMITTED SINCE	TOTAL	CURED	DIED	DESTROYED	TRANS SICK	REMAINING	REMARKS
11	58	69	-	-	1	56	12	

21-5-15.

(Sgd) J B Tapley Capt. A.V.C.
for Lieut AVC
O.C. 14th M.V.S.

No. 14. M.V.S. A.V.C.

Sick State of Horses for period from 21-5-15 to 27-5-15.

LAST RETURN	ADMITTED SINCE	TOTAL	CURED	DIED	DESTROYED	TRANS: SICK	REMAINING	REMARKS
12	48	60	-	-	1	43*	18	* Includes 3 mares-in-foal and two Section Horses.

28-5-15.

(Sgd) H.G.Y. Herrick
Lieut A.V.C.
O.C. 14th M.V.S.

121/6427

28th Division

A.D.V.S. 28th Division
Vol VI
From 1st to 30th June 1915

COPY

Army Form C. 2118.

WAR DIARY
or
INTELLIGENCE SUMMARY.

(Erase heading not required.)

Instructions regarding War Diaries and Intelligence Summaries are contained in F. S. Regs., Part II. and the Staff Manual respectively. Title pages will be prepared in manuscript.

Hour, Date, Place		Summary of Events and Information	Remarks and references to Appendices
WATOU	1=6=15	Closed the Advanced Collecting Post of 17 M.V.S.	FINE.
"	3=6=15 9 p.m.	Inspected all horses of the 28th Divisional Signal Co.	"
"	4=6=15.	17th M.V.S. moved to WINNIZEELE area. Inspected all horses Divisional Squadron Surrey Yeomanry, and the 83rd Infantry Brigade.	"
"	11=6=15.	Returned from 5 days' leave.	"
Westoutre	14=6=15.	Divisional Headquarters moved to Westoutre. Inspected all animals 58th Field Coy. R.E.	"
	17-6=15	Inspected all horses of the 28th Divisional Train.	"
	19=6=15.	Inspected all horses "A" How. Batt. 49th Brigade, R.F.A., with its Ammunition Column.	"
	20=6=15.	17th M.V.S. moved into WESTOUTRE area .	"
	21=6=15.	Attended parade of horses for casting by Remount Officer.	"
	25=6=15.	Inspected all horses 2/1st Field Co. R.E. & 84th Field Ambulance.	Wet.
	26=6=15.	Inspected all horses 146th Brigade, R.F.A.	FINE.
	29th=6=15	Inspected all horses 3rd Brigade, R.F.A., and sent two suspicious cases to skin disease to M.V.S. D.D.V.S., 2nd Army visited and examined these 2 cases and arranged for their evacuation to-morrow.	"
	30=6=15.	Inspected all horses of the 31st Brigade, R.F.A.	

WESTOUTRE, 2=7=15.

(Signed) J.J.B. TAPLEY, Capt., A.V.C., A.D.V.S., 28th DIVISION.

28th Division

107/6210

A.D.V.S. 28th Division

Vol VII   1 — 31.7.15.

War Diary for
month of July 1915.

J. Staples
A.D.V.S. 28th Division

[Stamp: A.D.V.S. 28th DIVISION Date 1-8-15]

WAR DIARY
or
INTELLIGENCE SUMMARY.

(Erase heading not required.)

Army Form C. 2118.

Instructions regarding War Diaries and Intelligence Summaries are contained in F. S. Regs., Part II. and the Staff Manual respectively. Title pages will be prepared in manuscript.

Place	Hour, Date	Summary of Events and Information	Remarks and references to Appendices
WESTOUTRE.	1.7.15 9.P.M.	Inspected all horses 28th Divisional Ammunition Column.	Fine. Hot.
do	2.7.15 9.P.M.	Inspected all animals 83rd Infantry Brigade.	Fine. Hot.
do	6.7.15 9 PM	Inspected all animals 85th Infantry Brigade.	Fine. Hot.
do	7.7.15 9 PM	Inspected all animals 84th Infantry Brigade.	Heavy Rain.
do	9.7.15 9 PM	Inspected all animals 28th Divisional Train.	Stormy. Hot.
do	10.7.15 9.P.M.	Inspected horses of A.49 Howitzer Batt. & Ammn: Col.	Fine. Hot.
do	12.7.15	Inspected horses of 2/1 Northumbrian Field Co. Y. R.E.	Wet.
do	18.7.15 9.P.M.	X 2nd Heavy Brigade R.G.A. and XII th Heavy Battery. Owing to the Division Made Veterinary arrangements for these units, & inspected all horses of the X.B. of	Hot.
do	20.7.15 9.P.M.	Took over Veterinary charge of horses 2nd Corps H.Q. & Signals. Visited Mr head.	Fine. Hot.
do	22.7.15 9.P.M.	CAPT. R.D. WILLIAMS. A.V.C. Left this Division to do temporary duty with 50th Division.	Fine. Hot. Showery. Hot.

Army Form C. 2118.

WAR DIARY
or
INTELLIGENCE SUMMARY.

(Erase heading not required.)

Instructions regarding War Diaries and Intelligence
Summaries are contained in F. S. Regs., Part II.
and the Staff Manual respectively. Title pages
will be prepared in manuscript.

Hour, Date, Place	Summary of Events and Information	Remarks and references to Appendices
WESTOUTRE. 24.7.15. 9.P.M.	Inspected all horses of Signals of H.Q. 2nd Corps. Attended demonstration given by LIEUT. HOBDAY in the intra-dermal half-ball method of malleinisation of animals.	Showery.
do 25.7.15 9.P.M.	Inspected all horses 12th H.Bty.Y.R.G.A.	Just. Showery just
do 29.7.15 9.P.M.	Inspected all horses 3rd Coy to H.Q. D.H.Q.M.G. and D.D.V.S. 2nd Army inspected 17 M.V.S.	Fine just.
do 31.7.15 9.P.M.	Inspected all horses of 3rd Corps Signals.	Fine just.

J. Stapley. Major A.V.C.
ADVS 2nd Corps

1/8/15.

Sick State of Horses for Period from 25=6=15 to 1=7=15.

In last Return	Admitted Since	Total	Cured	Died	Destroyed	Abandoned	Trans Sick	Remaining	Remarks
31 4 Abandoned	30 at last	61 4 Billet	4*	1ˣ	1°	1	41 1	16	* Includes 3 Mares in foal returned to Units x Pneumonia o Lame O.Shoul.

2=7=15.

(Signed) H.G.T. HERRICK, Lieut., A.V.C.,
O.C., No. 17, M.V.S.

A.D.V.S. 28th DIVISION

Army Form C. 2118.

WAR DIARY
or
INTELLIGENCE SUMMARY.
(Erase heading not required.)

Instructions regarding War Diaries and Intelligence Summaries are contained in F.S. Regs., Part II. and the Staff Manual respectively. Title pages will be prepared in manuscript.

Hour, Date, Place	Summary of Events and Information	Remarks and references to Appendices
WESTOUTRE. 24.7.15. 9. P.M.	Inspected all horses of Signals of H.Q. 2nd Corps. Attended demonstration given by LIEUT. HOBDAY in the intra-dermal palpebral method of malleination of animals.	Showery.
do 25.7.15. 9. P.M.	Inspected all horses 12th H. Batt. Y R.G.A.	Showery. 9 P.S.T.
do 29.7.15. 9. P.M.	Inspected all horses 3rd Corps H.Q. D.A.Q.M.G. and D.D.V.S. 2nd Army inspected 17 M.V.S.	Fine. 9 P.S.T.
do 31.7.15. 9. P.M.	Inspected all horses of 3rd Corps Signals.	Fine. 9 P.S.T.

1/8/15.

J.B. Taylor. Major A.V.C.
A.D.V.S. 28th Div.

Sick State of Horses for Period from 25=6=15 to 1=7=15.

In last Return	Admitted Since	Total	Cured	Died	Destroyed	Abandoned	Trans Sick	Remaining	Remarks
31 4 Abandoned	30 at last	61 4 Billet	4*	1ˣ	1°	1	41 1	16	* Includes 3 Mares in foal returned to Units x Pneumonia o Lame O.Shoul.

2=7=15.

(Signed) H.G.T. HERRICK, Lieut., A.V.C.,
O.C., No. 17, M.V.S.

A.D.V.S. 28th DIVISION

Sick State of Horses for period from 2=7=15 to 8=7=15

In last Return	Admitted Since	Total	Cured	Died	Destroyed	Trans: Sick	Remaining	Remarks.
16 1*	26	42 1	-	-	-	14	29	~~* Abandoned~~ * Abandoned at last Billet - Mare in Foal

9=7=15

(Signed) H.G.T. HERRICK, Lieut., A.V.C.,
O.C., No. 17, M.V.S.,

A.D.V.S. 28th DIVISION

Sick State of Horses for period from 9=7=15 to 15=7=15.

In last Return	Admitted Since	Total	Cured	Died	Destroyed	Trans: Sick	Remaining	Remarks
29	36	65	1	-	-	45*	19	* Includes 1 Mare with foal at foot

16=7=15.　　　　　　(Signed)　　H.G.T. HERRICK, Lieut., A.V.C.,
　　　　　　　　　　　　　　　　O.C., No. 17, M.V.S.,

Sick State of Horses for period from 16=7=15 to 22=7=15.

In last Return	Admitted Since	Total	Cured	Died	Destroyed	Trans: Sick	Remaining	Remarks
19	21	40	-	-	2	13	25	

23=7=15.   (Signed) H.G.T. HERRICK, Lieut., A.V.C.,
                                      O.C., No. 17, M.V.S.

Sick State of Horses for period from 23=7=15 to 29=7=15.

In last Return	Admitted Since	Total	Cured	Died	Destroyed	Trans: Sick	Remaining	Remarks.
25	41	66	3	-	1	32	30	

30=7=15.

(Signed) H.G.T. HERRICK, Lieut., A.V.C.
O.C., No. 17, M.V.S.,

151/6753

38th Division

ADM. 28th Division

August 15

Army Form C. 2118.

Capt. McMillan A/C
A.D.V.S. – 20th Division

WAR DIARY
or
INTELLIGENCE SUMMARY.
(Erase heading not required.)

Instructions regarding War Diaries and Intelligence Summaries are contained in F. S. Regs., Part II. and the Staff Manual respectively. Title pages will be prepared in manuscript.

Hour, Date, Place	Summary of Events and Information	Remarks and references to Appendices
WESTOUTRE – 12 Aug 15	Arrived at WESTOUTRE at 11 a.m. Took over duties of A.D.V.S. 20th Division from Major TAPLEY. Left for ENGLAND at 2 p.m. Took over one charger belonging to Major TAPLEY who brought up one horse with me from No. 13 VETY. HOSPITAL, BOULOGNE, an A.D.V.S. one now to be provided with two chargers instead of one to a motor car.	
" – 13 Aug. 15	Visited rest of Veterinary Officers performing duty in the Division, also A.D.V.S. of the 3rd & 6th Divisions. Lieut FORREST receives orders to leave this Division. Report to the C.O. 98th BRIGADE R.G.A. for duty.	

Army Form C. 2118.

WAR DIARY
or
INTELLIGENCE SUMMARY.
(Erase heading not required.)

Instructions regarding War Diaries and Intelligence Summaries are contained in F. S. Regs., Part II. and the Staff Manual respectively. Title pages will be prepared in manuscript.

Hour, Date, Place	Summary of Events and Information	Remarks and references to Appendices
WESTOUTRE — 13 Aug 15.	Veterinary Officers of 20th Division now consist of —	
	A.D.V.S. — Capt. K.W. MELLARD	
	1st M.V.S. — Lieut. H.G.T. HERRICK	
	INFANTRY. BDES. — Lieut. W.J. BAMBRIDGE	
	3rd BRIG. R.F.A — Lieut. F.R. ADAMS.	
	14 b " " — Lieut. T.M. MITCHELL	
	31 " " — Lieut. E.J. NICHOLSON.	
	DIV. TRAIN } Capt. R.D. WILLIAMS.	
	DIV. AMM. Col. }	
— 14 Aug 15	Visited 10th Bry Rca BAILLEUL workshop	
	2nd Cav. Signal — Owned charge of Capt.	
	GRASNETT R.E. to be destroyed — Mr. Brown M.F.	

(73989) W4141—463.   400,000.   9/14.   H.&J.Ltd.   Forms/C. 2118/10.

Army Form C. 2118.

WAR DIARY
or
INTELLIGENCE SUMMARY.

(Erase heading not required.)

Instructions regarding War Diaries and Intelligence Summaries are contained in F.S. Regs., Part II. and the Staff Manual respectively. Title pages will be prepared in manuscript.

Hour, Date, Place	Summary of Events and Information	Remarks and references to Appendices
WESTOUTRE — 15 Aug 15.	G.O.C. 20th Division inspected No. 17 Mob Vety. Sect.	
" 16 Aug 15	D.D.V.S. visited WESTOUTRE & gave me instructions	
" 17 Aug 15	re duties of A.D.V.S. Inspected horses of 31st Bing Bde. men sick horses to no care left behind by 37th Division	
" 18 Aug 15	Farms with cases of foot & mouth disease inspected near BOESCHEPE & put out of bounds for troops	
" 19 Aug 15	Inspected horses of 3rd King R.A. with Lt. Adams AVC	
" 20 Aug 15	Inspected 20th Divisional Supply & Post mortem on carcase of cow alleged to have died from eating chlorinated lime used from yards. P.M. showed cause of death to be infection	

WAR DIARY
or
INTELLIGENCE SUMMARY.
(Erase heading not required.)

Army Form C. 2118.

Instructions regarding War Diaries and Intelligence Summaries are contained in F.S. Regs., Part II. and the Staff Manual respectively. Title pages will be prepared in manuscript.

Hour, Date, Place	Summary of Events and Information	Remarks and references to Appendices
WESTOUTRE — 21 Aug 15.	Inspected horses at 2nd Corps Headquarters.	
23 Aug 15.	Inspected horses with 2nd Corps. Prepared for casting of three animals were not Veterinary Case.	
24 Aug 15.	Lieut Venrick granted 7 days leave home.	
25 Aug 15.	Inspected horses of the Corps. 3 granted to reck. Horse left with them by 37th Division	
26 Aug 15.	Copl. Mich. A.V.C. — clerk transferred to the H.Q. Office S.I.C.	
27 Aug 15.	Selected horses for heavy draught for S.O.S. trains.	
28 Aug 15.	Inspected Divisional train 70th Army Column — all these horses looking exceptionally well. Lieut W.J. Hambridge transferred to Woolwich. Taken over a motor 4 day Renown car.	
29 Aug 15.	Relieved by Lt. W. H. Bishop A.V.C.	

Army Form C. 2118.

WAR DIARY
or
INTELLIGENCE SUMMARY.
(Erase heading not required.)

Hour, Date, Place	Summary of Events and Information	Remarks and references to Appendices
WESTOUTRE – 30 Aug 15	Inspected 146th Heavy R.F.A. taken charge. Lieut. Mitchell A.V.C.	
31 Aug 15	Lieut Bishop AVC arrive from England Posted to P4 + 85th Infantry Brigade	
	31st Aug '15	William Boyd A.V.O. ADVS 20th Division

28th Division

121/7050

Confidential

War Diary

of

A.D.V.S. 28th Division.

From 1st Sept. '15
to
30th Sept. 1915

Vol IX

WAR DIARY
or
INTELLIGENCE SUMMARY.
(Erase heading not required.)

Army Form C. 2118.

Capt Hutherland A.S.C
a/s O.C — 2/1 Div ???

Hour, Date, Place	Summary of Events and Information	Remarks and references to Appendices
WESTOUTRE — 1 Sept 15	Capt Lieut A. H. BISHOP A.S.C. around his charge in the division, he arrived from England yesterday. He was placed in temp charge of the 1st & 2nd Nth Infantry Brigade. — Lieut BISHOP has — Canadian qualification (steam) who has had only 3 years experience of army work.	
2 Sept 15.	Inspected horses at Lord Boys Headquarters. Horses & cases to be evacuated to Mobile Vety Section	
3 Sept 15.	Inspected Infantry Brigade + Northumberland Field Co. R.E.	
5 Sept 15	Visited units of 146 Brig R.F.A. with Lieut MITCHELL. All horses look well with exception of those of the Ammunition Column, many of these are in poor condition	

Army Form C. 2118.

WAR DIARY
or
INTELLIGENCE SUMMARY.
(Erase heading not required.)

Instructions regarding War Diaries and Intelligence Summaries are contained in F.S. Regs., Part II. and the Staff Manual respectively. Title pages will be prepared in manuscript.

Hour, Date, Place	Summary of Events and Information	Remarks and references to Appendices
WESTOUTRE – 5 Sept 15	have reported to have recently fallen away in condition. to put it down to the water supply, as many of the fields are very low & the water at times has a bad Colour & smell. – Horses are now better elsewhere.	
" 6 Sept 15	Attained board – to purchase charger belonging to Capt. PARBURY R.F.A, the animal should have been sold to Government before leaving ENGLAND.	
" 7 Sept 15	Corporal DONOVAN A.V.C. arrived for duty as clerk in A.D.V.S. office. Inspected horses of 3rd R. Fusiliers (C's & D Coy Bny.) These horses are not in good condition Many of them are old respirent cheap jobs.	

WAR DIARY
or
INTELLIGENCE SUMMARY.

(Erase heading not required.)

Army Form C. 2118.

Instructions regarding War Diaries and Intelligence Summaries are contained in F.S. Regs., Part II. and the Staff Manual respectively. Title pages will be prepared in manuscript.

Hour, Date, Place	Summary of Events and Information	Remarks and references to Appendices
WESTOUTRE — 9 Sept 15	Sergeants Watkin Meuse arrive take over charge of 3 + 5 Infantry Brigade respectively from Corporal Lyall + Sapper A.V.C.	
" 10 Sept 15	Accompanied S/M & Spls on his inspection of the Pit Infantry Brigade.	
" 11 Sept 15	Inspected newly formed reserve of stores. Most of these consist an apparently award that have undergone a course of treatment at Vlamertinghe.	
" 12 Sept 15	Lieut. L. P. NICHOLSON sanctioned 7 days leave to ENGLAND. Inspected horses of Survey Company, 1st 85th Field Ambulance + the Divisional Signal Co. R.E.	

WAR DIARY
or
INTELLIGENCE SUMMARY.
(Erase heading not required.)

Army Form C. 2118.

Hour, Date, Place	Summary of Events and Information	Remarks and references to Appendices
WESTOUTRE — 14 Sept 15.	Attended 3rd Divisional Horse Show to judge horses.	
" 15 Sept 15.	Visited 146 Bde R.F.A. Ammunition Column. Some of their horses were in poor condition.	
" 16 Sept 15.	Accompanied Brigadier going to inspect the 9th Infantry Brigade. Inspected 3rd Division horses very poor but they are shortly due old horses (15-20) have recently been doing much hard work at night — taking rations &c to trenches.	
" 18 Sept 15.	Accompanied Bde Gnrl for inspection of the 24th Infantry Brigade — on the whole condition of these animals very good.	

WAR DIARY
or
INTELLIGENCE SUMMARY

(Erase heading not required.)

Army Form C. 2118.

Instructions regarding War Diaries and Intelligence Summaries are contained in F. S. Regs., Part II. and the Staff Manual respectively. Title pages will be prepared in manuscript.

Hour, Date, Place	Summary of Events and Information	Remarks and references to Appendices
WESTOUTRE – 19 Sept 15	Jams received that Division will shortly leave present area.	
20 Sept 15	Colonels Ryan & Ennis A.V.C. respectively transferred from 83rd & 66th Infantry Brigade to the Divisional (?) Mobile Vety. Section – Only 2 N.C.O's to the rank of Sergeant are now being left with Infantry Brigades & Artillery Units	
21 Sept 15	S.O.S.T. 2nd Army with A.D.V.S. of the 1st Canadian Division visited our area, as the Canadian Divn. are to relieve the 28th	
22 Sept 15	Evacuated sick of Division, & Division leaving for MERRIS to march 1/first to Divisional leaving for MERRIS	

Army Form C. 2118.

WAR DIARY
or
INTELLIGENCE SUMMARY.
(Erase heading not required.)

Instructions regarding War Diaries and Intelligence Summaries are contained in F.S. Regs., Part II. and the Staff Manual respectively. Title pages will be prepared in manuscript.

Hour, Date, Place	Summary of Events and Information	Remarks and references to Appendices
MERRIS – 23 Sept 15	Division moved to MERRIS & is now in reserve.	
" 24 Sept 15	Division most of Units of Division is in new Area. Horses of which are much scattered extending over country from BAILLEUL to HAZEBROUCK. R.A.V.C. N.C.O. in charge of different Units now very much so & not nearly sufficient for some of Veterinary Officers to visit each Units under their charge every day.	
" 25 Sept 15	Evacuated sick horses (8) from BAILLEUL	
BETHUNE 26 Sept 15	Division moved to BETHUNE & are now part of the 1st Army (1st Corps). Army troops on march owing to great battle in & about LA BASSEE	

Army Form C. 2118.

WAR DIARY
or
INTELLIGENCE SUMMARY.
(Erase heading not required.)

Hour, Date, Place	Summary of Events and Information	Remarks and references to Appendices
BETHUNE — 27 Sept 15	Corps now in camp in Billery distant round BEUVRY	
" 28 Sept 15	All camp in dry condition owing to heavy rain. Several casualties from shell fire in 3rd Howitzers.	
" 29 Sept 15	6 hours interrupted by enemy in headquarters interrupter centerslips. Very wet day and constantly changing billets	
" 30 Sept 15	Various units of Divisional which have not got thro attached Eden	

In the field
30 Sept 15

J W Melland Capt
A V C
A D V S
20th Division

A.D.v.S. 28ᵗᵉ Dn.
Oct.
vol. X

Army Form C. 2118

Lieutenant Colonel A.D.C.
A.D.M.S. 20th Division

WAR DIARY
or
INTELLIGENCE SUMMARY
(Erase heading not required.)

Instructions regarding War Diaries and Intelligence Summaries are contained in F.S. Regs., Part II. and the Staff Manual respectively. Title Pages will be prepared in manuscript.

Place	Date	Hour	Summary of Events and Information	Remarks and references to Appendices
BETHUNE		1 Oct 15	German aerial in rumour BETHUNE for about 5 miles. Much shrapnel R.A. units near SAILLY LE BOURSE	
"		2 Oct 15	Town of BETHUNE shelled all morning, but no casualties amongst troops. Inspected 31st Brig. Amm. Column. Units of Horsed Casualty away behind	
"		3 pm 10 Oct 15	Very few animals now being evacuated by M.V.T.	
"		5 Oct 15	Divisional Vanguards moved to BUSNES — the line of Division remained in action near SAILLY — most of them units resting near BUSNES.	
"		9 Oct 15	Visited Infantry Brigades of Divn with Brig. & told — many changes in forward of Infantry transport being & result casualties near EBOS.	
"		9 Oct 15	Saw the care of the sick & wounded evacuated from L. Rly K.T.A.	
"		1 pm 15	Inspected 130th Brig. K.T.A.	
"		10 Oct 15	Inspected 24th Brig K.T.A. Horsed & further Casualty evacuation	

1875 Wt. W593/826 1,000,000 4/15 J.B.C. & A. A.D.S.S./Forms/C. 2118.

WAR DIARY
INTELLIGENCE SUMMARY
(Erase heading not required.)

Army Form C. 2118

Instructions regarding War Diaries and Intelligence Summaries are contained in F.S. Regs., Part II. and the Staff Manual respectively. Title Pages will be prepared in manuscript.

Place	Date	Hour	Summary of Events and Information	Remarks and references to Appendices
BETHUNE	10/Oct/15		Arrane isolated by Lieut ADAMS V.O. in charge of party. One horse picked out 3 more cases — therefore new were taken from in-lying picket from skin of these horses. Reported Evng by D.D.V.S. 1st Army.	
BUSNES	11/Oct/15		Twelve 12th Bty R.F.A. in company with D.D.V.S. 1st Army. Instructions reached shipping of horses, working relation etc. All anxious cases to be evacuated by M.V.T.	
"	12/Oct/15		Inspected Divisional Ammunition Column, Royal Fusiliers. Head of Divisional Train.	
"	13/Oct/15		Inspected 40 newly joined remounts of Divison.	
"	14/Oct/15		Three Units of Divison Constantly moving, also required sufficient transport of Infantry - noticed inadequate lack of sufficient transport animals	
"	15/Oct/15		Divisional Headquarters returns to BETHUNE	

Army Form C. 2118

WAR DIARY
INTELLIGENCE SUMMARY
(Erase heading not required.)

Instructions regarding War Diaries and Intelligence Summaries are contained in F. S. Regs., Part II. and the Staff Manual respectively. Title Pages will be prepared in manuscript.

Place	Date	Hour	Summary of Events and Information	Remarks and references to Appendices
BETHUNE	17 Oct 15		Received the thanks of 13 Infantry Brigade billets about Order from BETHUNE.	
	18 Oct 15			
	19 Oct 15		M.O., moved to find billets (whiting work) inspected the 22nd Bty RFA. with D.D.V.S. 1st Army.	
	20 Oct 15		Confidential order received that Serbians would have to embark for abroad (SERBIA) in two days time. Arrangement were made by D.D.V.S. that all horses of 22 Bty R.F.A. going to recruit cases of mange were being left behind. Fresh horses taken over from another Division. (?)	
Entrain journey	21 Oct 15		Entrained at LILLERS Station at 6 p.m. that units of Division entrained here to this place near LILLERS Station	21 Oct 15 Capt. Williams (V.D.) AVC relieved of charge of D.A.C. by R Woods S/Sgt. AVC
"	22 Oct 15		Continued train journey to MARSEILLES via Paris, MONTARGIS	
"	23 Oct 15		Continued railway journey. Frequent stoppages for watering en route.	

Army Form C. 2118

WAR DIARY
or
INTELLIGENCE SUMMARY
(Erase heading not required.)

Instructions regarding War Diaries and Intelligence Summaries are contained in F.S. Regs., Part II. and the Staff Manual respectively. Title Pages will be prepared in manuscript.

Place	Date	Hour	Summary of Events and Information	Remarks and references to Appendices
MARSEILLES	- 24/10/15		Arrived at MARSEILLES at 2 a.m. All units of Division sent to encampment on new ground at PARC BORELY — sick horses were collected in Camp & evacuated daily to the Indian Veterinary Hospital. All Units on arrival here were replenished with drugs &c from advanced base Vety. stores	
"	- 25/10/15		All Units of Division with exception of Div. Ammunition Column have now arrived in Marseilles. Camp is rather congested owing to wet weather. Ground in a very muddy state.	
"	- 26/10/15		Major OLIVER arrived in MARSEILLES from L.H.Q. Met all Nos. of Division remarked that every Unit was properly equipped & gave instruction for special attention on board ship.	
"	- 27/10/15		Very wet Tuesday in Camp. Many cases of abrasion & injuries from recent 3 days railway journey.	

1875 Wt. W593/826 1,000,000 4/15 J.B.C. & A. A.D.S.S./Forms/C. 2118.

Army Form C. 2118

WAR DIARY

INTELLIGENCE SUMMARY

(Erase heading not required.)

Instructions regarding War Diaries and Intelligence Summaries are contained in F.S. Regs., Part II. and the Staff Manual respectively. Title Pages will be prepared in manuscript.

Place	Date	Hour	Summary of Events and Information	Remarks and references to Appendices
MARSEILLES	28/10/15		Telegram received from D.V.S. ABBEVILLE that a horse evacuated from the D.A.C. several days previous had reacted to Mallein test. Orders received to remit ADAMS to embark for ALEXANDRIA & proceed there to take over charge of a Veterinary Hospital. Thought that had been sent ahead.	
"	29/10/15		Major OLIVER inspected D.A.C. for glanders arranged for testing all the horses with mallein of D.A.C.	
"	30/10/15		Two horses in Tn1 section reacted to mallein, diagnosis verified by P.M. examination.	
"	31/10/15		Continued testing D.A.C. horses for glanders. Further reactions today	

J. Mellard Capt
A.V.S. A.V.C.
20th Division

1875. Wt. W593/826 1,000,000 4/15 J.B.C. & A. A.D.S.S./Forms/C. 2118.

www.ingramcontent.com/pod-product-compliance
Lightning Source LLC
Chambersburg PA
CBHW080809010526
44113CB00013B/2348

9781474514118